LIVING BRITAIN

Dedicated to the memory of

GORDON BENINGFIELD

good friend and
guardian of our countryside

LIVING BRITAIN

A Wildlife Celebration for the Millennium

PETER CRAWFORD

ACKNOWLEDGEMENTS

It is almost 15 years since I and my team at the BBC Natural History Unit produced the BBC1 series *The Living Isles* and I wrote the companion book which traced the natural history of the British Isles from ice age to motorway age. Part of that team – producer Mark Jacobs and some very talented cameramen – have joined me to produce the BBC2 series *Living Britain*. Together with producer Yvonne Ellis and a very dedicated production team – Sean Christian, Adam White, Victoria Simpson, David Beale, Tim Green, Alison Brown-Humes and Loulla Charalambous; consultants Paul Morrison and Sally Wilson; film editors Alan Hoida and Andrew Naylor – we have spent almost three years together planning, filming and editing this millennium celebration of Britain's landscapes and wildlife. Everyone is agreed that the fickle British weather has been our greatest challenge. I am indebted to all of these colleagues for their enthusiasm and support.

At BBC Books I have been encouraged and organized by a first-class production team: notably commissioning editor Viv Bowler, project editor Lara Speicher, editor Anne Gatti, art director Linda Blakemore and designer Janet James. This book is a great credit to their confidence and professionalism.

As every author knows, writing a book can be a lonely job. It is, though, satisfying in a very different way from making television programmes. I hope that the reader detects something of the passion and concern that I share with so many people in Britain for our landscapes and wildlife. Many people – from centuries back – have written about this natural national heritage. Their writings and thoughts have greatly influenced mine. I am especially indebted to author and friend John F. Burton who has meticulously read my draft chapters and made many helpful suggestions for their improvement. Individual chapters have been reviewed by others expert in their field – but any errors that survive are probably mine.

I have been particularly supported by the regional knowledge and field observations of the three principal photographers for the book: Niall Benvie from Scotland, Mark Hamblin from the Pennines and Colin Varndell from Dorset. Their influence on the style and content of the book has been considerable – and it has been a great pleasure working with them.

Much to her surprise, my wife Pat has become totally engrossed in this book project. Our house has been taken over by the research material and pictures from which we have distilled the structure and detail of each chapter. Month by month, she has provided me with an endless stream of factual information and then gentle, constructive criticism about my words. Without her uncompromising support, I would have enjoyed the writing of this book far less.

PETER CRAWFORD
Bristol • July 1999

CONTENTS

PREFACE 7

Shetland Islands

Orkney Islands

C. Wrath   Pentland Firth
      Duncansby Hd

Lewis

Outer Hebrides   Harris   The Minch

North Uist   Moray Firth   Kinnairds Hd

Skye   R. Spey

South Uist   North West Highlands

    Rum   L. Ness   R. Dee

Inner Hebrides   Coll   The Cairngorms

Tiree   Mull   ▲ The Great Glen

     Ben Nevis   Grampian Mts

Jura   L. Lomond   R. Tay

Islay   Firth of Forth

Arran   R. Clyde   R. Tweed   Lindisfarne

     Southern Uplands   Farne Islands

Firth of Clyde   ▲ The Cheviot

           R. Tyne

Mull of Galloway   Solway Firth   R. Tees

     Scafell Pikes ▲   North York
Windermere   Lake   Moors
     District   P   Flamborough Hd
      Yorkshire
      e Dales

Morecambe Bay   n
        n   R. Humber   Spurn Point
Liverpool   Peak District   i
Bay   R. Mersey   n   ▲ The Peak
Anglesey   e
   Snowdon   R. Dee   s   The Wash
   ▲ Snowdonia   R. Trent
           The Fens   The Broads
  Cader Idris
   ▲
Cardigan
Bay   Cambrian Mts   R. Severn   R. Avon   R. Nene
          R. Ouse
      R. Tywi   R. Wye
St David's Hd   Cotswolds   Chiltern Hills
Pembrokeshire Islands   Brecon
(Skomer, Skokholm and   Beacons
Grassholm)   R. Thames   North Foreland

Bristol Channel   Somerset   Salisbury   North Downs
Lundy Island   Levels   Plain   R. Arun
   Exmoor   South Downs
      The New   Dungeness Point
      Forest   Selsey Bill   Beachy Hd
Dartmoor   Lyme   Isle of
     Bay   Portland Bill   Wight
Land's End   Start Point
Isles of Scilly
   The Lizard

PREFACE

Seen from space, Britain is but a small speck on the globe. Yet, today, one in every hundred of the world's population lives on this archipelago. Bounded by the Atlantic Ocean and cut off from mainland Europe by the English Channel and the North Sea, the 1000 Isles of Britain are home to almost sixty million people, most of whom live in England. It is perhaps a surprise that there is any room for nature.

British people live an essentially urban life. We have little contact with the land and its wildlife in our day-to-day lives. What we see is buildings and roads, factories and schools – the infrastructure of our modern Britain. But as every returning holidaymaker or visitor from abroad can see as they fly in to any of Britain's international airports, there is a lot of green down there. Unlike a road map, in reality the roads and motorways are tiny threads that criss-cross a patchwork of fields and woodlands, and the towns and cities are very small in comparison to the open landscape. Even in England, concrete and tarmac and all the buildings in the land cover no more than 5 per cent of the country. In Wales and Scotland the proportion is even smaller. Despite being one of the most densely populated nations in the world, the vast majority of Britain is open ground.

Above Male red fox – great survivor from the prehistoric wildwood of Britain – at home on a landfill site in east London.

Most of this is what we call 'the British countryside' – a mosaic of fields and woodlands, downland and heaths, moorland and mountains, all linked together by a network of streams and rivers flowing down to the marshes and estuaries that form part of a varied and extensive coastline, 6000 miles long. The sea that surrounds us has a great influence on the nature of our islands – moderating their climate and bringing the moisture that makes Britain such a 'green and pleasant land'. No one in the country lives more than 75 miles from the sea, and for the British people, clifftops and beaches have a special attraction. It is here, at the margins of our island nation, that we encounter something of the original wild nature of our country. Most of the interior has been transformed over the last five or six millennia as our predecessors cut down the forests and tilled the soil. Only at the tops of mountains does any real wilderness survive.

And yet, despite 6000 years of continuous agriculture and all the other land development that has been needed to support our burgeoning population, the landscape mosaic of Britain has retained much of the diversity and vitality of its plant and animal life. Fragmented, impoverished and constantly undergoing change, the distinctive landscapes and wildlife of Britain continue to inspire and are still a source of national pride. Few comparable corners of the world have such diversity and beauty of scenery and such a conspicuous variety of plant and animal inhabitants. Whilst we all have come to recognize that this is no 'garden of Eden' and that much should and could be done to enrich and conserve our natural heritage, this book – and the television series it accompanies – are unashamedly a 'celebration' for what survives alongside us into the new millennium – and not a 'lament' for what has been lost from the nature of Britain.

Nothing is more characteristic of Britain than its well-defined seasons. Each has its special appeal. It is this seasonal rhythm which gives Living Britain its unique character. Each month has its own seasonal colours and sounds, pace and mood, arrivals and departures and the comings and goings of its wildlife – all set against the backdrop of our own lives. This book, chapter by chapter, sets out to track the course of twelve months in Living Britain – highlighting the natural events that are governed by the passage of the year.

At the dawn of a new millennium – the seventh since Britain became an island and the fifth since the beginnings of Stonehenge – the British people have much to celebrate. The transient Millennium Dome at Greenwich stands briefly as an icon to all that the nation has achieved so far. A more enduring symbol of the vitality and spirit of the country at large can be seen in the mosaic of its landscapes and the diversity and vigour of its wildlife. If future generations can look back at the end of the 21st century and recognise the same diversity, character and beauty of Living Britain, that would indeed be something very valuable and meaningful to celebrate.

Above Six millennia of continuous management and change have created the tapestry that is the British countryside – such as this view of West Dorset from Eggardon Hill.

'through the

darkest days

of winter'

January

Above Golden eagle – symbol of wilderness.
Left A brief moment of January sunshine illuminates a
stand of Scots pines in Glen Affric, Invernesshire – one of the
remnants of the great Caledonian pine forest.

On the first day of the year, dawn breaks late over the glens of the Scottish Highlands. It is almost nine in the morning before the winter light brings any colour to the scene. The sun remains low in the sky, struggling to spill over the rim of the high tops even at noon. Down by the loch, the ground, although not frozen, has a damp chill that clings to the dormant vegetation. The heather seems lifeless and withdrawn. Here in Glen Affric, one of the surviving remnants of the ancient Caledonian Forest, magnificent Scots pines stand sentinel as a reminder of how so much of Britain looked in earlier times. Beyond their noble silhouettes, to the immediate north, is the snow-covered peak of Carn Eige and to the east the River Affric tumbles towards its union with the River Cannich flowing from the neighbouring glen. Though only an hour by road from Inverness, these glens are truly wild places which retain a primeval quality, especially in winter.

High above the ridge to the north of Glen Affric, a speck appears in the morning sky. The ridge itself rises over 900 metres (3000 feet) and the newcomer is flying at twice that altitude. In wide graceful circles, the bird surveys its highland kingdom, acute eyes penetrating every forested glen and scouring the open moorland for signs of life. As it dips over the ridge, without expending a single wingbeat, the eagle catches another updraught and changes course. Its wings, spanning almost 2 metres (7 feet), effortlessly carry the eagle towards the high treeless plateau, mottled with patches of snow. Seen in flight, the golden eagle has a breathtaking majesty. When perched or on the ground, its powerful body with lethal hooked beak and talons engenders respectful admiration. Its head and neck feathers are indeed golden and its piercing eyes, deep-set beneath pronounced brows, speak of intelligence and confidence.

The female golden eagle, as with most birds of prey, is larger than her mate. The pair form a partnership for life. Each bird was probably four or five years old before they reached maturity and began to breed. If they escape premature death, they may live for 20 to 25 years, and produce at least one fledgling each spring during most of their breeding life. It is a lamentable but sobering fact that, at the last count in 1992, Scotland could boast no more than about 420 breeding pairs. Numbers are probably no higher now than a century ago when eagles were suffering direct persecution from gamekeepers and egg collectors. The reasons for today's low numbers are to do with changing landscapes and human intrusion. Despite their apparent self-assurance and mastery of the air, golden eagles need space and solitude.

Right In winter, red squirrels look their best – bushy-tailed with thick, deep-coloured fur and ears sporting distinctive tufts of long hair.

One of the delights of a Scottish new year is to witness red squirrels courting. These nimble inhabitants of the pine forest look their best in winter. Their deep, chestnut-red fur is softer and thicker than in summer and some develop a grey tinge down the sides of their bodies. Their tails are extra bushy and their pointed ears sport distinctive tufts of long hair. Their lives are spent mostly in the trees, leaping with great agility between branches. Sharp claws help them speed up and down trunks, and the tail is used for balance and as a rudder when airborne. On the ground, they run and leap in short bursts, pausing frequently to take stock of their situation. Nuts and pine seeds stored in autumn help sustain them through the winter and the spring until the new crop matures. Most of their brief morning activity is spent searching by smell for the caches of food hidden when the fruits of the pine forest were plentiful. January is the start of the main breeding season for red squirrels. The scent of a female in season provokes the territorial male to emit a loud sneezing sound which brings rival males from distant corners of the forest. They all chase through the trees until the female allows the leading male to mate with her. It is at this time, when the squirrels are so preoccupied, that they can best be watched from below. By the time their second mating season comes in summer, the birch and other deciduous trees are in full leaf, concealing the squirrels' treetop escapades.

Above This wildcat – probably a female – triggered this photograph by breaking an infra-red beam set at a fallen tree trunk crossing a mountain stream at 370 metres (1200 feet) in the highlands of north Perthshire. The stripes and strongly ringed, thick tail suggest that she is a fine example of a pure Scottish wildcat.

The Scots pine is native to Scotland but has been reintroduced to many other parts of Britain. Admired for its imposing shape and size and for its ability to withstand severe weather, it is seen as an enduring symbol of good fortune. Some specimens live for two centuries or more, before they finally succumb to lightning or a winter gale. Their flaky bark harbours many insects and grubs, and their cones provide winged seeds – all invaluable food for the birds of the highland forest. Crested tits are local specialities of a few Scottish woodlands, especially around Speyside, where they forage in noisy, trilling flocks picking insects and grubs from the pine and birch bark and teasing seeds from spent cones. More effective at extracting conifer seeds is the crossbill, a specialist finch whose sharp mandibles twist across one another as the bird becomes adult, creating the perfect tool for inserting into pine cones and slicing through, scissor-style, to extract the ripe seeds. Some hardy Scottish crossbills start nesting in January to take advantage of the profusion of pine seeds in early spring when the cones open naturally as the weather warms. For several weeks, the parent crossbills will feed their offspring with a pulp of partially digested pine kernels until they are large enough to probe the cones on their own.

Glen Affric is one of the haunts of wildcats. Solitary and elusive creatures, they range from the treeless mountains down to the pastures in the alluvial valleys where rabbits and other smaller mammals are plentiful. Winter forces them to seek shelter in woodlands where they hole up in fallen trees and rocky crevices. Normally a night hunter that sleeps by day, in winter a hungry wildcat will emerge in daylight to stalk unwary rabbits and hares – and red squirrels intent on their courtship antics. With feline stealth it creeps on its belly until near enough to pounce on its chosen victim which it bites in the neck and slashes with the long claws of all four feet. As with domestic cats, birds are fair game and a red grouse will certainly suffice for several days. When times are hard, a wildcat travels far in search of food, sometimes venturing near villages and roads looking for easier pickings. At this time of year, the males – especially younger ones – are seeking their own territories and mates. Though rare, the wildcat ranks along with the fox as Scotland's most effective mammalian predator – a true warrior of the ancient Caledonian wildwood.

The mountain hare is a native of the Scottish Highlands. Smaller than the brown hare found throughout much of Britain, its home is high moorland where it feeds mostly on heather. When winter comes, its coat, which is bluish-brown in summer, moults to white except for the ear-tips which remain black, presumably as signals to other hares when moving above the snow-line. Almost identical to the arctic hares of Scandinavia and the Alps, these so-called 'blue' mountain hares of Scotland are very much at home in snow over which they scamper leaving behind large footprints made by their long and furry hind feet. To reach the heather, they dig through soft snow but are thwarted by icy conditions and suffer high mortality in prolonged freezes. By day they lie low in scrapes, known as 'forms', made in the snow or vegetation, or take refuge in short burrows dug in the peat. These hardy mammals have found a highland refuge in Scotland since the rest of Britain became a more

Right In its light-coloured winter coat, the mountain hare blends with the snow-covered terrain. By summer, its fur moults to a bluish-grey, except for its distinctive darker tail.

temperate land. Ever since the close of the last Ice Age, they have nibbled at the heather, converting vegetation into flesh. Countless generations of foxes, pine martens, wildcats and other Scottish predators have the mountain hare to thank for their own winter survival.

With its back to the dark cliff edge and to the midday light, the eagle is almost invisible to creatures in the glen, even to the most keen-eyed. The jet-black pupils of its eyes focus their extraordinary powers on the distant scene below. From its form, scraped in the heather, a mountain hare moves cautiously across the overnight dusting of snow already dropping from the lower tufts. When stationary, the grey-white colour of its winter fur merges with the greyness of the ground. More than half a mile away, the eagle registers every movement of the hare as it seeks the youngest shoots of heather. Judging that its intended prey is engrossed in feeding, the eagle pushes off effortlessly from the ledge. Dropping away from the backlit rim, it flaps its wings twice to gather momentum for the silent, lethal glide. If not taken completely by surprise, the hare bolts for cover. Zigzagging across the mottled moor, it endeavours to out-course the dark, pursuing shape. With an occasional corrective wingbeat, the eagle anticipates the hare's every evasive move and finally intercepts. The end is brief. Viewed dispassionately, this life-and-death drama is a routine but essential component of the wilderness way of life.

Left Golden eagle feeding on a mountain hare. Despite their camouflaged fur, a hare moving across open country can be seen by the sharp-eyed eagle from a great distance – but, alerted by its companions, an agile hare will often outrun its pursuer.

THE CAIRNGORMS – PTARMIGAN COUNTRY

Running diagonally from Inverness on the east coast of Scotland westwards to Fort William at the foot of Ben Nevis, at 1322 metres (4406 feet) Britain's highest mountain, is the deep fault-line of the Great Glen. This impressive geological feature, 88 kilometres (55 miles) long, includes the well-known Scottish icons of Loch Ness, Loch Lochy and the Caledonian Canal, and sharply divides the Highlands. To the north are the glorious glens of Affric, Cannich and Strathfarrar and beyond those lie the even wilder landscapes of Torridon, with the awe-inspiring peaks of 993-metre (3309-feet) Ben Eighe and 1037-metre (3456-feet) Liathach. To the south-east of the Great Glen, beyond the meandering valley of the River Spey, is Britain's most extensive area of wilderness – the Cairngorms. The high plateau of this mountain range is a massif of rounded peaks rising above 1000 metres (3500 feet) and covering 414 square kilometres (160 square miles). Modest by European or North American standards, this wild landscape is spectacular in winter, when it reverts to its arctic character. Increasingly popular with summer hikers and enthusiasts of winter sports, there are roads and ski lifts which penetrate this wilderness. As you ascend to the treeless plateau, you pass through diverse areas of natural pine forest interspersed with open moorland and peaty bogs. It is one of the nation's premier nature reserves, home to many alpine plant species and to the summer herds of red deer

Ptarmigan – grouse of the high Arctic – are the only native birds of Britain to change colour with the seasons. In winter, they forage across the snow-covered ski slopes of the Cairngorms.

that controversially graze the precious flora. In the patches of ancient woodland, Scots pines, which escaped being grazed when they were saplings, reach great ages and heights. Some towering veterans are more than three centuries old. At their altitude limit of 640 metres (2100 feet) the pines, though ancient, are stunted and twisted by the wind and cold, hardly growing taller than 3 metres (10 feet). Beyond this tree-line – the only natural one in Britain – the juniper shrub gives way to open moorland carpeted with heather. In winter, this is too bleak for red deer but a herd of reindeer introduced from Scandinavia in 1952 grazes the Glenmore slopes, adding to the arctic look of the Cairngorms. During the months of snow, they scrape at the ground to reveal mosses that contain fatty acids vital to their survival in the bitter cold.

Ptarmigan live up here the whole year round. In winter, their plumage is almost snow white, an effective camouflage against predators such as the golden eagle. Their feet are covered by an extra ruff of feathers that acts as snow shoes as they forage in search of emerging shoots and leaves of heather, crowberry and bilberry. When the final snow packs melt in late May or early June, the ptarmigan will start their hectic breeding season. Brief territorial skirmishes are followed by a short period of incubation. When they hatch, the chicks leave the nest almost immediately and can fly within 10 days. If any single species emblemizes the arctic nature of the Cairngorms, it would surely be the ptarmigan.

The outpost of Britain geographically nearest to the Arctic is Shetland. This remote archipelago lies about 160 kilometres (100 miles) north of John O'Groats on mainland Scotland. Unst, the most northerly isle of Shetland, is further north than the lower tip of Greenland and on the same latitude as Anchorage in Alaska. But despite being only 523 kilometres (325 miles) from the Arctic Circle, these windswept, almost treeless islands have a relatively mild climate. Their saving grace is the sea. Here at the apex of the British Isles, there is a continuous replenishment of warm currents from the North Atlantic Drift giving Shetland more temperate conditions than its latitude suggests. The same currents carry nutrients from deep in the Atlantic, making the waters around Shetland among the richest in the world.

Though humid and salt-laden, the air in Shetland is invigorating. Being so flat, clouds race quickly by in the strong winds and rainfall is meagre. In winter, there is less snow than on mainland Scotland. Through the long days of early summer there can be cloudless skies and warm, gentle sea breezes. It is then that the islands' clifftops resound to the calls of thousands of breeding seabirds and inland its lochans and moorland echo to the haunting cries of nesting dunlin, golden plover, red-throated diver, whimbrel, curlew, red-necked phalarope, and other wading birds. Now in January, Shetland is a very different place which lives up to its reputation as the most northerly and remote part of Britain. Winter here is very long. Although not nearly as bitter as many parts of the Scottish mainland, it can be bleak. The enemy is the dark. Being so close to the Arctic Circle, daylight hours are depressingly brief. Some 23,500 Shetlanders live here, many of them in the main town of Lerwick but also spread over the seventeen inhabited islands. Their principal occupations were once crofting, sheep farming and fishing, but since the offshore oil boom of the 1970s, life has taken on a different rhythm. Shetlanders have always loved their homes and the latest riches from the sea have certainly made the incessant wind and winter darkness much more tolerable.

On the cliffs and shoreline of the isles you will frequently hear the deep resonant calls of ravens. Shetland is one of the strongholds of this jet-black bird, the largest of all the crow tribe. Closer observation of this intriguing bird not only reveals that its plumage is fired by a glossy iridescence of purples, blues and greens, but that it has remarkable and admirable attributes. As a species, the raven is one of the most widespread of all birds in

Above Shetland – Britain's most northerly outpost – is on the same latitude as Anchorage in Alaska. But the sea moderates its climate, and snow seldom stays for long.

Left The head and pick-axe bill of the raven look heavy in proportion to its shiny black body which it carries in a half-hopping, lumbering manner on soot-black, powerful legs.

the northern hemisphere, and also one of the most ecologically adaptable. It seems equally at home in the frozen Arctic as it does in deserts. It has been in Britain since the end of the last Ice Age and was probably one of the first 'pioneers'. When the first pioneering people came to Shetland five or six millennia ago, ravens must soon have learned to associate with them, scavenging their waste and feeding on the carrion of their domesticated animals, even on their own dead. No wonder that the all-black raven became a favourite bird of fable. People could see human attributes in its appearance and behaviour and the bird was regarded as a portent of omens and bad news and a messenger of gods. Excavations at Jarlshof on the southern tip of Shetland show that ravens lived in the ninth-century settlements of Vikings for whom they were sacred birds. The Norse war god Odin had two tame ravens called Hugin and Munin – 'thought' and 'memory'. Each day they flew around the world and reported back to him at dusk, sitting on each shoulder and whispering in his ear. To those Shetlanders, Odin was known as Raveneguden, the raven god.

Today ravens still benefit from the islands' hospitality. Even in winter, they enjoy an extremely varied bill of fare – from carrion to live prey such as small birds and mammals, frogs and shellfish. On calm days, they pick over the shoreline searching the seaweed for crustaceans and other marine delicacies and scavenging for dead seabirds washed ashore. They even tackle the corpses of seals and whales beached by storms. Later in the year when the cliffs abound with the eggs and nestlings of breeding seabirds, ravens have a bonanza. Not surprisingly, Shetland has one of the largest and most dense raven populations of anywhere in Britain. A recent survey counted more than 200 breeding pairs as well as some 400 or so 'flocking' birds that were not yet nesting. Ravens are amongst the earliest birds to breed in Britain. Even in Shetland, with its brief winter days, some pairs start their courtship in January. Like eagles, ravens form lifetime partnerships and for each pair their traditional nest site is a focal point all year round, as they also use it as a roosting site. They jointly defend it against all-comers and as the breeding season approaches, they perform their aerial displays above it. Soaring and diving, rolling and tumbling, the pair fly in unison, matching each other's mastery of the air.

Because of where it is, surrounded by ocean, Shetland can experience fierce storms. The seas rise up and beat the coastline with a fury which is rare on the mainland. In the new year of 1992, winds of over 320 kilometres (200 miles) per hour were recorded on Unst. When the gales blow, ravens and all other land-based birds take shelter and only the nimble fulmars, kittiwakes, petrels and shearwaters

Right Despite competition with the fishing industry, the grey or Atlantic seal is flourishing again in Shetland. Each can eat 10 kgs (22 lbs) of fish a day.

rise to the challenge, skimming through the spume looking for small fish in distress. On secluded beaches, female grey seals have begun to moult. Their pups are now two or three months old and have become very efficient hunters of fish and lobsters. During the nineteenth century, grey seals were hunted around the Scottish coasts, and Shetland was no exception, particularly as it has long been a centre for the European fishing industry. Seal blubber made oil for domestic and commercial fuel, and their skins made warm and waterproof boots. For centuries, fishermen have seen seals as serious competitors and despite a series of legal measures to conserve them, numbers continued to fall, aided by a disease much like the distemper suffered by domestic dogs. Today, in Shetland and around the coast of Britain, the grey seal is flourishing again – in some places to the continuing dismay of the coastal fishing industry. In contrast, the so-called 'common' seal is much less widespread. More appropriately known on the other side of the Atlantic as the 'harbour seal', it prefers calmer waters than the robust grey seal. Here in Britain, it frequents sheltered east-coast estuaries such as those of the Moray Firth on the east coast of Scotland and the Wash in East Anglia. On the exposed west coast of Scotland, only long sea lochs such as Loch Linnhe and its smaller neighbour Loch Sunart offer sufficient shelter from winter storms. Surprisingly perhaps, Shetland has a sizeable population of common seals, particularly around the isle of Fetlar where unusually they co-exist with a thriving colony of grey seals.

Above The otter is now one of Britain's most elusive mammals. They live in secluded fresh-water habitats such as lakes, rivers and streams – but also on some undisturbed coasts, such as the west coast of Scotland and in Shetland. Strong swimmers, they are as much at home on land as on ice, over which they venture in search of fish and crustaceans trapped in shallow sea pools.

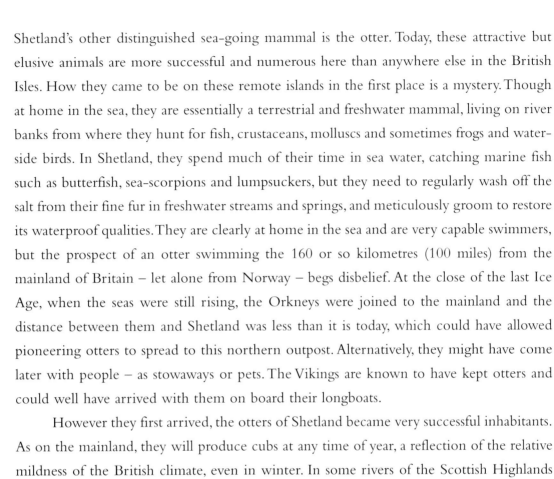

Shetland's other distinguished sea-going mammal is the otter. Today, these attractive but elusive animals are more successful and numerous here than anywhere else in the British Isles. How they came to be on these remote islands in the first place is a mystery. Though at home in the sea, they are essentially a terrestrial and freshwater mammal, living on river banks from where they hunt for fish, crustaceans, molluscs and sometimes frogs and water-side birds. In Shetland, they spend much of their time in sea water, catching marine fish such as butterfish, sea-scorpions and lumpsuckers, but they need to regularly wash off the salt from their fine fur in freshwater streams and springs, and meticulously groom to restore its waterproof qualities. They are clearly at home in the sea and are very capable swimmers, but the prospect of an otter swimming the 160 or so kilometres (100 miles) from the mainland of Britain – let alone from Norway – begs disbelief. At the close of the last Ice Age, when the seas were still rising, the Orkneys were joined to the mainland and the distance between them and Shetland was less than it is today, which could have allowed pioneering otters to spread to this northern outpost. Alternatively, they might have come later with people – as stowaways or pets. The Vikings are known to have kept otters and could well have arrived with them on board their longboats.

However they first arrived, the otters of Shetland became very successful inhabitants. As on the mainland, they will produce cubs at any time of year, a reflection of the relative mildness of the British climate, even in winter. In some rivers of the Scottish Highlands where there are still otters, they can produce cubs when snow covers the land. Not even freezing water is a barrier to these hardy animals which are able to make holes in the ice through which they disappear to hunt fish and crustaceans and dormant frogs and eels buried in mud. When winters are exceptionally severe in the Highlands, a female otter will move her family down to the coast where they can fish in warmer, ice-free waters – just like those in Shetland.

In a lifetime, most of us will never see a wild otter – but for Shetlanders there can be daily sightings, even in the busy, high-tech harbour of Sullom Voe. Here in the deep, sheltered sea loch, family groups of mothers with their growing cubs can be watched playing and fishing against the backdrop of the world's largest oil terminal. It is an extraordinary spectacle which is both heartening and reassuring – a fitting icon for this new millennium.

THE RETURN OF THE NATIVE

Of all Britain's wildlife, the otter is a creature of our times. As a nation, we almost lost this attractive and once widespread mammal as a result of habitat drainage and destruction, agricultural chemicals, hunting and gamekeeping, and persistent disturbance and intrusion into their reclusive lives. Protected by law since 1981, otters have become a focus for conservation efforts throughout the country and a barometer of our resolve and ability to turn back the clock.

Otters are perfectly adapted for a semi-aquatic way of life. On land, their four strong but short legs with their large, five-toed feet carry them close to the ground in a hunched, rolling gait – but they can be surprisingly agile in pursuit of prey. However, in water they are in their element. On the surface, they paddle with all four legs like a dog, but when needing a burst of speed, they tuck their front legs into their sides and use their broad, tapering tails to propel their sleek bodies through the water at speeds of up to 10 kilometres (6 miles) per hour – sometimes 'porpoising' along the surface to gain extra propulsion. Underwater, the sinuous, streamlined body, webbed feet and muscular tail, flattened at its tip, combine to propel the otter with agility and grace as it leaves a trail of silvery bubbles that escape from its dense, water-proofing and insulating fur. Long, sensitive whiskers help to detect prey, even in murky conditions and at night. Underwater its ears and nostrils are closed by special valves, but its eyesight is enhanced by unique muscles that adjust the focus to compensate for the visual distortion of the water. Just before it dives, the

This female otter with her cubs, out hunting near the oil terminal at Shetland, is a reassuring sign that these shy creatures can have a place in modern Britain.

otter takes a breath deep into its large lungs, often making an audible gasp. Being energetic in its pursuit of prey, the animal expends much energy and stays submerged only for short periods, typical dives lasting no more than 30 seconds. It prolongs its underwater chases by breaking surface to snatch another breath, before continuing its pursuit. Whether freshwater or coastal, the diet of otters is principally fish – although, in season, crayfish and amphibians are taken. The otter's eyes, set high on the head, are more effective when approaching prey from below which makes small mammals and birds swimming on the surface especially vulnerable. Water voles, coots and moorhens can be dragged beneath the surface by these surreptitious and opportunist predators.

Otters are at the top of their food-chain and have no serious competition from other wildlife. They have no natural predators to threaten their numbers – apart from humans and human activities. Of all the pressures on their habitats and food supplies, it seems that the use of organochlorine pesticides introduced in the 1950s had the most devastating effect on otter health and populations. Most injurious to wildlife were the powerful chemicals used extensively as cereal dressings and in sheep dips, that leached into the soil or ran off fields into freshwater habitats. Just like birds of prey, otters accumulated these contaminants in their tissues – leading to sterility or death. The real extent of the problem may never be known, but once the offending chemicals were withdrawn from general use, raptors

made a complete recovery and otters have come back almost from the brink of extinction.

Today, you may still never see an otter – but the chances of glimpsing this most elusive of our native mammals is considerably greater than it was in the 1970s. Since then, numbers have significantly recovered – especially in the 'Tarka country' of Devon and south-west England, in parts of west Wales and much of Scotland, particularly Shetland. The encouraging trend sees them spreading from these strongholds into the river systems of some of their former territories. There have been signs of otters – notably their droppings, or 'spraints' – in the centre of towns such as Exeter, Winchester and Salisbury, and sightings in industrialized South Yorkshire where the once heavily polluted River Don was thought beyond redemption. Even the upper reaches of the River Thames have been re-adopted as 'otter country'.

Throughout the country, thousands of volunteers have been helping to monitor the status of the otter, restore river channels and enhance freshwater habitats by creating artificial holts and places where these shy creatures can find rest and refuge. The Wildlife Trusts and other conservation organizations have encouraged landowners, industry, agriculture and water authorities to play a major role in this welcome 'comeback' – aimed at making every British river 'otter friendly' by 2010. However, the battle for the otter is far from won. There are new threats such as the synthetic pyrethroids now marketed as 'safe' alternatives for sheep-dipping. These leak into the water system where they are toxic to invertebrate life – the basis of the food-chain. The loss of mayflies, stoneflies and dragonfly larvae may not seem critical, but on them depend the fish, crustaceans, dippers, kingfishers and herons that are the more obvious and popular denizens of our lakes and rivers. The otter, though never likely to be conspicuous, is perhaps the most sensitive index of our success at restoring an enduring vitality to Living Britain.

Equally at home in the winter surf around the coast of Scotland's islands and mainland are eider ducks. The largest populations gather in the Ythan estuary just north of Aberdeen. The much-prized down of these ducks helps keep them insulated from the cold, and when breeding time comes in early April the females will pluck these soft feathers from their breasts to line their nests. Now in January, the drakes have just moulted to reveal their very striking breeding plumage with glistening white back, velvet-black belly and black cap to the head. Seen close, the light-coloured breast feathers are a delicate pink, and the nape an exceptionally beautiful almond-green. Out at sea, bobbing in the wind-lashed waves and diving for crabs and mussels, the rafts of eiders are already beginning preparations for their spring courtship. The ghostly cooing calls of the males drift across the water, as the birds rise and fall from view. Their breeding grounds

THE GLORY OF LINDISFARNE

The attraction of the Lindisfarne National Nature Reserve to wintering birds lies not simply in its position – an ice-free, sheltered haven within range of arctic islands to the north and Scandinavia and northern Europe to the east – but in its mud. Like all such estuaries and shallow bays, its irresistible attraction lies hidden in the silt – an inestimable natural wealth of invertebrate life that feeds on the algae and other micro-organisms filling every space in this gloriously nutritious, muddy mix of sand grains and particles of soil. Ragworms with their bristly fringes are delicacies for many wading birds as are juicy lugworms, the bait also sought by fishermen seen roaming the sandflats with their spades. When the worms emerge to exude their familiar wriggly sand casts, these industrious food-processors of mud are extracted from their U-shaped burrows by keen-eyed, swift-billed

Wigeon are ducks that graze on grass and marine plants such as eel-grass. In winter 30,000 flock to the mudflats of Lindisfarne on the coast of Northumberland.

waders. Relatively large molluscs such as cockles and razor shells filter nutrients from the silt and in turn make meals for any straight-billed bird that can deftly winkle them from their vertical burrows. An oystercatcher can even cope with a tenacious bivalve mollusc such as a mussel. If the two opposing shells gape only slightly, the bird stabs its robust, orange bill into the fleshy interior and hammers a hole into the other side of its tightly closing victim. Staggering numbers of much smaller worms and molluscs pervade the mud – in the richest parts there will be as many as 70,000 of them in the top 4 centimetres (1½ inches) of every square metre (10 square feet). No wonder Lindisfarne attracts 20,000 dunlin and 10,000 knot each winter, together with great numbers of other waders such as bar-tailed godwit, which appear regularly in flocks of 3,000 to 7,000.

are mainly in Scotland but in winter they can be seen off some coasts around England and also South Wales. A large number of eider ducks return each year to the Farne Islands off Northumberland, and the neighbouring island of Lindisfarne. Also known as 'Holy Island', this historic village with its ancient priory and castle can be visited at low tide by driving over a mile-long raised causeway, linking the small community twice a day to the mainland. As you cross, you can see the extent of the mudflats that lie in the lee of the island and sheltered by Guile Point to the south. Some 2500 hectares (over 6100 acres) of sand and mud are revealed at spring low tides, a veritable feasting table for the tens of thousands of geese, duck, swans and waders that overwinter in this North Sea refuge, making it a site of international importance in the bird world.

Wintering ducks also seek food and refuge here: mallard, pintail, teal and shoveler dabble on the surface, sifting through large volumes of water to filter out particles of food. The inside edges of the shoveler's bill have comb-like 'teeth' that trap the morsels as the water is forced through this very effective 'shovel'. In shallow waters and halfway up between the tidelines, eelgrass grows profusely and provides the main food for vast flocks of visiting wigeon and wild geese that graze along the margins of the mud. Eelgrass looks more like seaweed than the land-based flowering plants to which it is more closely related. It is a perennial which roots in the fine sand and grows in extensive meadows on the shallow sea-bed. Its fleshy leaves have evolved a thick outer membrane to help repel the salt, and its cell sap is concentrated to reduce water loss through osmosis. In summer the warmth of the water prompts these unique plants to produce flowers with pollen that is then carried by water currents to fertilize other clumps of eelgrass. In winter some 20,000 pale-bellied brent geese wing in from Spitsbergen in the Arctic Ocean. They come to feast on the eelgrass which sustains them, together with 30,000 wigeon, right through the winter. The seemingly limitless resources of this small bay also stretch to help

feed flocks of greylag geese and the largest herds of whooper swan to visit anywhere in Britain. From October onwards, family groups of these bulky birds, named for their distinctive trumpeting calls, wing in to Scottish lochs from their summer breeding grounds in Iceland and then, as winter progresses, many move south to milder coastal places such as Lindisfarne where they graze the eelgrass beds at low tide and agricultural grassland just inland.

Out at sea, apart from the eider, rafts of other diving ducks such as long-tailed duck and common scoter regularly spend all winter in the waters around Lindisfarne. In some years other colourful species of sea duck can be seen off the islands of Lindisfarne and the Farnes, often in dense flocks. Pintails, mergansers, goldeneye and scaup arrive to feed in the rich coastal water, but seldom come into the bay, let alone ashore. Here at Lindisfarne – just as in the many other estuaries and muddy bays around Britain's long, indented coastline – an immense number and variety of wintering wildfowl and waders are fuelled by the unseen riches of the coastal waters and the land between the tides. This is Britain's greatest natural claim to fame – the unsung glory of its endless mud.

Above After dark, on the last Tuesday of January, the people of Shetland gather in Lerwick for their Up-Helly-Aa celebrations, a revived Norse festival to mark the end of Yuletide.

Away from the sea, January can be a very different scene. Because the winters in Britain are comparatively mild, very few warm-blooded animals need to hibernate. Hedgehogs, dormice and bats take to their winter quarters for a long sleep, but even this dormancy is interrupted on warm days when the creatures will stir from their torpor and venture out in search of food. Moles dig deeper in frosty weather, to enable them to pursue earthworms which remain abundant. When they sleep, moles tuck up safely in their underground homes, almost immune to the worst weather. Being so small, voles and shrews need to feed almost constantly, especially as the temperature drops. The common shrew, one of the smallest and prettiest of Britain's mammals, restricts its movements to well-worn tracks along hedgerows and field margins, using its long, sensitive snout to test the air in search of food. Amongst dead leaves it expertly finds hibernating insects and woodlice. It spends much of its time underground and, like the hedgehog, thrives on earthworms. So energetic is this little shrew, and so voracious its appetite, that it must consume at least twice its own weight each day and eat something at least every three or four hours to avoid starving to death. The short-tailed or field vole is perhaps the most numerous of Britain's mammals. An aggressive and noisy creature, it is principally a vegetarian, consuming grass and the shoots of crops during winter. It digs underground burrows where it shelters from predators and the cold, and stores food. These passages link with a network of runs above ground that carry the voles unseen through the sparse vegetation. In deepest winter, this labyrinth is continued beneath the cover of snow so that the voles can still graze the shoots of the new season's crops away from the cold air and the prying eyes of predators.

Throughout Britain, January is the principal mating time for foxes and, at night, they emerge from their earths in search of partners. Since autumn, they have spent solitary lives – using their intelligence and acute senses to hunt and scavenge for food. Competing dog foxes now announce their presence with short, triple barks that resound through the night air. The vixens respond with chilling screams that can be scary to people unused to the sound. The fox, of course, has become as much at home in some of Britain's cities as in its more natural setting of the countryside. It is found in almost every corner of the land, from suburban gardens in the heart of the south-country to the bleak moorland of Scotland's Highlands and islands. For the fox, winter anywhere in Britain is the most testing season, and one in which it demonstrates its unmatched skills of survival and adaptability.

With the night screams of the fox and the calls of the raven, the new natural cycle has been set in motion. In Shetland, by the end of January, the days are perceptibly longer. There is an air of expectancy amongst the resident wildlife – and the islands' people. During the last century, the ancient Norse celebration of Up-Helly-Aa has been enthusiastically revived. Traditionally it marks the end of the yuletide celebrations that have distracted the community through the darkest days of winter. Now held on the last Tuesday of January, the event brings together islanders from all over Shetland. At exactly half past seven in the evening, an elaborate replica of a Norse longboat begins a procession through the streets of Lerwick. Shetlanders dressed as Vikings walk by its side, lit by flaming torches. Bands play and people chant the traditional Up-Helly-Aa song. At its destination, the great vessel that took weeks to build is set alight. Within an hour, it is totally consumed but the revelry continues through the night. At daybreak, a pallid light steals across the Shetland sky, and the last islanders return to their homes. On the cliffs the ravens stir. It is time that they, too, set about the earnest business of the new year.

'when nature

itself is

marking time'

February

Above Snowdrops – prelude to spring – pierce the soil or
snow to brighten gloomy February woodland.
Left Hoarfrost clinging to a line of beech trees. It will be May
before their leafy canopy closes overhead.

Though less than six weeks since the winter solstice, the first day of February in London claws back an extra 53 minutes between sunrise and sunset. In the city, on colder days, there are pink evening skies, and by the time the night clouds pick up the yellow glow of street lamps, the rumble of homebound traffic fills the winter air. Some 480 kilometres (300 miles) away on the Solway Firth, dividing Scotland from north-west England, the sinking sun illuminates one of the biggest skies in Britain. Slate-grey clouds, their undersides tinged with the same winter pink, roll in from the Atlantic and reflect the embers of the day in a vast, rippling expanse of mud. Silhouetted against this instant watercolour come the geese, noisily making their way home to the safe haven of Caerlaverock National Nature Reserve. For another night, these great flocks of barnacle geese together with pink-footed and greylag geese will roost on the foreshore before setting off next dawn to feed on nearby grassland. At dusk and dawn, the noisy flights of geese weave mesmerizing patterns across this natural masterpiece of sound and light.

Further north in Scotland, blizzards can white-out the ski slopes above Aviemore and bring traffic chaos to the Highlands. Throughout Britain, February can be the coldest month with the most snow. Traditionally, Candlemas, the second day of the month, was considered by farmers to be the halfway point of winter. Especially in hill country, a prudent owner of livestock would ensure that half his stores of hay and other feed remained in the barn. It may be late April before the last frosts are gone and the grass begins to grow. In contrast, the modern arable farmer is already looking ahead to spring. These days, most wheat crops are sown in autumn and by February, their shoots are well established and can better survive the cold and dryness of this wintry month. When weather permits, some fields are rolled and fertilized. Others which were ploughed in autumn have been broken up by frost and can now be tilled and smoothed by the harrow, in readiness for spring sowing and planting.

For many farmers, February is a mark-time month – a time for repairing fences and machinery and catching up with friends. For the rest of us who have less contact with the land, it seems a season

when nature itself is marking time, loath to come out while winter does its worst. But already snowdrops are showing. The leaf tips of this winter-flowering lily, sometimes called snow-piercer, are specially hardened and pointed to penetrate the frozen ground and the flowers are protected by a sheath-like spathe as they emerge. Also known as Candlemas bells, colonies of these snow-white blooms can appear almost overnight in both wild and cultivated places. They were probably first introduced to Britain into churchyards and monastery gardens from more southerly parts of Europe where winters are warmer and there are insects to help pollinate the flowers. Though widespread now, British snowdrops reproduce almost exclusively by dividing their bulbs rather than by seed. Their copious pollen attracts small flying insects that emerge on warmer winter days, and from their pollination a new generation of snowdrop seedlings can be spawned.

Left Barnacle geese spend winter on Scotland's west coast and estuaries. In October they wing in from Greenland and Spitzbergen to graze on the ice-free coastal grasslands. Flying in ragged, trailing flocks, they yelp like dogs – especially when taking off at first light to seek fresh pastures.

LAMB'S TAILS AND PUSSY WILLOW

On the bare twigs of hazel trees, the first brownish-yellow catkins which began to form in autumn now open and become creamy yellow. These 'lamb's tails' are the male flowers of the tree and produce clouds of dusty pollen. Carried by the wind, the pollen fertilizes the tiny bud-like female flowers, tipped with red hairs to receive it. Silver birch trees reproduce in a similar way. Their male catkins give the bare winter tracery a purple-brown hue in February and continue to grow until spring when the female catkins appear with the first flush of leaves. Later in the month, catkins of aspen trees and the closely-related grey poplar

On breezy early-spring days, the clouds of pollen that fill the air are produced by the male flowers of trees such as hazel (left) and goat willow (right).

add to the pollen in the air. In both species, individual trees bear either male or female catkins. Willows also produce catkins – the most common of which is the goat willow, known as sallow or 'pussy' willow because of its distinctive male catkins which are silky grey in February and then turn bright yellow with ripe pollen in late March. These attract early spring bees and butterflies by day and several species of moths at night. Sprays of sallow, heavy with both male and female catkins, decorate churches on Palm Sunday – especially when the Easter festival falls early in the year and few other wild plants are in flower.

In country lanes, especially in the mild south-west counties of Devon and Cornwall, hedgerow plants are stirring. Cow parsley is sprouting the new rosettes that will eventually spread into wayside umbrellas of white blooms. Yellow splashes of coltsfoot brighten the most unlikely places – even wasteland – and in damp woodlands, meadows and corners of gardens, swathes of lesser celandines catch the first warmth of the February sun. In hedgerows, the pale green spires of the arum lily thrust their way through the decaying leaves of winter. In time, the sheath unfolds to reveal a purple or yellow spadix which eventually becomes the familiar spike of poisonous orange berries. Its common country names of lords and ladies, red-hot poker, Jack-in-the-pulpit, cuckoo-pint and willy lily mostly refer to its suggestive shape. In late winter, its emerging furled spires act as beacons to blackbirds and thrushes attracted to the succulent corms from which the plant grows. When ripe, the spadix gives off the smell of rotting meat which attracts small flies. Some crawl down inside the sheath and become temporarily trapped below a circle of downward-pointing hairs in the folds at its base.

When they escape, having pollinated the female flowers, they leave past the now withered hairs, generously doused in more pollen. Another early-flowering pungent plant is stinking hellebore. Common in woodlands, especially beech, its base of stiff, long-stalked, evergreen leaves produces numerous flowers with lime-green petals. The whole effect makes the plant barely visible, but its odour attracts early bees and other woodland insects that emerge on warmer days and pollinate the plant while feeding on its nectar.

The flowers of dog's mercury are similarly green and smelly. Their spear-shaped leaves and insignificant spikes of small, greenish flowers carpet late-winter woodland floors and hedge banks. If walked on, they give off a fetid odour attractive to winter midges which pollinate their female flowers. This plant, a member of the spurge family, is an indicator of the antiquity of the woodland or hedgerow in which it grows. To people and livestock it can be deadly poisonous, giving it the traditional derogatory epithet 'dog' – to distinguish it from a similar-looking plant also called 'mercury' which had healing properties. The same prefix was applied to the two common forms of violet. 'Dog' violets which flower later in the spring are unscented whereas the sweet violet has a heady fragrance eulogized as the flower of Aphrodite, goddess of love. An oil distilled from its petals has been used since the times of ancient Greece in perfume making and also in herbal medicines.

The delicate sweet violet indeed has many virtues. As one of the first wild flowers to bloom, it is also attractive to insects on the wing in search of winter sustenance.

Right The sweet violet flowers early, along with primroses. Its heady scent contains iodine which dulls our sense of smell, quickly taking away the sweet sensation.

Above As spring progresses, the male blackbird perfects his song – developing a repertoire of musical motifs that improve with age.

The pace of woodland life is changing. As you walk across last year's leaf-litter and crackling twigs, you can detect a different atmosphere. At your feet new shoots are poking through and the woodland floor feels alive again. Especially in late afternoon, there is an urgency in the calls of woodland birds. Robins that sang alone through January are now joined by the energetic song of the male chaffinch. It is one of Britain's commonest birds with over five million pairs resident all year round. The glorious, liquid song of the blackbird becomes more sonorous as the month advances and its breeding time approaches. Raking noisily in the leaf litter for dormant insects and other invertebrates, it keeps a cocked eye on intruders. Taking to the air, its alarm call clatters through the wood, alerting others. Shy birds such as the wren and dunnock interrupt their singing practice and wait in suspense in case there is need for flight. As dusk falls, all these birds are reluctant to leave their chosen roosting places, their eyes less effective in the fading light.

The tawny owl with its familiar 'wise' face and proverbial 'to-whit-to-wooo' used to be called the 'wood owl'. It spends its day roosting in trees, usually sitting bolt upright in a hollowed bough or flat against a trunk, with its eyes half closed, waiting for darkness. If encountered by smaller woodland birds, there is great panic and chatter of alarm calls as some of them mob the roosting owl and others scatter through the wood. The tawny owl seldom ventures far in daylight. When it does, it is invariably accompanied by an excited mob of smaller birds. Its prey would certainly include them, but it also catches and eats small mammals such as mice and voles and will take young squirrels, rabbits and even weasels. Its soft plumage and specially shaped wing-feathers make it silent in flight and particularly efficient in the dim light of a woodland evening. The angry, 'chink-chink' alarm call of the ever-watchful blackbird might betray the presence of a tawny owl –

Right Tawny owl at roost in a pine tree – resting before its next silent night-time hunt.

THE WORLD OF THE BADGER

Badger-watchers describe how, on warm days at this time of year, the sow emerges to gather new bedding by scraping together piles of dry grass and bracken with her front paws and then, tucking them between her chin and forequarters, shuffles backwards over the surface of the sett and down the tunnel. Below ground, in the further reaches of the sett, she will have dug out a fresh chamber which she lines with this bedding. When they are born, the cubs are covered in silky-grey hair but the dark facial stripes are already evident. It will be five weeks before their eyes open, and well into spring before they venture from their underground world.

Female badger dragging fresh bedding backwards into the sett where, in a special chamber, she gives birth to her cubs. These attractive mammals start the new millennium surrounded by controversy.

The adult badger is perfectly adapted for digging. Its body is wedge-shaped, with very muscular shoulders and neck, and is carried low on the ground on short but exceptionally powerful legs. The feet, especially those at the front, each have five well-developed claws which it uses to rake at the soil and to remove roots and stones in the path of its digging. The loose material accumulates under the badger as it works. Now and again it moves the soil backwards by arching its back, and, when sufficient has accumulated, it backs up to the entrance of the sett. The sight of the rear end of a badger as it disgorges its spoils onto the woodland floor is sometimes the only glimpse we have of badgers in daylight.

To feed, badgers more usually venture abroad at night. Though they have large canine teeth, suggesting a flesh-eating diet, their menu includes a great variety of food, both animal and vegetable. They are true omnivores, taking full advantage

and then the cacophony rises as other birds join in. The owl, now detected, leaves its vantage point and sets off through the wood in search of less manic hunting grounds. Its excellent binocular night vision and acute hearing gives it great advantage. Dropping silently from a lookout perch, it swoops on small prey such as voles and wood mice and sometimes woodland birds. At this time of year, prey is becoming more plentiful and the vegetation is still sparse – ideal conditions for hunting and for raising young. Tawny owls are amongst the first woodland birds to begin their nesting, and by the end of February many already have eggs. Each is round and white, like a ping-pong ball, and the female starts incubating as soon as the first is laid, usually in a hollow tree. She lays her eggs – normally two or three but sometimes more – at intervals of a few days, so that the chicks are at different stages in the nest, thereby spreading the parental tasks for herself and her mate. The female seems to know of the seasonal productivity of their woodland habitat. Vast quantities of earthworms – together with slugs, beetles, bees and wasps, dead or alive rabbits, rats, mice and hedgehogs, birds' eggs, frogs, acorns and beech mast, bluebell bulbs, cereal crops, grass, roots and bark – all feature in the badger's catholic diet. Like foxes, badgers have been accused by sheep farmers of taking lambs, but they are probably not sufficiently agile and are content with scavenging for casualties. The farmers' – and the Ministry of Agriculture's – most vociferous complaint is that badgers contribute to the spread of tuberculosis between cattle. For decades the issue has threatened the welfare of Britain's 300,000 strong population of badgers. It continues to taint the reputation of this much-loved native mammal – and is political dynamite which regularly forces a showdown between farmers and conservationists.

There is no doubt that badgers contract and carry TB, but it does not appear to be a significant threat to the survival of the badgers themselves – nationally, their numbers are increasing. It is their lungs and kidneys which are most prone to the infection, which is why the bacteria is thought to be spread in their breath, droppings and urine. But it is by no means certain that the disease is transmitted between badgers in this way, nor that it is freely passed on to cattle in the field. Badger conservationists point out that it is more likely that healthy badgers rooting under cowpats for their favourite beetles might contract TB from infected and badly managed cattle. The essential dilemma is whether widespread culling of badgers has any real effect on the spread of TB in cattle. In the 1980s and 1990s, the Ministry of Agriculture authorized the killing of 25,000 badgers. In south-west England, where bovine TB was a widespread problem, post-mortems on the badgers culled in the early years of the scheme showed that less than 15 per cent of the badgers carried the bacteria. Despite the slaughter, TB continued to increase on the dairy farms of the south-west. Since then, the Ministry of Agriculture has changed its policy and culling tactics several times – and at the end of the 1990s, scientists seemed no wiser about the best way forward. In response to pressure from dairy farmers, the culling campaign continued. Greater understanding about the pathways of transmission, including other possible vectors of the disease, is central to the unresolved issue. Clearly, definitive research and an informed consensus of opinion is crucial if the badger – one of Britain's most ancient and distinctive mammalian inhabitants – is to flourish without regrets in the new millennium.

when food is less plentiful for she will lay fewer eggs. If the hardship comes after the chicks have hatched, the largest offspring will eat the smallest. By regulating its breeding patterns, the tawny owl remains adaptable – and successful. It is the most numerous and widespread owl in Britain.

As the owl goes about its night-time business, there are energetic stirrings beneath the forest floor. February can be the busiest time for badgers. Contrary to expectations, these hardy mammals do not hibernate and can survive long periods without eating. Their setts, excavated in banks and beneath the roots of giant trees, give them protection against the elements and a safe place to sleep during the coldest days of winter. The main chambers may be 3 metres (almost 10 feet) from the surface and it is here that the sow gives birth, often as early as this month or certainly by the end of March.

Dawn in February woodland is a surprisingly noisy and busy time. It is now that woodpeckers start their territorial drumming. Although all three native British species communicate this way, it is the lesser and the great spotted woodpeckers which are renowned for their early spring performances. Although both sexes drum, it is the male which advertises for a mate and marks out the extent of his territory with noisy proclamations. Striking the end of his strong beak rapidly on a resonant branch, he produces a succession of staccato sounds – sometimes hammering out as many as 20 blows a second. The great spotted woodpecker, also known as the 'pied woodpecker', is the size of a stocky blackbird and produces short bursts of very powerful drumming. The lesser spotted species, often called the 'barred woodpecker' because of its distinctive plumage, is barely larger than a sparrow. Its drum-rolls, although not as explosive as those of its larger cousin, are higher pitched and last for twice as long. Rare in Scotland and the very north of England, the lesser spotted was the more common of the two in Victorian times. Today they favour old orchards and seems to have benefited from the surfeit of dead and decaying elm trees left in the wake of Dutch elm disease – a small consolation for this plague. The green woodpecker prefers more open country, often feeding on the ground, using its long tongue to extract ants and other insects from ant hills and short turf. It is an appreciably bigger bird and makes an impressive sight when visiting

Above Male great spotted woodpecker – also called the 'pied woodpecker' – searching for dormant insects in the bark of an alder stump.

garden lawns and bird tables in winter. From February, its demonic laugh trails across the countryside as it stakes out its breeding territory and searches for a suitable trunk in which to chisel out a nesting hole. Although green woodpeckers rarely drum like their spotted cousins, both males and females are very efficient excavators of wood, chipping out at least one new home every spring.

Above this woodland drumming you might hear the alarm calls of one of Britain's most belligerent mammals – the grey squirrel. Although greys continue their courting into spring, it is now in February that they can perform their most extravagant arboreal antics. Like their red counterparts, it is the females who goad their suitors into frantic, noisy chases. Taking the lead, each leaves a perfumed trail through the treetops. Enticed, the males follow in hot pursuit, emitting short, sharp

barks. The female leads them on a merry dance, until she submits to the ardour of the leading male. As the day advances, they search for caches of acorns and other nuts hidden in the autumn, before retiring to the safety and warmth of their dreys. After mating, a female becomes very assertive and will drive out the males from her chosen nesting site. Sometimes she builds a special drey in which to give birth, or takes over an unoccupied woodpecker's hole if large enough. The female grey squirrel makes a perfect mother, tending diligently to her helpless young. After raising a litter in early spring, she may mate again and produce another family in the summer.

St Valentine's Day on February 14th was commonly thought to be the day by which all birds had chosen their mates. Surprisingly many have – but for others it is still too early to be sure of a successful partnership. Many species are dependent on insects to feed their young. Until the real warmth of spring arrives, a union would

Above The barred plumage of the male common partridge, or 'grey partridge', is more striking than that of the hen, but both have an orange-brown face.

be premature. Some whose incubation periods are prolonged affairs will pair up long before the end of winter. Some native grey partridges have been pairing since the middle of January. Each morning, no matter how frosty, the cock birds gather in sheltered field corners to challenge each other, performing running battles to establish seniority and territory. The courtship in February also takes

AMOROUS AMPHIBIANS

Worldwide there are more than 4000 species of amphibians; in Britain there are merely six that are truly native – the common frog, the common and natterjack toads, the common or smooth newt, the palmate and the great crested newt. There are a few others which have been intentionally or accidentally introduced – such as the notoriously noisy marsh frog, rampant in Romney Marsh. All Britain's amphibians spend much of the winter out of sight, in hibernation. Frogs are first to emerge towards the end of February when they congregate at traditional freshwater breeding sites. On mild, rainy nights they may travel more than half a mile, leaping with their long and muscular hind legs. The males arrive first and strike up their croaking chorus to attract the contingent of females who are gracelessly grabbed as they reach the spawning site. Jumping on a female's back and wrapping his front limbs around her smooth-skinned body, the ardent male hangs on with specially developed horny 'nuptial pads' on each of his 'thumbs'. In this inelegant but functional position, the pair take to the water where she lays her eggs which he simultaneously fertilizes. Each egg is enveloped in a layer of jelly which swells to insulate the embryo from the water and give a measure of protection from predators, creating the masses of frogspawn familiar in late winter from which the speckled tadpoles emerge two or three weeks later.

Male and female frogs swim in tandem, often for several days, until the female releases as many as 3,000 eggs which are simultaneously fertilized by her partner. Frogspawn forms great clumps, whereas toads lay eggs in strings.

Toad migration and spawning can be an even more spectacular affair. Over the course of just a few days, hordes of these warty-skinned amphibians leave their dry hibernation sites in walls and banks, compost heaps or under logs, and head for the communal mating grounds around favoured lakes and larger ponds. The males set off first, usually at night, climbing walls and crossing roads with determined fervour that seems unstoppable – except by traffic. Despite many casualties, the males and then the larger females, their abdomens distended by eggs, reach their common goal. Some males adopt a cunning tactic by waiting in ambush along the route and completing their journey as passengers, hanging on to females with their nuptial pads. Other males wait in the water, croaking loudly. The cacophony rises as more females arrive and are mobbed in a toady scrum. Larger males can dislodge smaller rivals from their mounts – and males which tackle other males are warned off by a brief but insistent chirp. The deeper this 'release call', the larger and more tenacious the toad already in possession.

Compared to the migration and pairing, toad spawning is a more leisurely affair, and may take a few hours as the female expels her strings of eggs and her smaller companion sheds his sperm. As they move together through the vegetation, the toadspawn is wrapped around the aquatic vegetation where, like that of frogs, the jelly protects the infant amphibians from the worst ravages of their watery world. But, toad tadpoles have a distinct advantage. Their jet-black skin contains toxins which, like adult toads, make them unpalatable to many predators. This is probably the main reason why, in summer, many toadlets emerge from fishing lakes whereas mating frogs and newts seek out the security of smaller ponds and ditches.

The smooth or common newt is the most numerous of the three British species and because it favours chalky water, it is found principally in the south. The small palmate newt prefers more acid water and is more common in the north and west of Britain. As its name suggests, the great crested newt is the largest, growing to 15 centimetres long (6 inches), but this species has become increasingly rare, despite the fact that its warty skin produces protective toxins. The males of all three newts develop more intense markings and colouration, especially on their abdomens to enhance their courtship displays, and the great crested and the smooth newts sport a conspicuous crest along their head and back. Newt fertilization takes place within the female's body. After an elaborate courtship ritual, the male deposits a packet-like 'spermatophore' on the bed of the pond or stream which the female, enticed by his colour and performance, picks up in the vent at the base of her tail. She then lays the eggs singly, rolled in the underside of water plants. Newt tadpoles are tiny and take until late summer to develop into miniature adults, and two or three years before they are fully mature and ready to return to the pond of their conception to take part in the annual affairs of our amorous amphibians.

the form of running chases, the cock and hen taking turns to be the pursuer. When they lay, the females often share nests, accumulating collective clutches of up to 40 eggs. By the time they hatch, healthy field margins will be harbouring the insect caterpillars and other high-protein invertebrate larvae that the chicks need for growth. In fields that are indiscriminately sprayed with insecticides, partridges are rare. The great shooting estates of places such as East Anglia, mindful of the welfare of their game, cease shooting soon after Christmas and take care to leave unsprayed field margins. Other birds, such as lapwings, also benefit. It is now that you can admire the tumbling aerial displays of the males as they twist and dive over arable land, accompanied by throbbing wingbeats and their distinctive 'peewit' song. This handsome bird, also known as the 'green plover' in recognition of its glossy green back, is the farmer's friend, consuming wireworms and other pests of root crops. Flying high across winter farmland, the flocks flicker black and white as they rove in search of better pickings or a safe roost for the cold night.

East Anglia can be very cold. Easterlies blow unimpeded from Siberia, tipping the mercury well below zero. Combined with the flatness of the landscape, the chill factor can make this most continental region of Britain feel more like the Arctic than a temperate, maritime land. When the weather comes from the north-east, blizzards can envelop the countryside overnight, transforming fenland and the Broads into a wonderland of reedbeds and frozen water. Efficient drainage has ensured that the large tracts of grazing are no longer overwhelmed by winter flooding. The dykes and ditches that once criss-crossed the land between the 40 or so shallow freshwater Broads – the relics of flooded medieval peat diggings – have mostly lost their appeal to wildlife. Even frogs have become rare because of lack of spawning grounds. Only where fenland and marshland have been purposefully set aside for wildlife and landscape conservation can you see how much of this region must have looked before the advent of modern drainage and agricultural techniques. Thanks to conservation groups, there are such refuges in the Norfolk Broads and they come into their own in late spring and early summer. But they are mostly small and piecemeal. The former splendour of East Anglia needs scale to be appreciated – by wildlife as well as by people. One such place is the Ouse Washes – and it is perhaps seen at its best in deepest winter.

The Wash itself – that shallow inundation of the North Sea – creates a dramatic meeting-place of fenland and salt water. The Ouse Washes that drain the hinterland offer the finest marshland habitat anywhere in Britain. Canals and dykes are everywhere, making the landscape seem orderly and in many ways monotonous. The discipline of the system, devised over centuries of management, belies its inherent wildness. At the Isle of Ely – for more than a millennium a place of physical and spiritual refuge – it is easy to forget that much of the surrounding fenland is below sea level. With ingenuity and tenacity, generations of fen people have reclaimed and nurtured the Fens to create the richest and most lucrative growing-soils in Britain. The elegant cathedral spire of Ely is a monument to that success. But their other accomplishment is the creation of the network of wet wilderness that lies between the artificially dry land. There are many now famous wildlife reserves in the region – such as Wicken Fen, Woodwalton Fen and Holme Fen – but the flood meadows of the Ouse Washes in Cambridgeshire form a wetland of international proportions and importance. In summer the meadows are grazed by horses, sheep and cattle; in winter they are intentionally allowed to flood. This creates the perfect wintering grounds for vast numbers of duck and wild swans, including both the whooper and Bewick's species. Very similar in appearance to the whooper swans that visit

Lindisfarne and other wetlands in northern Britain, Bewick's swans come from breeding grounds in the remote tundra of northern Siberia mainly to southern Britain. They were first recognized as a distinct species in 1830 and named in honour of the respected naturalist and wood engraver, Thomas Bewick, who had died two years previously. They differ subtly from the whoopers in size and bill pattern – and in their calls. It takes an expert to tell them apart unless seen together, but for anyone with an eye for wild beauty, the sight of these long-distance travellers taking off and landing on the wintry waterscapes of the Ouse Washes is a thrilling experience.

When a cold snap comes, many animals, already under pressure, finally succumb. The rigours of winter stretch their resilience to the limits and diminish their food supplies. Keeping warm takes much of their energy. For some small, warm-

Above Whooper swans. The yellow patches on each side of their bills are larger and more pointed than those of Bewick's swans.

blooded creatures even a single night below freezing is terminal. Wrens and long-tailed tits will roost snugly together in small crannies and in last year's house martins' nests beneath the eaves. They have been seen to flock into postboxes, upturned flowerpots and, sensibly, into nestboxes intended for their use in the spring. Sometimes as many as 50 birds have been counted as they tumble in from the cold. For seed eaters such as finches, grain and other cultivated seeds provide welcome supplements to the remnants of wild fruits and berries that still hang in the hedgerows. Song thrushes and redwings quickly succumb during hard spells and will eagerly visit garden feeding stations for proffered fruit. In the hedgerows, a few hips and haws remain to be discovered, and berries of ivy and mistletoe provide a mid-winter bonus. The mistle thrush, as its name suggests, feasts on these winter fruits and is largely responsible for spreading their seeds. The sticky seeds of the parasitic mistletoe are introduced to a new host tree when the bird wipes its beak on the bark. Then, as if in jubilation, the

cock bird will fly to the highest point and announce its presence with a ringing song that cheers even the most punishing February day. Deservedly known as the 'storm-cock', this hardy thrush will sing in the foulest weather.

In upland England and Wales, the winter character of February is even more apparent. Although none of the hills are high by continental standards, they can be very bleak. The North York Moors run down from Urra Moor at 455 metres (1489 feet), the highest part of the Cleveland Hills, to meet the bracing east coast at Whitby and Robin Hood's Bay. Biting winds from Scandinavia and beyond can whip across the North Sea bringing dramatic drops of temperature to the moorland. The red grouse that escaped last autumn's guns rely on the heather for shelter and food. Like the ptarmigan of the Scottish Highlands, they are extremely hardy birds and will burrow into fresh snow to reach the best shoots of heather. If the snow persists for long, they move down to lower moorland and sometimes to farmland. The systematic winter burning of the heather on a controlled 10–15-year cycle is the key to a healthy moor. It creates a patchwork of heather of different ages and ensures that the grouse have food all year round, and year after year. Moorland habitats were originally created by felling and by fire, and need to be maintained that way. Many other species benefit, such as golden plover, lapwing and curlew that return in spring to breed. But now, the stoical grouse have these moors to themselves. For predatory birds such as merlins, peregrines and hen harriers there is insufficient prey in winter. By the time they and other birds return to establish their spring territories, the red grouse will be well underway with their own breeding schedule and will have first pick of nesting sites. The male grouse proclaim their territories with their insistent 'go-back, go-back, go-back' call that is the hallmark of early spring across the heather-clad northern moors – from the coastal hills of Northumberland and Yorkshire, through the Pennines to the Peak District of Derbyshire. Now still in the grip of winter, it is hard to imagine how these bleak uplands of the North Country will become transformed into the gentle purple moors of summer.

Above Male red grouse. Those in Britain form a sub-species of the Northern Hemisphere 'willow grouse'.
Right The corrie lake and glacial ridge at Cader Idris were created as the ice sheets melted.

The landscapes of Scotland and the rest of northern Britain were shaped by ice. The freezing and defrosting of successive Ice Ages shaped and re-shaped their contours, gouging their valleys and scraping away their soils. The elongated lochs of Scotland and the snake-like lakes of Cumbria are graphic relics of that surprisingly recent era. It is a mere 20 millennia since the ice began to melt, and less than half that time since the new shape and contours of Britain were eventually revealed. A hard winter in upland Britain is a rough reminder that this land has only just emerged. The highest mountains outside Scotland are the peaks of Snowdonia in north-west Wales. To visit them in winter is to be transported back to the end of the last Ice Age. There are 14 peaks over 900 metres (3000 feet) high, clustered around their bastion, Snowdon, which rises to a majestic 1085 metres (3560 feet). Known as Yr Wyddfa in the Welsh language, this highest point of Wales looks down over a wild and much revered landscape known as 'Eryri' by the Welsh-speaking community that lives within its gaze. Designated a National Park, the term 'Snowdonia' now embraces many other lesser peaks to the south, including the impressive relic glacial ridge and corrie lake at Cader Idris. There can be few places in Britain where the might of those Ice Age glaciers is more apparent. In bleakest February, when blizzards howl around the shattered ridge, that long winter seems like yesterday.

'the harbinger

of spring'

March

Above Kingfishers remain in Britain all year round. Some move
to the coast for winter, but return inland to breed.
Left An English churchyard in early spring – carpeted with lesser
celandines and festooned with equally yellow blossom of forsythia.

This irascible month, they say, enters like a lion and leaves like a lamb. Its weather can be blustery and cold. Storms are a frequent feature and there is a risk of frost almost every night. But there can be glorious sunny days when air temperatures climb dramatically and puffy, white clouds dash across crystal-clear, blue skies. The spring equinox, when daytime and night are of equal length, falls on the 21st and sets the pattern for spring. Even Easter – that most moveable of feasts – is calculated from this immutable astronomical event and spring is set to follow. March is a month that determines the schedule and tempo for the entire growing and breeding season in Britain. By the time the lion has mustered its final winter roar and made way for the gentler days that are April, the look of the land has been transformed and its life awakened.

An old English word for spring was 'Lenct' – a Norse term which has survived as 'Lent', the 40 days preceding Easter when the days noticeably 'lengthen'. Throughout much of Britain this first hint of the coming season was characterized by the flowering of the Lenct or Lent lily – that glorious harbinger of spring we know as the wild daffodil. Writers from Elizabethan times describe how it grew in great profusion in damp open woodland, heathland, commons and meadows. In March, country women came to the heart of London selling armfuls of the blooms, bringing a vivid splash of spring colour to city lives. Then mysteriously, towards the end of the nineteenth century, the flower immortalized by Wordsworth declined, particularly in central and eastern England. Like its cultivated form, the plants survive being cut or picked, although that is now outlawed because of the rarity of the wild form. The places where it continued to flourish were mystifyingly disconnected: south Devon, the Black Mountains of Wales, parts of the Sussex Weald and, a little later in the season, parts of the Yorkshire Dales and the Lake District. One special place retained its reputation as the prime March Mecca for daffodil-watchers – the area around Newent on the Gloucestershire-Herefordshire border.

Left Truly wild daffodils – once widespread in Britain – now bloom in only a handful of sites. Their appeal is their simplicity.

Known as the Golden Triangle, the region had long been famous for the yellow swathes that graced its banks and hedgerows, orchards and copses, churchyards and gardens. But when word spread that this national treasure was in decline, the Great Western Railway ran weekend 'Daffodil Specials' to carry Londoners to witness this dazzling spring spectacle.

The cultivated daffodil varieties that brighten city flower markets as early as February come mainly from the Isles of Scilly, where they flourish on specially prepared soils and are stimulated to bloom by the mildness of the islands' winters. Many end up in florists and flower stalls of Wales in time for March 1st, St David's Day. Why and how the daffodil became the national emblem of the principality has been the subject of much debate. Paradoxically, the flower, in its wild form, is far more rare in Wales than in England. There is, however, a daffodil peculiar to Wales which can claim pride of place. At the end of the eighteenth century, a distinctive daffodil with short stems bearing exquisitely uniform, floral trumpets was discovered growing wild along the coastal region of South Wales near Tenby in Pembrokeshire. Probably an accidental cross centuries ago between the once familiar 'Lent lily' and an unknown cultivar, this hardy hybrid shot to fame as 'the Tenby daffodil', and is still celebrated on St David's Day as one of the botanical curiosities of Wales – even regarded as a distinct species in its own right.

Above Gorse flowers almost all year round – but the blooms seem more vivid at the end of a long winter, when they attract emerging insects.

Yellow is the prevailing colour of early spring. Its vividness catches the eye, especially on sunny days. The yellow part of the spectrum seems to attract insects on the wing this early in the year. The flowers that are first to bloom signal their bright message that they are ripe with pollen and nectar. In return for supplying food for pioneering spring insects, the flowers are pollinated. It is no coincidence that pollen itself is pigmented yellow. The lesser celandines and coltsfoots continue to provide a welcome source of pollen and nectar for mice and voles as well as for active insects such as early bees and butterflies. Even when snow still covers the ground, the brilliant golden flowers of marsh marigolds light up meadowland and damp woods. Also known as kingcups, these luscious plants with glossy foliage are among the most ancient native plants of Britain, survivors of many glacial periods. Like the wild daffodil, they are now in decline but the reasons are less of a mystery. The drainage and 'improvement' of water meadows is to blame. More resilient is the primrose, the 'first rose' of spring. Although they, too, prefer damp conditions, clumps of primroses spread quickly on well-drained motorway embankments and along avenues and rides cut through woodland. Although they can grow in shady corners of ancient forest, they do need regular bursts of sunlight to flower. Primroses flowering in early March, when there are few insects to transfer pollen from one plant to another, successfully set their own seeds. Those that are cross-pollinated later by insects produce seeds that are fleshy and sticky. Ants and other foraging creatures attracted by this nutritious 'packaged' food, carry them away, often over great distances. This way Britain's 'prima rosa' is dispersed across the land.

On the south coast of Wales is a network of small lakes created two centuries ago by the damming of an estuary and the three limestone valleys that fed into it. Known as the Bosherston Pools, this area has become one of the most interesting wildlife areas in west Wales. Later in the spring, the drowned valleys become fringed with a dazzling display of yellow iris and in early summer the water is covered by beds of white lilies, for which the reserve is well known and attracts many visitors. In March the place has a different beauty. Wintering wildfowl such as coot, goldeneye and pochard dive and swim through its maze of reedbeds. Grey herons stealthily stalk their prey and kingfishers dart from the steep-sided, tree-clad shores to hover briefly over productive patches of water or to alight on favoured lookout branches. In flight, which is low, straight and swift with rapid wingbeats, kingfishers appear as a flash of iridescent cobalt blue or emerald green according to the incidence of the light. When perched, their orange-chestnut underside and cheeks become apparent, set off exquisitely by the white patch on the throat and on each side of the neck. With matching bright red legs, the adult in full breeding plumage is indeed the most tropically coloured of all British birds.

From its hovering position or from one of its lookouts, the bird dives headlong into the clear, cold water, seizing its quarry scissor-fashion in its pointed, open beak. Then, rising from the water with whirring wings, it alights on the most convenient perch to swallow its prize. Minnows, bullheads and sticklebacks are the kingfisher's favoured catch. Large or spiny individuals are usually despatched and softened by the kingfisher, by bludgeoning their bodies against the branch before turning the fish

Above By March, many herons already have chicks waiting hungrily in their colonial nest-sites. The adults take turns to fish – waiting patiently before striking with their sharp bills.

Right Emerging with a writhing eel calls for strength, agility and a large gullet, if the prey is to be swallowed and then regurgitated back at the nest.

round in its bill and swallowing it head first to avoid any problems with the scales and spines. Other food taken from the lake or stream includes frog tadpoles, small molluscs and crustaceans, and the larvae of caddis and mayflies. But small fish are clearly considered kingfisher delicacies – at this time of year, a male kingfisher frequently offers his catch to his partner as part of their ritual spring courtship.

The male three-spined sticklebacks are now also in their bright breeding livery. Their red bellies almost glow. From March until the end of June each will defend his chosen territory against all other males. He builds a tunnel-shaped nest out of sand and fragments of vegetation which he glues together on the bed of the shallow lake or stream with a secretion from his kidneys. To this underwater bower, the ardent stickleback entices a succession of females with his erotic zigzag dance. Holding his mouth open, he quivers against her flanks, inducing her to spawn in his tunnel. He then fertilizes the eggs and immediately drives away the obliging female. Having successfully wooed several other females, his nest can contain 1000 eggs. These he pugnaciously guards against predators and fans with his tail to enhance the flow of oxygen-rich water while they grow. When the eggs eventually hatch, the ever-attentive father watches over the shoal of tiny fry as they feed on small aquatic insects and crustaceans. If they wander too far from home, he sucks them into his mouth and spits them back into the nest. Within a couple of weeks, they become independent and leave their industrious father to raise several more broods before high summer.

Left The male three-spined stickleback in breeding colours entices the egg-laden female to his nest.

THE CURIOUS CASE OF THE CADDIS

Caddis flies – known to anglers as 'sedges' – are common moth-like insects of rivers, streams and lakes all over Britain. There are nearly 200 species – all of which are rather small and drab, with hairy wings and long antennae held straight ahead when the insect is at rest. Their larvae, however, have a distinctive fascination of their own. They live on the beds of the rivers or lakes above which the adult caddis flies mate and into which the females lay their eggs. When they hatch, the larvae feed on leaves and other detritus and, as they grow, their soft, caterpillar-like bodies become easy targets for fish and other predators such as the adults and larvae of the great diving beetle. To disguise and protect themselves, the larvae of many caddis fly species encase them-selves in protective tubes built from fragments of vegetation or small stones and grains of sand

The larvae of caddis flies can be seen crawling over the beds of ponds and streams, protected by their portable 'homes'. It will be a year or more before they emerge as the 'sedges' familiar to anglers.

dredged from the pond or riverbed. Different caddis larvae employ different materials and techniques according to the water conditions, using a sticky silk extruded from a special gland to cement together their favoured building materials. Relatively safe in their houses, they add to the front of their tubular homes as they grow.

It is possible to identify a specific caddis from the components of its larval case, and the way that it is constructed. There are cases of caddis larvae covered in tiny shells, others apparently decorated with shiny, mineral particles. Their collective name has its origins in the 'caddis man', the country pedlar who carried his wares of pots and pans pinned to his jacket. Unlike its namesake, the curious ornate case of the caddis fly larva is not intended as an advertisement, but for protection and disguise.

Making its ancient way from the source in the Cambrian mountains of central Wales, the River Wye is one of the least adulterated rivers in Britain, with no dams and few artificial embankments, and relatively little industrial or agricultural pollution. For this reason it remains one of Britain's finest for fish. The annual run of salmon starts early in the year and continues until late May. Throughout this spring season mature salmon return to the river of their birth to journey upstream to the shallow spawning grounds. Their first three or four years are spent in the Atlantic Ocean living on a saltwater diet of herring fry and sand eels which makes their silver bodies firm and sleek. Now drawn back to their ancestral breeding grounds, the mature fish stop feeding and prepare for the strenuous journey against the current to reach the cool and shallow headwaters of the River Wye where in autumn large numbers of salmon will congregate to spawn.

The timing of the 'run' and the month of spawning varies river by river. In Scotland, on classic salmon rivers such as the Spey, Dee and Tweed the run takes place between July and November and spawning is an early winter event. What is so intriguing to biologists and anglers alike is the fidelity that each salmon has not only to the river of its birth but to the detailed location of its nursery. Pausing occasionally to rest in holding pools, the fish forge their way upstream. On rivers with waterfalls, salmon have been seen to leap from the water to heights of 3 metres (10 feet) or so. The effort is so exhausting that a fish can lose half its adult weight from its exertions. During the upstream journey, the salmon's skin becomes thickened and rough, and develops a pink breeding hue which fades after spawning. Some fish are so debilitated after the breeding season that they succumb to disease and fail to reach the sea again. Others return to the ocean where they recover to become healthy, silver salmon. After a further year or two at sea, some come back again. Growth rings on their scales have shown that about 7 per cent of the salmon that spawn in the headwaters of the River Wye will make this remarkable spring pilgrimage twice in their lives.

On the steep slopes of the Wye Valley, there are tangible signs of spring. Leaves are beginning to return to the ancient woodland, and so is the sound of birdsong. In early March, you can often hear, and might sometimes see, female robins enticing their mates to feed them. The high-pitched squeaking call is very similar to the cries that will be uttered later by their chicks. The cock robin that responds to this sound by bringing food will clearly make an ideal father. This way the female 'tests' his parental instincts before allowing him to mate with her. By the end of March, they will have established their partnership and begun the business of nesting and rearing their first spring brood.

Lamentably in decline, particularly on farmland, is the dunnock, sometimes misleadingly called a hedge sparrow. This dainty little bird makes up for its drab plumage with its high-pitched, warbling song, a refrain rather like that of the wren, but less insistent. Both species, being so small and largely dependent on insects, suffer a high mortality in severe winters but the wren, in particular, seems to have the capacity to bounce back rapidly. In woodland and gardens, the wren's explosive song belies its small size and is often the only sign of its presence. Skulking by nature, it goes about its early spring activities with great diligence. As soon as the weather permits, the male bird builds a selection of ball-shaped nests from which his mate chooses one which she lines with down and lays up to eight minuscule, white eggs speckled like herself. Wrens are prolific breeders. Starting early in the year they raise two broods by the end of the season, compensating for the heavy toll of winter. In favourable years, this little, brown bird with the big, colourful song can build up to a total British count of seven million pairs, making it the most common breeding bird in Britain.

As March progresses, the other resident birds join in the spring chorus. Through winter all you hear of the blackbird is the cock bird's metallic 'plink, plink, plink' alarm call as it keeps sentinel on behalf of the woodland community – and in gardens warns of the passage of cats. Now in March it can be forgiven for its repetitive persistence as the male develops his rich and fluty song. Rivalling the nightingale in melody and virtuosity, the territorial and courtship performances of the cock blackbird are one of the most distinctive and welcome sounds of spring. From the tops of trees or television aerials, they proclaim their message, and as spring turns into summer, the song becomes more convoluted and voluptuous. For many fans of the British blackbird, its song outshines that of all the warblers and other migrants which soon flock in from distant lands to stake a claim in a corner of Britain. The chiffchaff is the first to arrive. Its two-note song gives this familiar spring bird its English name. The 'chiff' syllable is high-pitched – the 'chaff' is lower, but the two notes are uttered in random order and carry a long way through the crisp air of a March morning.

Above Unlike the willow warbler which it closely resembles visually, the chiffchaff's two-note call is unmistakable, carrying far from high in the leafy canopy.

Blown in by March winds, migrant birds and butterflies from the south make landfall along the English coast. The Isles of Scilly are famous for the early sightings made by dedicated bird-watchers who flock to the island of St Mary's at the first signs of spring. More than 50 low islands and islets make up the archipelago that represents the most southerly tip of Britain, some 48 kilometres (30 miles) west of Land's End. Buffeted by the Atlantic Ocean they act like a beacon to migrant birds coming up from the Bay of Biscay. From their wintering grounds in west and southern Africa, many birds cross into Europe by way of the Strait of Gibraltar and then, hugging the coasts of Spain and France, cross the eastern approaches of the English Channel. Exhausted and hungry, many make landfall on the Scillies. Other prominent touch-downs along the south coast include the Lizard Peninsula and the clifftops of Prawle Point and Start Point in Devon.

THE DECLINE AND RISE OF THE PEREGRINE

Sharp-winged and sharp-eyed, with an immensely powerful frame and formidable talons, the peregrine is a true falcon. To witness this raptor make a kill – either from the cliffs around the coasts or inland across open country – engenders admiration and excitement. This raptor is perfect in every respect, a prince among birds.

To see one flying effortlessly over the sea in pursuit of its prey is an awe-inspiring sight. Like an arrow, it heads off for a distant speck – a passing pigeon or wader. In level flight, the peregrine has the rapid wingbeats of all falcons, but it can soar and glide with exceptional grace and agility. Climbing above its prey, the falcon pauses then 'stoops' with wings pressed to its sides. As it plummets, a stooping peregrine can reach breathtaking speeds, often exceeding 160 kilometres (100 miles) an hour. The 'strike' can be directly from above, or in an arching swoop that impacts from below – the victim being struck by a hind toe of the peregrine and impaled by its lethal, leading claws. Many stoops can miss their target and

From its stronghold in the south-west of England, the peregrine is spreading back to its former haunts, such as the clifftops of Portland Bill overlooking Chesil Beach.

the peregrine will give up the chase. When successful, the bird returns to the cliffs where it plucks its prey, often in preparation for sharing with its family. To the amazement of summer visitors, the clifftops and coastal paths of west Wales, Cornwall, Devon and Dorset as well as those in Scotland can be strewn with feathers, as the young peregrines learn to master their parents' aerial skills – perfecting the art of being a 'bird of prey'. The July 'killing fields' along many of Britain's clifftops are witness to the recent welcome comeback of one of Britain's most impressive wild birds.

The cliffs and crags of western Britain – from the south-west peninsula, through Wales and Cumbria to the Highlands and islands of Scotland – make perfect peregrine country. Secluded nest sites are abundant and smaller birds are plentiful as prey. Pigeons – wild and stray homing birds – are favoured quarry, but species as large as mallard, shelduck, waders and auks, including puffins, will be intercepted, as will smaller birds such

as finches, thrushes and sparrows. In Scotland, the red grouse is fair game to the peregrine. Understandably, the peregrine – like all falcons – has had a poor track-record with gamekeepers and pigeon-fanciers. Throughout the nineteenth century, the gamekeeper's onslaught on the peregrine was unremitting and continued through the twentieth century. The carnage was greatest on the famous shooting areas of northern England and Scotland, but eyries close to pheasant and partridge shoots were seldom spared. From Victorian times, collectors raided peregrine nests for their beautiful eggs which show great variety of colour and patterning, and the rise of popularity in racing pigeons added to the peregrine's decline. During the Second World War, when homing pigeons were employed to carry naval messages, more than 600 peregrines were officially exterminated along the coast. With such prolonged persecution, it is perhaps surprising that the species survived at all.

Ironically, it was Britain's pigeon-fanciers and racers who, unwittingly, alerted the government to the bird's impending population crash. Their petition to the Home Office, complaining that peregrines were impeding their sport, prompted a national survey of peregrines in 1961 which showed that the falcon's numbers had plummeted to almost half their total population at the beginning of the Second World War. But the principal agent was not direct killing – it was poisoning by agricultural chemicals, notably DDT and the related organo-chlorine group of pesticides. The use of these persistent chemicals,

especially as dressings for cereal seeds to control insect crop pests, had intensified in North America and Europe during the 1950s. They were toxic to much wildlife, especially seed-eating birds. In turn, the toxins were picked up by birds of prey which, being higher up the food-chain, concentrated the poisons in their bodies. Some died from poisoning, others were impaired in their breeding. Those that did lay clutches often failed to raise chicks because the eggs had thin shells which broke.

The peregrine suffered particularly badly and its numbers crashed wherever such pesticides were employed. Although the species fared somewhat better in Britain than in several other industrialized countries – notably the USA, Germany and Scandinavia – if the decline had continued unchecked, it is thought that the peregrine would have become extinct in Britain by the end of the 1960s. The voluntary ban on DDT and other harmful pesticides, urgently introduced in the spring of 1962, began to turn the tide. Slowly, the peregrine populations recovered some of their lost ground in Britain, especially in Scotland and the West Country from where they are still spreading along the south coast. Year by year the peregrine has reclaimed its territory around Britain and is spreading into areas where it did not breed previously. Ominously, however, as more and more peregrine-watchers see for themselves piles of plucked pigeon feathers – the evidence of recent peregrine kills – there is now renewed pressure from sporting interests to legalize the culling of this prince of falcons.

Weekend bird-watchers are treated to the spectacle of passerine birds such as pipits, wheatears, chiffchaffs and other early warblers festooning the wind-sculptured hawthorn and gorse bushes that offer these early arrivals their first shelter and chance of food. Once rested, the hordes move on. Just to the east, at Slapton, the first wave of migrants touch down on the shingle beach and brackish ley to bed-and-breakfast on their way north. A similar welcome awaits them at Portland Bill, the high limestone spit that thrusts into the Channel. Below lies Chesil Beach and the Fleet, another combination of shingle bank and a brackish lake that provides the migrants with a drink and tasty pickings. Less welcoming are the pairs of peregrine that patrol the Dorset coastline. An exhausted bird of passage makes easy prey and the perfect parcel for the tiercel to present to his mate as a sign of his continuing commitment. By the end of March, she will be sitting on eggs. From their ledge on Portland Bill, a pair of peregrines scan a wide horizon for the next flock of immigrants.

Behind the sprawling towns of Poole, Bournemouth and Southampton, lie the fragmented heathlands of Hardy's Wessex. Now in March they are ablaze with the yellow blooms of gorse. In the mild winters which seem to have become the recent norm in the south of England, this evergreen shrub often flowers early in January. Its dense spiny foliage affords secure nest sites for birds such as linnets, whinchats and stonechats, and for that denizen of southern heathland, the Dartford warbler. This jaunty long-tailed bird with russet chest and bushy, grey head is uniquely loyal to Britain, remaining resident when other warblers migrate to warmer winter quarters. It relies on insects and spiders for food, and in severe winters its already small and pressured populations can be decimated. With the current effects of global warming, fortunes for the Dartford warbler are improving – and would be even better were it not for the continuing loss of its heathland habitat. A secretive bird, it is heard more than seen. In March the male bird begins to sing its musical, chattering song, staking its own territorial claim before its warbler cousins return from abroad. It scolds intruders with a rasping rattling call, and then flits into the cover of the yellow gorse. When all is clear, it emerges to continue its chattering proclamation and then takes off across the heath in a bouncing flight, still singing.

Above The Dartford warbler is mostly restricted to the heathlands of Dorset and Hampshire, but has established itself in pockets of dense scrub outside its ideal habitat.

Above It is thought that many 'mad March hares' seen 'boxing' are reluctant females fending off their suitors.

Across the open arable lands of the Midlands and East Anglia, March can blow chill winds. From the North Sea and the continent come biting easterlies, threatening sea defences and sending shock waves of winter deep inland. Most wheat crops were sown in late autumn and are now well established as rippling fields of short green stalks. A green winter is one of the hallmarks of contemporary Britain. Only in years when there are heavy snow falls does the farming countryside take on a more traditional winter look. Milder temperatures and changing agricultural cycles have radically altered the winter scene. Mad March hares that once frolicked across bare snow-driven furrows still waiting for shoots to emerge, now perform their extrovert performances against a verdant backdrop – but the spectacle is still one of the highlights of this month and April.

Unlike the rabbit, the brown hare is essentially a solitary animal that lives exclusively above ground. Through the winter, the hare keeps itself warm with the help of its thick coat of brownish fur which is whitish underneath. During the day, it shelters in a narrow 'form' which it digs in the soil with a deeper end to accommodate its bulky hindquarters and long hind legs. With its back to the wind, it sits out the bleakness of winter. At dusk it emerges to forage over grassland and crops.

MUSKY MUSTELIDS

The native otter, badger, pine marten, stoat, weasel and polecat – together with the introduced mink – all belong to a family of long-bodied, short-legged, mainly carnivorous mammals with some 70 species worldwide. One feature common to them all is a gland at the base of the tail which produces a musky odour – and gives them their collective family name, Mustelidae. Notorious for its stink is the skunk of North America – and here in Britain, the odour of the polecat can be almost as pungent. By contrast, otters, which mark their territories with 'spraints' scented by this gland, leave behind an odour which devoted otter-watchers describe as being like new-mown hay or camomile tea.

Both the stoat and the smaller weasel are fierce predators. Their slim bodies allow them to squeeze into crevices and burrows in search of prey – especially weasels which can pursue small rodents such as mice down their burrows. Given a chance, they will eat almost anything they can overcome, including birds and their eggs. Still regarded as vermin by gamekeepers and poultry farmers, a single female weasel will catch and kill hundreds of mice in a year to feed herself and her offspring. In Britain, weasels have two breeding seasons. Males and females normally live in separate territories, but in the early spring, males are attracted to females in season by their specific musky scent, and the female gives birth six weeks later. Later in the year, she mates again, by which time the youngsters from her first litter are mature enough to breed. Weasels live in the 'fast lane' of life – hunting continuously, breeding frequently and prolifically.

The stoat is considerably larger than a weasel and will tenaciously tackle a rabbit six times heavier than itself. Its varied diet enables it to survive almost anywhere in Britain.

The sensitive nose and top lip seek out the most succulent shoots and, like the rabbit, hares re-digest their soft droppings to maximize the nutritional value of the plant. Their large eyes and mobile ears detect danger and their long powerful hind legs give them an impressive head start over predators such as foxes, stoats and dogs, and even over patrolling birds of prey.

Normally a retiring creature, the brown hare, round about March, throws caution to the wind. Although, like rabbits, brown hares breed prolifically at any time of year, it is in early spring, when the days lengthen, that their full repertoire of sexual antics can be seen in broad daylight. The Jack-hares are ready to mate in early January, long before the females – also known as 'Jills' – are receptive.

Stoats are larger mustelids, eat larger prey, breed less often and give birth to smaller litters. They live life at a slower pace and normally survive longer than weasels – often for ten years or more. They mate in summer and, following delayed implantation of the embryo, the females make their dens in rock crevices or an abandoned rabbit burrow and give birth the following March or April – timed to the season when prey is becoming plentiful. In the Highland areas of Scotland, just as in the other alpine regions of Europe, the fur of an adult stoat is creamy-white in winter with the exception of the black tip to its tail. As the snow melts, the white hairs moult and the ermine coat reverts to the normal, red-brown colour with an off-white underside. Throughout the year, stoats are very effective killers. For this reason they have gained a wicked reputation with gamekeepers and poultry farmers whose snares and shotguns have taken a devastating toll on numbers over the last few centuries. The species' survival is largely due to the fact that the individual stoat is highly adaptable and can live for so long.

The stoat's near relative, the much larger polecat, has suffered even greater persecution and is now restricted to a few parts of central Wales, where it is a protected species and making a conspicuous comeback. Hunting mainly at night, it is also a ferocious killer, known to tackle turkeys and geese as well as game birds. The response

of gamekeepers is perhaps not surprising. Polecats that avoid the snares and traps illegally set for them, and survive the rigours of winter, perform their boisterous courtship in March and April, and the jills give birth to their kittens in early summer. Polecat families can be very sociable, grooming and playing with each other and remaining as a group until autumn. Polecats were reintroduced into Cumbria in the 1970s and there are signs that they have been expanding south into Lancashire and eastwards into County Durham – to a mixed reception.

But gamekeepers and wildlife conservationists are united in their antagonism towards the mink, a mustelid imported from North America early in the twentieth century. Bred for its fur in special mink-farms, the alien proved to be an artful escapee – and by the 1950s was breeding in the wild. Like its stoat and weasel cousins, the mink is a voracious killer. Although not as accomplished at swimming as the otter, it takes readily to the water in pursuit of eels and water voles. In winter, when furry animals are scarce, it turns to waterfowl, especially coots and moorhens. The prospect of eradicating the mink from Britain is negligible – unless a humane and safe genetic control can be developed. Fortunately, there is no evidence that mink and otters seriously compete for food, but conservationists remain alarmed at the damage that an expanding mink population can do to bird life.

Like buck rabbits, Jack hares pursue females with frenzied determination, chasing them in circles and often standing upright on their strong hind legs, pawing at unreceptive females like boxing kangaroos. In self-defence, the Jills may also 'box' away their suitors. Apparently oblivious to any outside dangers, the hare community becomes consumed by this spring fever. By the end of March, most adult females will be pregnant and those that were persuaded to mate in early January will already have a litter of two or three leverets. Born above ground, they are much more advanced than new-born rabbits and within a couple of weeks or so will be grazing on their own by night, lying low by day and capable of outrunning most predators.

Despite a century of modern agricultural revolution, the hare is still a feature of East Anglia. It has an affectionate place in local culture and even in the hearts of arable farmers. Norfolk, in particular, is pheasant country and any game is treated with respect. For generations, gamekeepers have declared open war against stoats and weasels and have attempted to banish the fox. The same intolerance has been meted out to birds of prey and carrion crows. Rabbits and hares have been beneficiaries of this selective culling of predators aimed at maximizing game birds such as pheasants and partridges. Other ground-nesting birds have also been helped – species such as lapwing, which in March are setting up their territories. Some parts of East Anglia such as Breckland also play host to the stone curlew, a migrant wader that arrives in March from the warmer south. Its plaintive 'cooeee' cry resembling that of the curlew was formerly heard widely over the downland and heaths of southern and eastern England. Its large, yellow, ring-like eyes, bright yellow legs and white wing-bars are the stone curlew's most distinctive features. If surprised, it freezes pressed tight against the ground with neck stretched forward. If flushed, it seems reluctant to take flight, preferring a dash to safety across the open ground.

Above The nest of the stone curlew is a scrape in the ground, sometimes lined with small pebbles or scraps of vegetation. Males and females have very similar plumage and share the incubation.

Another special East Anglian bird that rarely takes to the air is the bittern. Once fairly common in marshy areas of Britain, this large, brown-buff heron is now a rarity. In the early nineteenth century it was a target for wildfowlers and became extinct as a breeding bird. Migrants from European marshes re-colonized parts of Britain in the early twentieth century and by the 1950s the celebrated spring 'booming' of the male bittern had become a feature of many counties. The deep, resonant note is repeated three or four times in succession and carries for over a mile, advertising the male's presence at the breeding season. During the daytime, bitterns hide in reedbeds where their

Left Cock pheasant displaying. Though not native, this is Britain's most colourful and widespread game bird. It was introduced from Asia in the Middle Ages for its tasty meat.

barred and mottled plumage makes them almost invisible. If alarmed the bird stands motionless with its bill pointing skywards. If provoked it will run through the vegetation and, as a last resort, it lifts into the air and flaps owl-like across the marsh.

The Norfolk Broads remain one of the bitterns' last refuges in Britain. Other reserves where it survives include Minsmere on the Suffolk coast and Leighton Moss on the coast of Lancashire. Originally a tidal arm at the north end of Morecambe Bay, it was cut off in Victorian times by an embankment and sluice gate. For almost a century it was drained and farmed until, in the early twentieth century, it was allowed to become a freshwater marsh fed by several streams. This small, attractive wooded valley now surrounds one of the most interesting areas of fenland in northern Britain with abundant birdlife as well as red deer and otters. By the end of March at Leighton Moss, you will hear the drumming of snipe as these long-billed waders perform their splendid aerial courtship displays. Both male and female climb with strong, rapid wingbeats in towering circles above the marsh. They can reach a height of several hundred feet from where they dive with wings half open and their outer tail feathers widespread. As they plummet towards the ground, the air-stream vibrates the two outermost feathers, creating a drumming sound reminiscent of a bleating goat. A raised railway line runs along one side of the reserve. The rumble of the distant train mingling with the drumming of the snipe and the sonic boom of the bittern is the classic spring call-sign of this small reserve – and a reassuring reminder that the clock can be turned back.

Inland from Morecambe Bay lie the Pennines, the spine of northern England. At the more southerly end of this range, between Manchester and Sheffield, lie the modest peaks of Bleaklow Hill and Kinder Scout, both just over 600 metres (2000 feet). These are the highest points in the so-called Peak District which in reality is a plateau of peat-covered moors divided by deep, limestone dales. By the end of March the Dales are alive to the song of migrant chiffchaffs which spread quickly from the south. One week they are seen for the first time on the south coast of England; the next they can be setting up home in the heart of the Peak District. The chances are that the mature adults now returning to breed were last year's offspring reared in the same dale. Close behind them come migrant wheatears. These smart-looking members of the thrush family inherit their name from the Anglo-Saxon words 'hwit' and 'oers' meaning 'white' and 'rump' – which is the most noticeable feature of the male as he flits close to the ground. He alights frequently on stones and fence-posts, bobbing his head and flicking his tail. Some wheatears move on further north as the weather improves. Those that stay will soon pair and nest in rabbit burrows or in the crevices of limestone walls here. By the time that April arrives, their courtship songs will be heard in almost all the upland country of Britain – a sure sign that spring is on the way.

Some years Easter falls before the final gales of March have blown their full course. A complicated ecclesiastical formula directs that Easter Day itself should be celebrated on the Sunday immediately following the first full moon after the spring equinox – unless that day itself is a Sunday which delays Easter by another week. The earliest that Easter Day can fall is March 22nd – the latest is more than a full month later, April 25th. Year by year Easter takes the British people by surprise and further confuses the threshold of spring. For a nation preoccupied with talk of seasons and the weather, the real red-letter day for celebration is the day the clocks go forward. Overnight the gloom of winter is banished and there is an instant feeling of well-being.

Right Male wheatear with food. One of the earliest summer migrants to arrive in Britain, the wheatear soon moves north to the uplands where its brief but vigorous warble heralds the arrival of spring.

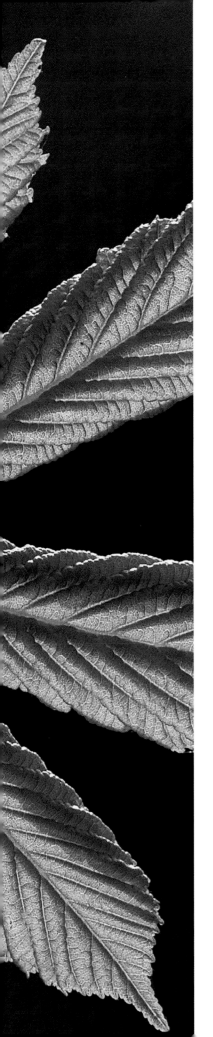

'the exuberance

of birdsong

elevates the mind'

April

Above The nodding, yellow flowers of cowslips were once as
familiar as buttercups. Happily they still spring up in clumps along the
embankments of motorways cut through chalk landscape.
Left Newly unfurled horse chestnut leaves.

Spring is a tentative time of year. As the sun begins to strengthen and to release winter's grip on the land, the soil warms but the air is still cold. This bittersweet mixture brings fine spells of sunshine followed by squally showers. The nights are still frosty, but just as the days seem to be more settled, a deep depression whistles down from the Arctic, bringing sleet and snow. The name of the month derives from the Latin 'aperire', to open. From the Mediterranean to southern Scandinavia, April sees the opening of buds to reveal spring-green leaves. Bud-burst and the greening of the countryside is one of the joys of living in a temperate part of the world where the seasons are so distinct. Here in Britain, the flush of spring moves northwards up the length of the land, at walking pace – from the Isles of Scilly to Shetland. But even at the end of May there are places in northern Britain still waiting to shake off the hard, drawn-out winter.

The New Forest in Hampshire is a magnificent example of ancient, southern woodland. Lying between the suburbia of Southampton and Bournemouth, it is an area of almost 390 square kilometres (150 square miles) embracing a mosaic of deciduous woodland, heathland and farmland. Its status as a royal hunting forest was won under the patronage of William the Conqueror, who clearly valued its beauty and natural wealth. That this expanse of English landscape was designated as a 'new forest' almost a millennium ago is testament to William's foresight. While, all around it, the centuries have taken their toll, this mature but managed tract of southern England is one of the few places in the densely populated south country that has retained a feeling of the original wildwood. To explore it in April, when the canopy is beginning to turn green, is to be transported back to a time in our country's natural history when the woodland way of life prevailed. Here you can find many of the native plants and animals that shaped the nature of Britain.

Right A New Forest beech wood in spring – haunt of fallow deer.

CROWNING GLORY

Up and down the country, all the larger species of deer, including the fallow, sika and red deer, shed their antlers by spring. It is an undignified process leaving some animals temporarily lopsided. Where they detach from the crown of the head, each antler leaves a circle of bloody tissue which heals over to form a bump from which the new one will grow. It seems an extravagant process which must drain the males of energy and nutrients. For this reason, in parts of Scotland with impoverished soils, some red deer stags develop small antlers or none at all. Contrary to expectation, some of the finest heads of red deer are found in the south of England, in such places as Exmoor and the Quantock Hills of Somerset. The fallow deer, which is predominantly southern in its distribution, has less difficulty with its nutrition and the bucks can grow very impressive antlers.

During May and June, the rudimentary antlers are covered by special skin matted with short, fine hairs. This 'velvet' is rich in blood vessels which carry the minerals and oxygen to the fast-growing bony sculpture within. At least, in spring, there is an ever-increasing supply of nutritious fresh leaves and shoots to nurture the deer to their prime. When a young male fallow deer is about a year old, it develops a pair of slender, unbranched prongs, which give it the name 'pricket'. The following year it grows a pair of antlers, each of which is branched into two

Fallow deer bucks shed their palmate antlers between March and June.

tines. Year by year, the complexity of the antlers increases until, at about the fifth spring, the full head of palmate antlers is achieved. In subsequent years, extra finger-like forms called 'spellers' are added to the main body of the antler. It is this palmate shape which easily distinguishes the fallow buck from the red deer stag who sports a distinctly branched pair of antlers.

Whereas in Scotland it is the red deer that holds pride of place, in woodlands of southern Britain, the fallow deer is by far the more common of these two species. Free-roaming herds have lived for centuries in the ancient forests of southern England – places such as the Forest of Dean that borders the River Wye, Epping Forest just north of London, and the New Forest. A herd of fallow deer moving silently through such woodland at the beginning of spring, before the leaves have shut out the light, is a memorable sight. These large mammals prefer to forage at dawn or dusk and are best viewed from the 'high-seats' which are often a feature of such places. To climb up onto one of these viewing platforms before first light, when breath mingles with frosty air, is to experience an English wood at one of its timeless moments. The shapes of the deer emerging from the morning mist have a classic quality which instantly transports you to another, more ancient Living Britain.

Above Wood anemones flower on the forest floor before the canopy of leaves closes above them, shutting out the light.

The wood anemone is one of the most reliable indicators of ancient woodland. It flowers from March until May, depending on how far up the country the warmth and light of spring has reached. So sensitive to light are these plants that they raise their drooping blush-pink heads at the first hint of sunshine. When clouds or dusk return, they nod demurely towards the soil. Here in Britain, its seeds are rarely fertile. Instead, it spreads imperceptibly across the woodland floor through the growth of its root system – at a rate of perhaps no more than 2 metres (7 feet) every 100 years. If you find a large patch, you can be sure that it has been growing there for centuries. Where you discover the flowers growing in the open, such as on the edge of meadowland or hedge banks, you can be equally sure that the delicate anemones are living relics of wildwood long since felled.

Despite being rich in nutrients the forest floor is not the ideal place for plants to grow. As spring advances and the canopy closes, the ground is shaded and many species cannot thrive. Many species

THE BRIMSTONE – THE ORIGINAL BUTTER-FLY

Most plants depend on insects of some kind for their pollination. The chief pollinator of woodland primroses in much of Britain is the brimstone butterfly. So common and distinctively butter-coloured is this insect that it was probably the first to be called a 'butter-fly' – a term which, in time, was used for all species. The name 'brimstone' also refers to the sulphur yellow of the upper side of the males' wings. The undersides of both sexes are greener and veined like leaves, which allows them to merge with vegetation such as the ivy in which they hibernate. Their ability to overwinter as adults ensures that the brimstone is one of the first butterflies to re-appear in spring. As early as February – sometimes January nowadays – this large and strikingly coloured butterfly can been seen flying powerfully through woodland

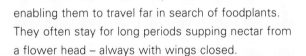

Although the adult brimstone butterfly sups nectar from a variety of flowers through the year, its caterpillars are entirely dependent on the leaves of two foodplants – the buckthorn and the alder buckthorn.

and along hedgerows. The females lay their eggs on the leaves of our two species of buckthorn trees, the principal foodplants of their caterpillars. Unlike many butterflies which lead brief lives as adult butterflies, the brimstone can live for almost twelve months. When the primroses have wilted, the adult moves to other plants for nectar. In late summer, brimstone butterflies can been seen probing their long tongues into the purple flowers of thistles and knapweed, and buddleia bushes in gardens. Paler brimstones could be mistaken for the cabbage white butterfly – but the flight of the brimstone is much more powerful and direct, enabling them to travel far in search of foodplants. They often stay for long periods supping nectar from a flower head – always with wings closed.

for which woodland is their natural home survive by flowering early in the spring or in the more open glades and margins of the forest. Plants such as orchids often flourish where trees have fallen through lightning strikes and gales or simply through old age. April is a good time to see them, although many woodland orchids continue to flower through to June. The early purple orchid, not surprisingly, is the first to appear. This handsome orchid with glossy, blotched leaves can grow to more than half a metre (1½ feet). When in flower, it fills the air with a feminine lily-of-the-valley scent which belies the masculinity of the pair of root tubers beneath each plant, a common characteristic of orchids. Later in the summer, other orchids enliven the gloomy woodland floor, but by then other ground vegetation often obscures their beauty and they bloom unseen by us.

Left For most of the year, adders are very sociable, hibernating or lying together in groups of males and females. At spring mating time, the males challenge one another in a bizarre test of dominance in which they rear up as if dancing, and then twist around each other in a strenuous trial of serpentine strength.

In the rides and glades of the New Forest, the warmth of April breathes new life into dormant snakes. Britain's largest snake, the grass snake, passes the winter in safe places beneath the roots of trees or under brushwood. Usually several associate together, entwined in intricate knots. Cool spring mornings are the best time to see them after they emerge from hibernation. It takes several hours of basking before they can move with any speed, and, with the vegetation still low, they are much easier to spot. The same applies to adders, distinguished by the dark zigzag down the backs of both sexes. The design does, however, make adders more difficult to see against the dappled forest floor. Both species are sexually active soon after they wake from hibernation. Snake courtship is a very energetic business, perhaps none more so than that of adders. The females emerge from hibernation a couple of weeks later than the males and soon after, usually in mid-April, the competing males perform the so-called 'adder dance'. In the vicinity of a female, two male adders approach each other and suddenly rear up together in a sinuous and synchronized set of movements. Twisting around his rival, each male strives to reach higher and higher in a sequence of violent movements. When they can rise no farther, they untwist and start again. The 'dance' sometimes continues for more than an hour. It is one of the most bizarre rituals of any reptile in the world. Finally one of them – usually the smaller – submits and makes an escape. He is pursued briefly by the victor, who then approaches the female and begins his equally elaborate courtship which involves much rubbing of bodies and flicking of his forked tongue. Mating itself takes a further two hours, by which time the brief April day has almost passed, and the cool evening air subdues the ardour of these splendid creatures.

An April morning can be enticing. The freshness and clarity of the air, and the exuberance of birdsong invigorates the eyes and ears, and elevates the mind. In town and country alike, this is a very special time of year. In towns it is often the trees which help us trace the progress of the year. Whether they are native, like the oaks of Greenwich and other city parks, or long-established introductions like the sycamore and lime, the magnificent horse chestnut and the ubiquitous London plane tree, all trees are a window on the seasons. Because of the heat generated by cities, the buds of urban trees usually open earlier than in the countryside. Introduced trees, however graceful, are not as attractive to native wildlife as the species that made up Britain's ancient woodlands. They and the wildlife they support have had a long, shared natural history. If, on a sunny April morning, you stop and observe a native birch tree, for example, you will see and hear that it is alive with birds and insects.

The birch was one of the first pioneering species to become naturally established in Britain, in the wake of the retreating glaciers. It is still a pioneering species today. Given a chance, saplings will shoot up in gardens and on rough ground and wasteland. Hardy by nature, the birch can grow in difficult conditions, forcing its way through the rubble of an abandoned city site or quickly becoming established if planted along the kerbsides of new housing estates. In April the more conspicuous male catkins of the birch produce great quantities of pollen which are carried by the wind in yellow clouds to pollinate the female catkins of other birches. The ripe, heavily laden catkins attract insects which in turn are a magnet for insect-eating birds. Acrobatic blue tits and great tits flock to birches – sometimes with goldfinches, redpolls and siskins – calling excitedly as they probe catkins and developing leaf buds. It is now prime breeding time for long-tailed tits. These minute birds often build their elaborate, oval nests in the dense shrubs on urban wasteland. As many as a dozen chicks can be waiting to be fed, as their parents flit energetically on whirring wings from tree to tree in search of small insects and spiders. Their long-tailed profile and bouncing flight is unmistakable, and a glimpse of these minute but extrovert birds going about their spring business is a real treat.

MORE SILENT SPRINGS?

April in Britain is a month blessed by birdsong. From rooftops and fences, treetops and hedges, in town and country, you can hear an astonishing variety of territorial and courtship calls. The most beautiful of these are delivered by some of our most familiar garden songbirds : thrushes, blackbirds, robins, chaffinches, dunnocks and wrens. Out in the country, the dawn chorus is amplified by other songsters such as skylarks and yellowhammers, turtle doves and reed buntings. The list goes on. We think of their songs as an essential and enduring part of spring.

The reality is that, for the last quarter of the twentieth century, most of these bird species have been in decline. Only the robin, chaffinch and wren have held their numbers. The problem is not an urban issue – it is rural. The culprit is modern farmland and the way it is treated with chemicals. A report to the government published in 1997 graphically demonstrated that many familiar and much-loved songbirds were disappearing from farmland at an alarming rate. Some species, such as song thrushes, tree sparrows, turtle doves and skylarks, were down by more than 50 per cent – sometimes much more – compared with their populations 25 years earlier. Other farmland birds such as lapwings and grey partridges had suffered similar devastation. The common factor

Song thrushes – like many other birds – feed their nestlings almost exclusively on caterpillars and other insect larvae. Pesticides are often applied at peak breeding time for many farmland birds – killing the grubs and starving the chicks.

was the increased use of pesticides on crops and other intensive practices that reduced the food available to these birds – particularly in spring and early summer when they are feeding their newly-hatched youngsters. Some, like partridges, are primarily seed eaters when adult, but their chicks need the high protein content of insects and other small invertebrates. It is these bugs and beetles, weevils and aphids that are targeted by the farmers' insecticides. The result is that on farmland sprayed by these chemicals, many young birds starve to death.

In many ways, the report echoed the warning issued 35 years earlier by the American ecologist and writer, Rachel Carson. In her shocking but bestselling book, 'Silent Spring', she drew the attention of the USA and the rest of the world to the damage being inflicted by organo-chlorine insecticides such as DDT and by other powerful chemicals which were being used so profligately to promote crop production, by killing plant and insect pests. The ecological downside of the increased financial yields was the direct effects of the poisons on other harmless wildlife. Many birds and other creatures were either killed directly by poisoning or, as

with peregrine falcons and other birds of prey, DDT accumulated in their food-chain and thinned the shells of their eggs. Rachel Carson's damning prophecy of a 'Silent Spring' for the world helped ban DDT and restrict the use of similar chemicals. It seemed that a brighter future for the wildlife of farmland was assured.

Today's agro-chemicals are much more selective in their action – but are also much more powerful. There has been a revolution in their production and application. But their purpose is still to kill the plants and insects that compete with or damage commercial crops, and the victims, whether intended or not, are often the mainstay food for young farmland birds. The effect of modern pesticides is more insidious than the pesticides of Rachel Carson's time, but their impact on the numbers of many songbirds and other inhabitants of farmland is no less real. Rough calculations show that recently about one million birds have been lost each year from the British breeding population. Unless the farming and agro-chemical industry, in tandem with the government, changes some of its policies and practices, much of twenty-first century Britain will be heading for another silent spring.

THE FOX – GREAT SURVIVOR FROM THE WILDWOOD

Since Aesop wrote his fables, 'Reynard' has endured a chequered reputation. To many sheep and poultry farmers, and most gamekeepers – even to some wildlife conservationists – the fox is seen as a pest. To the rest of us, it is one of the most charismatic native creatures of our country.

At the end of each winter, there are perhaps a quarter of a million foxes in Britain. Only 14 per cent of these live in our cities. The rest are rural foxes – just like they've always been. Each spring, the population increases by some 425,000, when the cubs are born, but each year about the same number of foxes die from one cause or another. In 1995, at the time when the issue of fox hunting featured high on the national agenda, it was thought that between 15,000 and 20,000 foxes were killed each year by registered hunts and maybe the same number again by unregulated groups hunting on foot with hounds and shotguns or rifles. A further 100,000 were killed by gamekeepers and landowners on the grounds that foxes prey on their pheasants and other livestock. To this toll, we should add a further 100,000 deaths caused by us as a direct result of being hit by our vehicles. That suggests that roughly half of each year's deaths are due to natural causes, such as disease or starvation, or simply old age. It is interesting that the total fox population in Britain appears to be stable. Like some other mammals, if conditions are unfavourable for bringing up cubs, a pregnant vixen will re-absorb the embryos of her unborn litter. If food is scarce or competition high because of a marked rise in the fox population, natural controls seem to adjust the numbers of offspring born each year. This is one of the reasons why many experts believe that artificial fox control has very little effect on the overall numbers of foxes in Britain.

What is more influential is the character of the landscape and the availability of food. This is the main reason why foxes are doing well in many of our cities, and also why they are on the increase in many upland areas such as central Wales. Here forestry plantations offer them good cover in which to find shelter and to rear their young in spring. The time when the fox cubs are being weaned coincides with the time when hill sheep are producing lambs. No wonder sheep farmers grazing their livestock in upland areas feel most at risk. But it is revealing that very few of them have ever witnessed a fox killing a lamb. Many lambs die from exposure at that altitude – easy pickings for a vixen with cubs to feed. Few people would begrudge the fox this spring-time bonus, and to the farmer, the fox is doing a service as a refuse collector.

It is when foxes turn their attentions to treasured wildlife that passions run high. On coasts such as north Norfolk, they have been proved responsible for the decimation of tern colonies at breeding time, and on hills and moorland they are known to prey on the eggs and chicks of ground-nesting birds such as lapwings, red grouse and snipe. In upland Wales, the fox is thought to be a major contributor to the drop in numbers of black grouse, and in Scotland, the fox has been proved to raid the nests of the rare capercaillie that breed on protected nature reserves. For the conservation organizations, such as the Royal Society for the Protection of Birds (RSPB), responsible for the management of these special areas, the fox problem is a thorny dilemma.

Throughout history we have admired the adaptability and resourcefulness of the fox – which was here in Britain before the last Ice Age, alongside sabre-toothed tigers.

At first light, wasteland in cities can become a playground for young foxes. These days you are more likely to encounter the red fox, Britain's largest land carnivore, in an urban setting than in the open country. During the second half of the twentieth century, foxes have become an accepted feature of several major conurbations – notably Bristol, Birmingham, Brighton, Bournemouth, Nottingham, the West Midlands, some boroughs of London, and Edinburgh. The garden suburbs built between the wars seem to create ideal fox habitat, supporting higher densities of animals than in the countryside beyond the city limits. But most of Britain's 240,000 adult fox population still lives a traditional rural life, never venturing far away from the security of woodland and fields. Town fox and country fox are one and the same species, although their general appearance and behaviour often sets them apart. Diet and habitat may be very different, but their biology and social life is very similar. Watching a family at play on a derelict city site reveals just as much of the essential nature of the fox as observing their more retiring country cousins.

As in the country, peak mating time for urban foxes is January. A vixen's pregnancy lasts a little under two months, by which time she has selected an earth in which to rear her cubs. The raised sheds of gardens and allotments or the space beneath the floorboards of a house are favoured sites for dens. Some vixens dig fresh earths in railway embankments or in parks, cemeteries and private gardens. It is here that the cubs, usually three to six in number, are born on the bare soil; unlike the badger, the fox does not drag bedding into its den. Cubs as young as three weeks may peer from the entrance of the earth, their eyes barely open and still very wobbly on their legs. Now in April, the outside world has much to attract them, and over the next few weeks they venture out into the open to explore and play. The watchful vixen performs most of the parental duties, but the dog fox may visit the den and play with his offspring. The chances are that elsewhere he has at least one other family. By the end of April, the cubs are large and confident enough to be taken hunting by their mother.

Out in the open country, rising temperatures and lengthening days bring a white-out of blackthorn blossom. This large shrub, almost a tree, is native throughout Britain. It forms thorny thickets which provide other plants with shelter from browsing and grazing animals, and secure nest sites for many birds. For the same reason, it is planted as a hedging shrub, to contain livestock and deter trespassers. Blackthorn flowers early when easterly winds can still bring severe weather. Traditionally known as 'blackthorn winters', these sudden cold snaps remind us that April is indeed a fickle month. The wise saying 'Ne'er cast a clout ere May is out' refers not to the month of May but to the blossom of the May tree, known also as hawthorn. When its white flowers adorn hedgerows, spring is here to stay.

Left Unlike any other bird, the dipper seeks its food by diving and walking underwater along the beds of shallow streams. Head down against the current, its broad back takes the strain and keeps its feet on the ground. It raises young in April and May, mainly in upland country with clear, fast-flowing streams.

In upland areas of Britain, the uncertain nature of April is even more apparent. In the Welsh hills, lambing is often not complete until the end of the month, which is just as well because even at these modest altitudes, snow can fall until well after Easter. These cold snaps delay the growth of the grass, which is why hill farmers put their ewes to the ram much later than in lowland regions. The five-month gestation period is timed to ensure that the lambs are born when the weather is less severe and when the hill grass has started to grow. Before this can happen, the soil must reach the critical temperature of 6 degrees centigrade. The higher the altitude, the later and shorter is the productive growing season. Even a 40-metre (130-feet) increase in altitude takes a week off the time. The brevity of the summer in hill country sets an urgent pace for all the processes of nature. Where possible, some bird species start their courtship rituals early in the year, to ensure that no time is wasted when the weather becomes more benign and their young can be nurtured. Black grouse are found, albeit sparsely, in the hill-country of central Wales. Their haunts are the wooded fringes of moorland where they make use of a variety of habitats for feeding on insects and vegetation. The cock bird has splendid glossy, blue-black plumage, a distinctive lyre-shaped tail and red wattles above his eyes. Known as the 'blackcock', he is one of Britain's most distinguished native game birds. Scotland has the largest numbers, but black grouse also inhabit the moors of Wales and the Lake District, Dartmoor, parts of the Pennines and in Northumberland. What is special about these birds is the way they perform their communal courtship on a display ground known as a 'lek'. An annual competitive display of male egos takes place on these specially designated open arenas, some of which are known to have been used by successive generations of black grouse for more than 50 years. The males are polygamous and there is great rivalry between them for the attention and favours of the rather dull-coloured hens. The senior males establish territorial patches within the lekking arena, with the top bird occupying centre stage. Those blackcocks that are successful at defending their patches, stand a better chance of winning the attentions of hens visiting the lek – and a better chance of mating.

The blackcocks' aggressive posturing changes to one of competitive 'dancing' when ladies are present. With hoarse cries, they leap into the air in their attempts to win attention. If a female seems impressed, the male adopts a more deliberate and less frenetic exhibition of plumage display, designed to charm the female into submission. All this male exhibitionism is accompanied by curious whirring calls. Both sexes are highly promiscuous, males attempting to mate with any female that enters his patch by design or accident. For their part the females seem to find any energetic male totally irresistible. The object of all this exercise at the lek is to ensure that sufficient young black grouse are produced to maintain the population. In recent decades, however, the species has dramatically declined in Britain – sadly a reflection of the loss of wildness in our hill-country.

By the close of April, the vanguard of spring has reached the lowlands of Scotland and is advancing on the Highlands. South of the Great Glen that cuts its narrow diagonal rift across the Highlands, lie Glen Tanar on Deeside, the Black Wood of Rannoch in Perth and Kinross, and Abernethy Forest on Speyside – all vestiges of the ancient pine forest. These are magical places, particularly in the turning-times of spring and autumn. Now at the end of April, it is in some of these precious remains of the 'Wood of Caledon' that you might hear, and even see, one of Britain's most spectacular birds – the capercaillie. This large and very handsome game bird took up residence in the primeval forest as soon as the native pines became established in the wake of the last Ice Age. The forest was probably at its peak 7000 years ago. Now, through climate change and felling, a mere 1 per cent remains. This relentless loss of habitat and the appeal of the capercaillie as a game bird, contributed to its demise. By the late eighteenth century the last few birds had been shot for the pot and the species became extinct in Britain. The present stock is mainly descended from birds reintroduced from Sweden in 1837. Since then, at this season, they have celebrated their ancient Caledonian birth rights in spectacular style.

The male capercaillie's iridescent, blue-black dress gives it a military look, enhanced by the metallic-green gorget across its neck and breast, and white epaulettes on the shoulders. Above each eye is a long, vermilion wattle. With its fiercely curved bill and legs feathered almost to the toes, it seems confidently ready for battle. The encounters between rival males usually take place before

dawn. There is an earnestness about this bird which commands respect. Unlike the black grouse, each cock has his distinct patch of forest. At night he roosts on a pine branch overlooking his territory. From here, before first light, he flaps noisily to the ground to deliver his territorial challenge into the cold morning air. Strutting slowly round the invisible margins of his terrain, he pauses now and again to feed

Left The cock capercaillie is famous for his aggressive courtship display and extraordinary 'clip-clop' vocalizing. The name derives from the Gaelic 'capullcoille' meaning 'horse of the woods'.

from the forest floor. Then, as if suddenly prompted, the capercaillie lifts his neck and head in a very upright, military carriage and calls out into the silent forest. The guttural sound he utters resembles the hollow 'clip-clop' of horses' hooves, which accelerates to an explosive climax. All the time, he holds his tail feathers in an impressive fan with his wings drooping slightly on each side of his taut body. Slowly turning his head from side to side, the cock bird surveys the dawn forest around him, his eyes and ears alert to signs of a rival. Any male intruder is met by a ferocious assault. The occupier of the territory at first falls ominously silent, then with much flailing of wings, head and feet, launches his attack until the interloper flees. Such displays and routs often go unnoticed by the hen birds, but, sometimes, in the pine trees, as if viewing from the gallery of a theatre, female capercaillies gather to witness this exciting dawn performance, before dropping to the ground and offering themselves for mating.

For most bird species in Scotland, May and June will be prime breeding time. The pair of golden eagles high on the crag are still incubating their precious clutch of two eggs. Through all of April, the female has done most of the sitting. Perhaps sensing the nearness of her mate, she rises up from the eyrie with powerful ease, and wings effortlessly along the glen. As if on that signal, the male golden eagle appears from beyond the upper ridge and joins her in the sky. As they glide in unison, you can see that he is distinctly smaller. The two soon separate, the female continuing on her purposeful course, perhaps in search of prey, or simply to stretch her wings after her day-long confinement on the nest. The male heads back with majestic, unhurried wingbeats and drops down on the eyrie to begin his vigil. His mate has reached the head of the glen. On a damp mountain ledge high above the scree, the closely packed flowers of purple saxifrage are forcing their heads through a recent fall of snow. This brilliant splash of colour is the only relief in a bleak, grey scene. To reach the High Tops, the walking pace of spring has still some way to go.

Meanwhile, in the south of Britain, summer visitors have arrived from Africa. Over farmland, swallows are hawking for early insects, and in towns, the welcome scream of swifts cascades from a blue, late-April sky. Across the wooded areas of lowland Britain, male and female cuckoos have taken up residence. The males are already displaying and noisily announcing their availability while each female keenly defends her chosen territory where, in late May, she will perform her infamous deeds. For us, the instantly recognizable call of the cuckoo marks the end of that uncertain time when winter is reluctant to bow out, and spring stays in the wings.

'heady scents

pervade the

woodland air'

May

Above Roe deer fawn in spring

Left Of all spring flowers, bluebells capture the character of
the season, when warmth has returned but the canopy of leaves
has not yet closed – such as in this young beech plantation.

The name 'May' probably derives from the ancient Sanskrit word 'mah' which means 'to grow'. More recently, in classical mythology, the name 'Maia' was given to the brightest of the seven heavenly sisters that made up the star constellation of Pleiades, a conspicuous feature of the night sky at the beginning of May in southern Europe. In Britain, however, dawns in early May are often characterized by fog which descends as moisture-laden breezes from northern Europe and condenses over much of the land. Because so many May Day celebrations are likely to be dampened by fog, towns and villages often postpone their events until later in the month. The offset in season can be squarely blamed on Pope Gregory who introduced his new Gregorian calendar to Europe in 1582. Designed, quite correctly, to lose 11 days from that year to make up for previous unaccounted leap years, the effect was to drag the first of May back earlier in the season. In Protestant Britain people rioted, claiming that they would lose 11 days from their lives. It would be another 70 years before this country fell into line and accepted that May Day, over here, would forever come too soon.

At Magdalen College, Oxford, there is a medieval bell tower standing within the college grounds. On the first day of May, just before sunrise, cassocked choristers climb the narrow, stone stairs which open to the roof. Here, high above the city, the view can be spectacular. More often than not, on May Day all you see is fog. On the last stroke of six o'clock, the pure sounds of the choir sing a joyous chorus in celebration of spring. Beyond the spires, now emerging from night, the rising sun slowly burns away the gloom and heralds the start of another May.

To the immediate south of the tower is an extensive meadow, a rare and valuable asset here in the heart of the city. For centuries, it has been a haven of tranquillity for scholars of the college and an oasis for wildlife. Surrounded by a spectacular variety of trees, this low-lying pasture often floods in winter. By April, like all such wet meadows, it begins to dry out and to bloom in a succession of spectacular spring and early summer wild flowers. The most famous of Magdalen's floral displays is that of snake's-head fritillaries. This exquisite plant once graced most ancient flood meadows across the south and east of England. The timing of the hay making was critical. If the grass crop was cut too soon, many species of flowering plant were unable to produce their seed. Where the fritillary survives, it does so only because traditional practices have been deliberately retained. Several sites in Oxfordshire are famous for the flowering of these rare botanical beauties, and one meadow at Cricklade in Wiltshire contains 80 per cent of the nation's fritillary population. As the first rays of May Day streak across the Magdalen meadow, most of the fritillary blooms are past their prime and have set seed. Nevertheless, a few late-flowering heads open their delicate, chequered, purple and white blooms to greet the sunlight. Unlike modern fields of grass, this meadow will not be mown until all the flowers have matured. The choristers' dawn chorus from the tower and this fading field of fritillaries are evocative relics of another, bygone Britain.

As the Oxford day progresses and the air warms up, screaming mobs of swifts recently arrived from tropical Africa, dash between the college towers, diving in pursuit of swarms of flying insects that rise in clouds above the busy city. Soon the swifts will start to build their nests in the holes and crevices of buildings. This is the only time in their hectic lives when they stop flying and touch down. Feeding, drinking, mating, and even sleeping, are accomplished on the wing. If forced involuntarily to the ground, their tiny, fragile legs make it difficult for them to struggle back into the air. They are masters of the sky, out-flying even the most agile birds of prey. At dusk, as May advances, gangs of these aerial revellers can be seen and heard soaring ever higher in pursuit of another meal, until they disappear from sight, leaving a trail of summer sounds.

Equally tireless are the swallows that return in April and early May to rear their

Above The chequered purple flowers of the snake's-head fritillary, once common on water-meadows across southern England, now bloom in only a handful of protected sites.

families in Britain. More evident in the open countryside, they, like swifts, are dependent on a plentiful supply of insects. If you walk downwind of a reservoir or lake on a balmy May evening, you will be surrounded by hundreds of swallows, swooping for flying insects that have just emerged from

their aquatic larvae. Males and females court each other with extravagant aerial displays and preening on the ground. The pair construct their nest in barns and farm outbuildings, even under the roofs of open porches and garages in villages. Never far from people, they probably shared caves with the earliest inhabitants of Britain. Like the screams of swifts, their twittering warbles are a sure sign that summer is here to stay.

House martins, close relatives of swallows, arrive a little later. They make great use of our homes and outbuildings for nest sites. A pair will return faithfully to the same house to repair the nest they built the year before or to construct a new one next to it. The house martin must have been exclusively a cliff and cave dweller before our ancestors settled down and built homes with convenient, overhanging eaves. Collecting beakfuls of mud from the edges of ponds or field puddles, the industrious pair lay down successive layers, reinforced with plant fibres, until the deep saucer-shaped nest is complete. The entrance hole is small enough to exclude even an inquisitive sparrow. In the security of this immaculate home, lined with feathers, the pair will raise their family. For those privileged people whose homes are chosen by house martins, the close presence of such diligent and dedicated birds is a constant source of summer entertainment.

The only member of the swallow family to visit Britain that retains its independence from us and our buildings is the sand martin. As its name suggests, it excavates tunnels into sand or gravel faces, often in quarries or road and rail cuttings. Like swifts and swallows, sand martins are very sociable and a colony may consist of hundreds of pairs nesting close together. Each bird burrows with its beak, scraping away the loose sand with its tiny feet, before lining the end of the tunnel with a litter of dry grass, straw and feathers. By the end of May, many pairs have chicks and the colony becomes a hectic place. The adult birds constantly commute between their burrows and nearby feeding grounds where insects are plentiful. By the end of June most chicks have fledged and left the colony to join their parents in the great flocks that are a feature of our summer sky.

Above Spring sweeps northwards and upwards. The hill-country of northern England responds to the warmth and longer hours of daylight, such as in this wild flower meadow in the Peak District of Derbyshire.

Right Sand martins live up to their name – nesting colonially in burrows that they excavate in sand quarries and other vertical sand-banks in cliffs or river sides.

THE BUGS OF MAY

Two insect specialities of May that carry the name of the month are the mayflies and may bugs that emerge at the first hint of real warmth. Mayflies are the freshwater insects described by the poet Shelley as creatures 'gathered into death without a dawn'. He was referring to the ephemeral nature of their beautiful adult form which flies for just a day. In contrast, their larvae, known as 'nymphs', live unseen beneath the water for a year or more, feeding on the vegetation in lakes, streams and rivers, and moulting as they grow. Finally, in late spring, they swim upwards and struggle through the surface tension to reach the air where they shed their larval skin. The winged insect that first emerges is not the adult form. This is what fishermen call the 'dun'. Its entire body, including its wings, is encased in an opaque skin which, within hours, is moulted, revealing the exquisitely delicate adult mayfly. This is the 'spinner' that excites fishermen and trout alike. They swarm in vast numbers above the surface of the water, the males rising and falling as they perform their marvellous nuptial dance. Attracted by this mass display of masculinity, the females join them, and mating follows in the air. Dropping to the water, the females lay their eggs, and then die. Exhausted from their frenetic aerial ballet, the male spinners also drop to the water where, trapped by the surface tension, their struggles attract the attentions of trout that rise to liberate the mayflies from their dying throes.

The trout fisherman casting his hand-spun spinner, imitates the mayfly's final curtain call, and beguiles his quarry. To him, more than anyone, this annual event on the famous trout-streams of southern England is one of the finest natural wonders of May.

May bugs are very different. They are the large, strong-flying beetles which appear at dusk during May and swarm around trees and bushes. Attracted to lights, they alarm children by colliding with their bedroom windows at night. If the window is ajar, the alien can fall stunned on the sill, then writhe on its back, emitting a loud, threatening buzzing sound. Cockchafers, as may bugs are more properly called – along with their relatives, the stag beetles – are the largest beetles in Britain. Measuring up to 2.5 centimetres (1 inch) long, their black, horny bodies are covered with short grey hairs, which form dense, white triangles on each side, and their wing-cases are a shiny, chestnut brown. The tip of the abdomen is spiked and the male's head carries an impressive set of fan-like antennae. The may bugs feed on fresh leaves, principally oak, on which they can inflict considerable harm. Their night-time May swarming leads to mating, after which the female digs into the soil to lay her eggs, a dozen or so at a time. When they hatch three weeks later, the grubs tunnel through the soil for two complete years, feeding destructively on the roots of grasses and cereals and even killing young shrubs and trees.

Common cockchafer taking off from oak leaves. Known as 'maybugs', these large beetles can emerge in great swarms, buzzing around the tops of trees at dusk and colliding with lit windowpanes.

In woodlands and gardens, our resident birds are dependent on a plentiful supply of caterpillars and other insect larvae for feeding their young. Whereas the adults of many familiar species have a varied diet, their growing chicks need the easily digestible, pre-packaged protein provided in the form of insect grubs and caterpillars. The timing and abundance of such insect larvae is governed by the leafing of the trees and other vegetation and sets the breeding schedule of nearly all Britain's woodland birds. The leaves of the common oak, for example, unfurl in May. Caterpillars of certain moths, such as the green oak tortrix moth, infest these succulent new leaves before they turn bitter-tasting with tannins. The way the female moths, after laying eggs, fold together the sides of the oak leaf using their own silk, gave them their older name, 'oak-rollers'. Hidden from the view of birds, the caterpillars feed on the inside of the rolled leaf. As May progresses, millions of these caterpillars and those of other species munch away at each oak tree, sometimes completely devouring its first green flush of leaves. If you stop and listen carefully in a spring oakwood, you may hear the incessant pitter-patter of caterpillar droppings falling like rain through the canopy and then down onto the woodland floor. This is why so many oaks can look bare in June – but they recover to produce a second flush of leaves, by which time the surviving tortrix caterpillars have pupated, stopped eating and hatched out into adult moths. The breeding schedule of the great tit, and other insect-eating woodland birds, is synchronized to this May 'flush' of oak moth caterpillars. During this month, a sharp-eyed great tit can snatch 300 of these larvae in a single day – most of them destined for the gaping mouths of its chicks. Oak trees support a host of other insect species, including 200 different kinds of moths and butterflies, many species of aphids and various bugs and beetles. Together, they make up the staple diet for many other insect-eating birds and carnivorous insects such as ladybird larvae, and spiders. Each tree species, as it comes into leaf, hosts its own intricate food web. Birches and beeches, ash and alder, hazel and hawthorn, all have their own insect armies that march across their leaves. Leaves become insects, become birds.

Above Blue tit feeding a caterpillar to nestlings inside a hollow tree. Nest-boxes add to their breeding success.

In May, many of our woodlands are carpeted with bluebells, perhaps Britain's most famous and charismatic plant. The Atlantic climate bestows relatively mild, wet winters on the land, especially near the coast. On the continent of Europe, where winters are cold and dry, bluebells are very rare. In Britain, they are so ubiquitous and popular that they could well be regarded as our national flower. Confusingly, however, many Scots call the English bluebell a 'wild hyacinth' and reserve the name 'bluebell' for the summer flower that south of the border is called a 'harebell'.

Other woodland plants now in flower include wild garlic, also known as ramsons. Like the bluebell, it favours shaded woods, and the two plants often flower together above great swathes of foliage which temporarily shades out other plants. The deep blue hue of the bluebells and the heady aroma of the ramsons seems to define a British wood in springtime. Both species are conspicuously members of the lily family and are good indicators that the woodland is ancient. Other wild May lilies include herb paris, a plant that favours chalky soils. The 'paris' of its common name refers to the symmetry of its strikingly beautiful but unpleasant-smelling flower, all the parts of which are on a 'par' with one another. Lily-of-the-valley, the familiar plant of cottage gardens, is a native species which grows wild in some woodlands and springs up spontaneously in unexpected places such as roadside verges and car parks.

Far left Ramsons, or wild garlic, is a lily that carpets the floors of shaded deciduous woodlands throughout Britain. Its name comes from an old European word meaning 'rank'.

Left By May, badgers born in January or February are growing fast, and emerge from their sett after dark. These three siblings will soon venture into the woodland.

As evening approaches, a rich mix of May-time scents pervades the woodland air, to the accompaniment of songbirds closing their day. It is the time for the day shift to retire, and leave the woodland to the creatures of the night. The badger cubs which were born in February are now exploring the surface of their woodland home. For weeks they have been confined to the labyrinth of the sett. Even for a nocturnal animal and one that spends most of its life underground, curiosity about the outside world is undiminished. The sow, still heavy-looking with milk, emerges first. When the night air is mild and the ground not soaked in recent rain, her keen sense of smell is at its most acute. She lifts her head, testing the air and listening to the sounds of the woodland. With her snout raised, she sniffs in all directions, watching for movement with her small, short-sighted eyes. Satisfied that all is well, she allows the cubs to emerge. For some time they remain close to the entrance, playing tentatively with each other. The sow licks them, searching for ticks and other skin parasites that take hold when underground. Much of the cubs' play is with their mother, testing their strength against hers, and practising their field skills. Between bouts of play, they drag leaves around and dig little holes in the ground. At the slightest unfamiliar sound or prompted by their mother, the cubs bolt back underground. But if all is quiet in the wood, everybody scratches.

By the middle of May, much of the British countryside is snowy with the blossom that takes its name. The small, white flowers of the hawthorn, with their bittersweet scent, form billowing ribbons of may blossom as far as the eye can see. This is one of the great natural events of our landscape, but one that has its origins in our social history. The lines of white blossom mark what little remains of the 320,000 kilometres (200,000 miles) of hedgerow planted in the eighteenth and nineteenth centuries. The Enclosure Acts of that time created much of the patchwork of fields and hedges that we recognize today as the quintessential English countryside – and hawthorn was its mainstay. Quick-growing, tenacious and covered in thorns, the tree made the ideal basis of a hedge intended to contain livestock and delineate ownership. Left untrimmed the hawthorn will grow into a substantial tree, reaching up to 14 metres (46 feet) and was one of the features of the wildwood. Cut back regularly, it becomes an impenetrable bush. For much of the year the humble hawthorn is just a 'quickthorn' hedge but now, at the beginning of summer, it bursts into an unbridled glory of its own. Hawthorn was one of the most conspicuous victims of the seventeenth-century adoption of the new calendar in Britain. In the good old days, its blossom heralded the beginning of the month, and everyone knew that, at last, 'the may was out'. Now it blooms when the month of May is almost halfway through.

Left The Uffington white horse carved in the Berkshire downs dates from the Iron Age. Today, in May, it is surrounded by rape fields in flower, another sign of the times.

Above Meadow buttercups are tenacious survivors. They normally bloom between May and July – but in some exceptional years they flower until autumn.

Despite the recent agricultural revolution that continues to strip the countryside of hedges and transform the colour and the very nature of the land, May reminds us that not all is lost. Throughout the country you can still be dazzled by a more traditional blaze of yellow – a field of buttercups. From May through to July, sometimes later in exceptional years, buttercups bloom across Britain. These hardy meadow plants are great survivors. They seem resilient to ploughing and to weedkillers, to the blades of the mower and the rasping teeth of cattle. Nothing seems to keep them down. But year by year, as pasture and hay meadows become uneconomical, buttercups are being marginalized and those glorious fields of swaying, shiny, yellow heads may join those meadows of fritillaries in the annals of folklore.

THE CANNY CUCKOO

The only view that most of us will ever have of a cuckoo is a glimpse of it in flight, hastening on a straight and level course, with its sharp wings held below its body and its long tail trailing. It always seems a very purposeful bird. Its manner and its plumage, slate-grey and barred on the underside, make it look much like a sparrowhawk. Even sparrows and other small birds share in this confusion, as they chase and mob each passing cuckoo. Perhaps they know that every female cuckoo has a lethal mission. Whatever we think of the parasitic lifestyle of these visitors from Africa, it is difficult not to admire them. At every stage of their brief summer visit to Britain, they reveal themselves as distinctly canny.

The males arrive first and throughout the season they are the most conspicuous – in voice, if not in view. They display excitedly, sometimes in male parties. Perching like parrots with two toes each side of the branch, they sway side to side and bob up and down, cockily fanning their large, decorative tails. Swelling their throats and leaning forwards, they utter their distinctive 'cuc-koo' call. The female, for her part, is highly territorial. When she arrives, she keenly defends her patch of British soil, announcing her presence with her own style of 'cuckooing' and also a distinctive bubbling call. She surveys her territory for signs of unsuspecting victims on which she can impose her own offspring. It is a devilish strategy which she inflicts on species smaller than herself – reed and willow warblers, wagtails and pipits,

even dunnocks and robins. All her life, if possible, a female cuckoo will return to the same kind of habitat and select the same host species. Uncannily, the eggs she lays in the nest of her 'victim', often bear a striking resemblance to those already there. She does this after several days of judicious watching to ensure that she lays each egg in a nest with an incomplete clutch. Bird-watchers who have witnessed this extraordinary event

The adult cuckoo can be mistaken for a bird of prey. Its parasitic way of life is no less predatory – depriving its British 'hosts' of their own eggs and chicks, and substituting its own.

say that the female cuckoo chooses the late afternoon to perform her deed. Her host will have laid her own egg in the morning, and will now be feeding away from the nest. Taking the victim's egg in her ample beak, the hen cuckoo turns around on the nest and deposits one of her own, flying away with the stolen egg which she drops or even swallows. In all, she repeats this process a dozen times or more, usually on alternate days and always in a different nest – there is no point having her own chicks competing against one another. When her final egg is laid, the female cuckoo takes no further part in the future of her offspring to which she remains a total stranger. The male plays an even smaller role. The more flamboyant will mate with several females, spreading his genetic message as widely as possible before flying back to Africa. The adult cuckoos are the earliest of our summer visitors to leave our shores. Their mission accomplished, they leave in July.

Back in the nest, the cuckoo's egg is incubated by the pair of unsuspecting host birds. It hatches with the other

eggs, sometimes earlier if the female cuckoo has been accurate with her observations. Whether the cuckoo chick hatches first or not, it instinctively removes all future competition. When barely eight hours old, in a monumental feat of strength, the blind, naked hatchling ejects the other eggs or chicks one by one. Sinking down into the bottom of the nest-cup, it manoeuvres each object into a special hollow in its back, and then, heaving with its featherless limbs, it disgorges its cargo over the rim of the nest. It is an instinctive response to any pressure on its back and the cuckoo chick does not rest until all the eggs or defenceless chicks are removed. Exhausted, it sinks back into the nest and waits to be fed by its two bemused but totally devoted foster parents.

The host birds attend to every need of the alien chick as if it were their own. The parent cuckoo was careful to choose the nest of an insect-eating species for her offspring, to ensure a plentiful supply of the grubs and caterpillars which are also a cuckoo's preferred diet. A few species, such as spotted flycatchers and blackcaps, seem to have become resistant to parasitism by cuckoos. They immediately desert their nests if an alien egg appears. It is fascinating to ponder why, over evolutionary time, more species have not become immune to this onerous victimization which, for the foster parents, can wipe out a total breeding season. The adopted chick rapidly grows much bigger than them, and they are often forced to perch on the youngster's back to satisfy its gaping mouth. It soon outgrows the nest and perches nearby, constantly clamouring to be fed with insects. For the parents it seems a thankless task. All their efforts are a genetic waste of time.

When four weeks old, the cuckoo fledgling leaves its foster parents and sets out on its independent life. It feeds on the insect bounty of a British summer until strong enough to set off in late August or early September, when it follows the route taken weeks earlier by its real parents, back to Africa. How it does this, completely on its own, is uncanny – even for a cuckoo.

Above Yellow flag iris, adopted by Louis VII as his crusading heraldic emblem, became known as the 'fleur-de-lys', a corruption of 'Louis'.

Britain's ponds and streams celebrate the arrival of summer with displays of the showy flag iris. If not carefully handled, its sharp-edged and pointed leaves can cut flesh, giving the iris another common name, sword flag. The spikes of these robust plants emerge early in the year at the edge of open water, along ditches and in damp meadows throughout Britain. By mid-May, they tower above the other vegetation to open their vivid yellow flowers. Less conspicuous, but no less beautiful, are the finely marked blooms of the cuckoo flower, so named because of its appearance at the time when cuckoos call. Other local names include lady's smock, milkmaids and May flower. But in some years, the cuckoo bird and the cuckoo flower make their first appearance considerably earlier in spring, heralding the arrival of fine weather.

On the warm winds from the south come other migrants. Their arrival coincides with the abundance of insects in our woodlands and countryside. Bird-watchers notice that in a cool or damp spring, the bulk of the summer migrants arrive later. It is as if they are forewarned en route through the Mediterranean and southern Europe that Britain is not yet ready to receive them. Most of Britain's summer visitors start to arrive from their African winter quarters in mid-April – species such as swifts and swallows, blackcaps, whitethroats, reed warblers and willow warblers, and the nightingale whose exquisite song usually graces woodland and copses by May Day. Then follows the final influx of birds including wood warblers and grasshopper warblers, pied and spotted flycatchers, lesser whitethroats and redstarts. Nearly all of these immigrants have distinctive songs which add new tones and volume to the May dawn chorus. One of the delights of the month is to rise before the sun in time to hear the crescendo of songbirds as they usher in first light.

Among the special places where you will be certain to hear many of these summer migrants are the oakwoods of central Wales. As in many regions of Britain, oaks once covered much of the principality. Today only fragments of that wildwood remain. In the higher areas, the oaks themselves are different from those of lowland England. The pedunculate or English oak has large branches which arise from a short trunk to form the characteristic massive crown. Its leaves are almost stalkless but when the acorns form, they do have stalks – hence the awkward name 'pedunculate', meaning 'growing from a stalk'. Our other native oak has branches arising at different levels up the long trunk, to create a fan-shaped crown. Its leaves have stalks but its acorns sit directly on the outer twigs, giving this oak the equally unromantic name 'sessile', meaning 'stalkless'. This species of oak is found more commonly in upland areas of Britain where it tolerates shallow, acid soils. In central Wales, ageing stands of sessile oaks cling to the steep sides of valleys. These 'hanging' oakwoods are very atmospheric places. Because they have been grazed by sheep for the past century, they have little trace of regenerating trees and shrubs. Instead of struggling through undergrowth, you walk on an open, mossy sward. Above is a dense, mature canopy that hosts vast hordes of insects. It is for this May bonanza that the foreigners flock to Wales. Pied flycatchers, redstarts, chiffchaffs, willow and wood warblers, and tree pipits arrive to stake their claim, competing with the resident birds, such as great tits and blue tits, robins and nuthatches, for the insects and for nest sites.

Left The scratchy musical song of the male whitethroat, proclaimed from the depths of a field hedge or from the top of a garden shrub, announces that these warblers have arrived from their wintering grounds south of the Sahara.

May is a month when wildcats give birth to their kittens. This distinct feline species (*Felis silvestris*) was once widespread across the forests and steppe country of Europe, Africa and much of Asia. It probably never reached Ireland, but was formerly found through much of mainland Britain. As its scientific name suggests, it is essentially a creature of the forest. A millennium ago, when Britain was still a wooded country, the wildcat was feared as a predator and favoured for its skins. Austere medieval nuns were forbidden from wearing any fur of value greater than commonplace lamb or wildcat. As the forests were cut down for fuel, timber and to create agricultural land, *Felis silvestris*, like so many creatures of the 'wildwood', was driven to the more remote corners of the country. By the beginning of the twentieth century, it had reached its lowest population in historic times, and naturalists feared that, like the wolf, beaver, brown bear and wild pig, it would become extinct in Britain.

The First World War took gamekeepers away from the land. When the survivors returned, the fox became their 'enemy number one'. No longer in the forefront of persecution, the wildcat began to re-colonize some of its old haunts. Surveys in 1946 and 1962 showed that it continued to make new ground. Today, the species is still associated with Scotland where it favours deciduous and coniferous woodland and scrubland, especially near moorland and hill-country where it can more readily catch rabbits, hares and other small mammals. The true wildcat is noticeably larger, and certainly more powerful, than most domestic and feral cats. The body of the male can weigh up to 7 kilograms (15 pounds) and is distinctively striped. The spine has a dark line of fur running down to the short, stocky tail which has a series of black rings or bands. The chin and chest area usually has hints of lighter fur.

Males and females are solitary hunters and go their own ways for much of the year. Like domestic cats, the female calls when on heat, and the act of mating prompts her eggs to be released into her womb. Unlike domestic cats, this happens at distinct times of year, usually March, so that the kittens are born when food is naturally plentiful. A litter can be as little as two when times are hard, but three or four seems more normal. The female gives birth in a secret, secure place, and supports her blind offspring on her milk for a week or two. When their eyes open, she brings them prey until, perhaps at the age of ten or twelve weeks, they can accompany her on summer hunting trips. In the autumn, fully grown, they disperse to make their own way in the wilder places of Scotland.

When a year old, the new generation is ready to breed. They sometimes cross with feral cats – domestic cats living wild in the countryside. The resulting hybrid can often be hard to distinguish in the field, in looks and behaviour, from a true wildcat. For similar reasons, any large striped feral cat can be mistaken for its wild cousin. The spread of Felis silvestris is therefore difficult to track, but experts believe that it is making an impressive comeback in Scotland. It seems a suitable case for re-introduction to other parts of the country. Helped by the creation of new forests, a new generation of gamekeepers, and a rebound of the rabbit population from the ravages of myxomatosis, this is probably the first time for more than a millennium that the wildcat has expanded its range in Britain.

Wildcat suckling her kittens. With the more tolerant attitude of gamekeepers and the return of the rabbit, the species is expanding its range – perhaps no longer just in Scotland.

Right From May to July, thrift adds splashes of colour to clifftops and saltmarshes around Britain's coasts, and to mountain ledges in Scotland and northern England.

A far cry from the remnant wildwood of central Wales – in character but not in distance – are the 'seabird cities' of Pembrokeshire. Isolated from the mainland by a narrow but treacherous channel is the rocky island of Skomer and, beyond that, the island of Skokholm. Through early spring, their rocky terrains bloomed with a spectacular display of heathland plants and pink clifftop thrift. Now in May, the islands have been commandeered by the seabirds that come to nest there, notably guillemots and razorbills, fulmars and kittiwakes, and on Skomer, 6000 pairs of puffins. Skokholm is remarkable for the way it attracts Manx shearwaters and storm petrels. Both these species spend most of their lives gliding over ocean waves in search of food, but they have to touch down to rear their young. Clumsy on land, they nest in burrows to give protection from marauding gulls. Some use vacated rabbit burrows; others excavate their own nesting chambers. During daylight, the adults take turns to fly great distances to feed, returning only under the cover of darkness. In the safety of their burrows, the storm petrels purr and the Manx shearwaters emit the most extraordinary wailing sound that has frightened the life out of stranded sailors and inspired legends about underground trolls. Each year, Skokholm alone is host to 40,000 of these weird-sounding ocean fugitives.

Further out to sea is Grassholm, the spring and summer home to some 30,000 pairs of gannets that began to arrive from their ocean feeding grounds in late winter. After St Kilda off the north-west coast of Scotland, Grassholm is the second largest gannet colony in Britain and the third largest in the world. The incubation period for gannets is 45 days – the longest of any bird nesting in Britain. By May, most eggs have hatched and the nests have hungry chicks. The parents take turns to fish, plunging from great heights in pursuit of the shoals that mass around the Pembrokeshire coast in early summer. This isolated gannetry has expanded dramatically over the last century – almost tenfold. By contrast, the puffin colony on Grassholm has dwindled as the birds' extensive network of burrows has collapsed from the sheer pressure of numbers. Happily the colony of these jaunty little birds on nearby Skomer has fared better, although the British population is declining overall.

Top The British Isles are a seasonal breeding home for most of the North Atlantic gannets. By May they have established their colonies.
Above The puffin's triangular bill can carry as many as 10 sand eels.

By the end of May, throughout the length of Britain, colonies of seabirds are well established in their breeding timetable. On the coast of Yorkshire, at the towering limestone cliffs of Bempton that overlook the North Sea, every ledge and crack is now occupied by the nests of eight species of seabird, including 20,000 guillemots and other auks, and 80,000 kittiwakes. Further north, the seabirds of the Farne Islands are also in full cry. As the weather improves, these islands also become a Mecca for bird enthusiasts. From Easter to mid-summer there is great activity on the stacks and cliffs, as nineteen species of seabird perform their courtship rituals and rear their young. Across the border, in the Firth of Forth, the colony of gannets on the Bass Rock and vast numbers of other seabirds on the Isle of May have embarked on their hectic breeding season. As the summer progresses around the entire coast of Scotland and its outer islands – from St Kilda far out in the Atlantic to Noss in Shetland and remote Fair Isle – we are left in no doubt about the importance of the British Isles at this time of year as breeding and feeding grounds for vast numbers of oceanic birds.

Away from the long and beautiful coastline of Scotland, the pace of life also accelerates towards the end of May. In the glens, roe deer fawns are born in the cover of woodland, sometimes as twins. Red deer hinds also give birth then, usually just to a single calf. The young of both species are at risk from predators and scavengers, such as foxes and crows as well as from golden eagles. For the first few days of its life, the fawn has no scent, and remains hidden in vegetation where it feeds from its mother two or three times a day. The youngster then joins her as she grazes the fresh spring grass and heather, pausing now and again to suckle her offspring. Up here in Scotland, the spring season is sometimes a full month behind the south, but it is surprising how soon after making landfall on the south coast some of the bird migrants from Africa arrive in the deciduous woodlands north of the border.

High in the glen, the pair of golden eagles also have young. The two chicks that hatched at the beginning of May are still covered in white down. Soon their first dark feathers will appear, giving the growing eaglets a piebald appearance. They are very vulnerable to extremes of weather, even in the shelter of the eyrie. Until they are strong enough to tear up prey for themselves, the female must stay at the nest, attending to their needs. The male bird does most of the hunting at this stage, scanning his familiar terrain for the unwary, and returning to his dependants with regular bounty. It will be July before their offspring are ready to fly. Until then, as the days become warmer and other new life ventures from the safety of their natal homes, there will be good hunting.

'the blowsy

generosity of

nature'

June

Above Skylarks sing from song posts as well as high in
the air – ascending vertically in a hovering flight and filling
the summer air with its warbling song.
Left Ox-eye daisies grace summer roadsides.

Whoever invented the calendar served Britain well. For the peak of the natural year to fall in any month but June, the middle month, would be a travesty. In other parts of the world, this month is simply mid-winter or mid-summer, the coldest or the hottest time of year. Here in Britain, on the Atlantic edge of Europe, June is a gentle blend of the luxuriance of spring and the warmth of the summer still to come. As the northern hemisphere heads towards the longest day, the people of Britain have time to relish the blowsy generosity of nature and to marvel at its splendour.

Nowhere epitomizes this colourful abundance more than the hedgerows and lanes of southern England. Like lines of bunting, they welcome the return of summer. The more established the hedge and bank, the more species of wild flower you are likely to find there. But even recently created hedgerows and verges become spangled with wild flowers in June. Just as yellow and white and blue were the predominant colours of April and May, now in June, Britain's lanes and roads are fringed with a floral apron of white and red.

Along every country lane, as cars sweep by, the massed flowers of cow parsley foam like breaking waves. Beneath the umbrella-like canopy of these aptly named 'umbellifers' shelter other white flowers. The large star-like flowers of greater stitchwort are still evident as are the long-stalked flowers of white campion. Like its close relative, the red campion, this common and handsome hedgerow plant was wound into improvised garlands to crown 'champions' at summer village games. But of all the white-petalled flowers of June, it is the ox-eye or moon daisy that is the most eye-catching. With its wide solitary bloom and dazzling centre of vivid yellow, this tenacious giant daisy frequently graces roadside verges wherever it is given a chance. Even from the central reservations of motorways, the brilliance of these pioneering plants delights the eyes of passing motorists, as their tall sturdy stems sway defiantly in the wake of commuters hurrying home to enjoy the long evenings of June.

The byways of Britain bloom in a succession of red flowers. One of the earliest is ragged robin, a pretty plant with unevenly divided petals that give it that unkempt look. Similarly coloured is herb Robert, a name possibly derived from the Latin 'ruber', meaning red. The shape of its flower identifies it as a member of the geranium family – as does the strong smell of its hairy leaves. But it is also said that the eleventh-century French monk Abbé Robert, who founded the Cistercian order in Britain, used the leaves for healing a great variety of ills.

The June hedgerow hues of red and white combine in one outstanding early-summer flower –

Above As spring turns to summer, traditional meadows and hedgerows display a procession of wild flowers — here ragged robin with buttercups.

Below right The dog rose — unofficial emblem of England — takes its name from the Latin, Rosa canina.

the dog rose. These wild roses became a symbol of Tudor England. In time, they also provided the horticultural stock for many garden varieties and their hardy roots are still used for grafting. Through spring, the arching stems of this tenacious climber, armed with prickles shaped like miniature shark-fins, scramble towards the sunshine. If spared the hedge-cutter's flail, each stem, up to three metres long (ten feet), emerges triumphantly above the heads of other roadside plants, as a cascade of large and delicate pink flowers. The pastel hue of most individual blooms comes from the way their five notched, white petals are tinged with red. Some flowers are pure white, others pure pink. The overall effect is like a warm blush as the face of the countryside colours up for summer.

THE SWALLOWTAIL
Relic of the Ice Age and Harbinger of Global Warming

Just a short drive northeast of Norwich is one of Britain's most revealing nature reserves. Set up and run by the Norfolk Wildlife Trust, the Broadland Conservation Centre features a floating gallery and information centre which, together with the living exhibit of Ranworth Broad itself, tells the dramatic story of the Norfolk Broads – a natural history that spans many thousands of years. You can explore Ranworth Broad by way of a boarded trail that conducts you through a classic broadland scene illustrating the entire succession of plant life by which wet fenland is, with time, transformed into mature oak woodland. You pass by the small surviving patches of fringing reedbeds and through the typical reed fen that

Swallowtails – perhaps the most elegant of British butterflies – survive in fragmented pockets of the Norfolk Broads, and are entirely dependent on one plant, milk parsley.

each year is cut for its sturdy crop of Norfolk reed, prized by thatchers. Here the peat accumulates and, over centuries, dries out to create a firm footing for alder scrub, which eventually is succeeded by the climax woodland of mature oaks. This is a process which started at the end of the last Ice Age and still continues today. At Ranworth, you can witness the whole process in an afternoon, just by strolling along a simple boardwalk. It is a graphic passage through time.

If you visit in late May, June, July, or some years in August, you will be treated to a visual bonus – the spectacle of Britain's largest and, some would say, most beautiful butterfly. The swallowtail breeds nowhere else in this country except in Ranworth and one or two other pockets of the Norfolk Broads, but it was much more

widespread in the past. Its story shadows that of fenland itself and can be traced right back to the last Ice Age – perhaps even further. As the ice sheets formed to the north, sea levels were lowered. Whereas today England and Wales are bounded by the English Channel, the Irish Sea and the North Sea, vast areas of fenland and saltmarsh formed, linking this land with the rest of Europe. In time, some fenland matured into woodland – just as can be seen at Ranworth. It is thought that, during warmer interludes in the prolonged Ice Age, the swallowtail butterfly colonized England from its continental homeland. When conditions deteriorated again, the species retreated south, except for a substantial population that managed to survive in the mosaic of fen and woodland that stretched across the southern part of what is now the North Sea. Here they flourished in isolation until dense forestation and increasing cold forced them to adapt to living on coastal fens and marshes, the only ice-free places where they could continue to breed in Ice Age Britain. It was in these coastal refuges that each May the adult butterflies took to the wing, mated and laid their eggs on the only plentiful foodplant that was suitable for their caterpillars – the milk parsley.

Much further south in warmer continental Europe,

where wildlife escaped the extremes of the Ice Age, the mainstream swallowtail populations still enjoyed a variety of habitats and a greater selection of parsley species on which their caterpillars could feed. As the centuries passed, the two races evolved independently. Today, the continental race of the swallowtail is found in a great range of habitats and its caterpillars feed on many kinds of plants all belonging to the carrot and parsley family (Umbelliferae). Here in Britain, the butterfly is restricted to just a few broadland refuges – and is still almost totally dependent on milk parsley. So different are the habitats and habits of the two races that they have been allotted distinctive names. On the Continent the swallowtail's scientific name is *Papilio machaon gorganus*. Here in Britain it is distinguished as a separate subspecies *Papilio machaon britannicus*. The two races rarely, if ever, meet – although in warm summers, the continental form migrates north across the Channel in small numbers and invades the south coast from Kent to the Isle of Wight. If global warming continues, who knows what might happen to the integrity of the British race! Meanwhile, those flotillas of magnificent butterflies sailing over the fenland of Ranworth Broad are a telling reminder that the nature of today's Britain owes much to the last Ice Age, and to the rise and fall of the sea.

Left Silage-making has replaced hay-making in most parts of the country.

As the days lengthen and the June sunshine warms the soil, other plants are coaxed into flower. Beyond the hedgerow, many fields were traditionally managed for hay, as winter feed for livestock. Each meadow would have a distinctive natural mixture of grasses and meadow flowers, dictated by soil and region. Cutting normally took place just as the grasses themselves were coming into flower, so that the stems retained more of their protein content. By June, many meadow flowers were in bloom, and ripe hayfields were a riot of colour. More often, today, winter fodder is provided by fields of specially cultivated grasses which are fertilized with nitrogen and sprayed with herbicides to keep the wild plants at bay. In place of hay, the farmer makes silage. Less labour intensive than haymaking, this method of growing grass often reaps the reward of two or three crops a year, especially in the south. But despite the vivid, almost artificial green of these modern fields, they still harbour insects and other invertebrate life such as slugs and snails, which in turn become food for other creatures. You just have to watch the silage harvester working its way up and down a field on a warm June day to witness the hidden wealth. As if bidden by the farmer himself, rooks and crows tumble from the air to scavenge the cut grass in search of easy pickings. The good news spreads. From further afield tramp flocks of gulls to tug at the roots in pursuit of worms and beetles. Then high in the air, circling on the midday thermals, come the buzzards. No field vole or grasshopper is safe from their penetrating gaze. Even bold rooks and crows make way, as these masters of the summer skies take their undisputed place at the emerald green table.

Throughout the country, buzzards are thriving again. They were once very common, but ruthless gamekeeping and irrational fear of their impact as predatory birds, drove them from their familiar lowland haunts to remote hill-country. Now that much of the British countryside is enjoying more enlightened times, these adaptable and resourceful birds have made a comeback. In some parts of southern England, they patrol in confident 'gangs', descending on the farmers' fields, as if they knew that persecution is a thing of the past. Though heavy, almost ungainly in build when standing

Above Buzzard 'mantling' prey. These handsome raptors have extended their range in recent years and, in some parts of the country, it is not unusual to see several circling lazily on summer thermals, watching for signs of potential prey. Their somewhat feeble, mewing 'kiew' belies their grandeur – especially when seen on the ground, arching their wings over their prize.

Above Group of young fallow deer, in early morning, feeding in Powerstock Forest, Dorset. Introduced to England by the Normans for the 'chase', they have become part of the English scene.

Left Male sparrowhawk on alder stump. The short rounded wings of this small hawk give it great advantage when hunting in woodland. Its power and flying skills out-manoeuvre most birds fleeing through the forest.

on the ground, the buzzard is truly handsome. Its large size and general appearance makes it look much like an eagle, a quality which must have contributed to its downfall. As much a scavenger as a hunter, the buzzard feeds on beetles and earthworms in cut grass and cereal stubble. In spring and autumn it follows the plough to pillage the freshly turned soil. But, now in June, when many pairs have two or three hungry youngsters waiting in their bulky treetop nests, adult buzzards will pounce on small mammals, including young rabbits. From the field, they rise with a slow, lumbering flight, especially when burdened with their winnings. But when they soar, on the lookout for food, they are masters of the air. Their rounded wings held forward, they lift and tack, wheel and soar without visible effort. Beneath them, each field, each hedgerow and each woodland has its special place as providers of food and shelter.

Above Eggardon Hill, that enduring feature of the west Dorset landscape, you can often see buzzards circling the ancient ramparts of this Iron Age settlement. Below them, the patchwork of fields reaches as far as the eye can see. On the horizon, to the south, is the glistening water of Lyme Bay. When the hilltop fort was built, perhaps 3000 years ago, the buzzards of that time would have looked down on a great expanse of forest. Such was the pristine character of most of southern Britain. In time, as more trees were felled and more soil was tilled, the look and the nature of the land was transformed into the mosaic of fields and hedgerows that we know and appreciate today. Just to walk around Eggardon – or any other surviving Iron Age feature of our landscape – is a reminder of that extraordinary process by which generations of people, working the land, have created the living tapestry that is the British countryside.

From a vantage point on the north-west corner of Eggardon, you can look down at a rare and small patch of old deciduous woodland. Still grandly called Powerstock Forest, these few acres of gnarled and stunted oaks represent the last vestige of the vast, prehistoric forest that once spread inland from the south coast until the highlands and colder climate of the north country restrained their growth. This was the ancient wildwood of Britain that gave our land its distinctive character. We are, despite appearances, a country of woodland plants and animals. Some species have adapted well to the open fields and grasslands created over time; others have become confined within the boundaries of their dwindling woodland home. One notable avian survivor of that wildwood is the sparrowhawk. During the twentieth century, the fortunes of this dashing bird of prey have dramatically fallen and risen, with the demise of woodland and hedges, and the widespread use of DDT and other poisonous pesticides in the late 1950s and 1960s. Happily, today they have almost regained their former glory as one of our most widespread and cosmopolitan birds. Powerstock Forest is home to several pairs, and by June each has several chicks to feed in their bulky nests in the tree canopy. Their manner of hunting is perfectly suited to this dark and secretive place. The sparrowhawk's short, rounded wings are ideal for threading a course through the stunted oak trees and undergrowth, giving the bird the advantage of surprise. Silently, it dashes towards its prey, a tree sparrow or perhaps a finch. To a chorus of frantic alarm calls from other woodland birds, this agile, yellow-eyed predator nimbly twists and turns until it out-manoeuvres its victim and brings it down to the forest floor.

Beneath the stunted boughs of this shrouded woodland, another successful forest creature is rearing young – the fallow deer. Woodland deer are one of the great wildlife success stories of Britain. There are deer in every county, and Britain is unique in Europe in having six species living wild in its countryside. Only the red and roe deer are truly native, but fallow deer lived here before the last Ice Age edged them out. Reintroduced from the Continent by Norman settlers, they have become re-established in a spectacular way. Dorset is one of their strongholds and those in Powerstock Forest are direct descendants of stock released there for King John's hunting parties. These darker forms are known as Old English Fallow, but at Powerstock there are also several white individuals that run with the herd. In June, the females drop their fawns in the seclusion of the dense woodland. The most dangerous time for a fawn is later in the summer, when it runs with its mother making feeding forays away from the shelter of their woodland home. Cars cause the premature deaths of many fawns which leap in front of unsuspecting motorists. But despite this carnage, fallow deer are thriving in Britain, in deer parks and in the wild, and they often venture out into fields and gardens. During the summer months, the bucks and does keep apart until the autumn rutting season. By then, the fawns will be well grown, and run as confident members of the herd.

Left Fallow deer can vary in colour. White forms, such as these on Powerstock Common, stand out against the landscape.

FAST BREEDERS, RUNNING WILD

As we start a new millennium, it's worth reflecting that the rabbit – now so much a part of the British scene – has been in Britain for less than 1000 years. Since there is no mention of rabbits in the Domesday Book, historians conclude that they were introduced from continental Europe by the Normans, for their skins and as a luxury food. Bred in captivity in warrens, 'coneys' (as adult rabbits were then called) were so prized for their pelts and meat that they were the exclusive prerogative of nobility. When they inevitably escaped into the open countryside, these fast-breeding vegetarians ran amok. It may have taken some time, but they changed much of the British landscape. Nibbling their way across the lowlands of England and then across the entire British Isles, they became one of the most widespread mammals in Britain and Ireland. By 1900, they were also considered to be among the most destructive, vying with the house mouse and brown rat (also historical introductions) as public enemy number one. They not only devastated crops but, through their relentless grazing, transformed vast areas of countryside into open grassland. The beneficiaries were the stoats and weasels, the foxes and birds of prey for whom rabbits became a favoured food. Many plants also benefited. The short sward of southern downland and the close-cropped turf of many other regions of Britain were created and maintained by these voracious nibblers, allowing orchids and other sensitive plants to flourish.

Until the 1950s much of Britain was shaped by the activities of rabbits, and much of its wildlife was largely dependent on them. All that changed with the introduction of the myxomatosis virus which, like the rabbit itself, was introduced from France. Carried by the rabbit flea, the virus reduced some rabbit communities by 99 per cent. On the downland of southern England, scrub returned and orchids disappeared. Birds of prey and mammals such as foxes were forced to find new sources of food, often at the expense of other wildlife.

By the winter of 1956, the rabbit was almost extinct in Britain. It is a credit to the resilience of 'old Brer' that they have made some kind of comeback. Those rabbits survived had either developed an immunity to the virus or had perhaps avoided it by changing their habits. It is thought that this is the reason why so many rabbits in Britain no longer live under ground where their communal living was a breeding ground for their fleas – and for the deadly virus. Today the sight of healthy rabbits munching buttercup stalks in June belies their turbulent, unnatural history.

Despite the ravages of myxomatosis, the rabbit has made a dramatic comeback. During its first millennium in Britain, it has endured a chequered history.

Eggardon Hill, like so much of the chalk downland of southern England, owes its enduring character to the animals that graze its vegetation. Were it not for the constant nibbling of countless generations of sheep and rabbits, shrubs and trees would grow in place of the open grassland. The growing points of grasses are at ground level. As every gardener knows, close-cropping of a lawn encourages its growth and keeps down other plants. Where downland turf is kept short by sheep, fine textured grasses thrive; species such as sheep's fescue, red fescue, hair-grasses and oat-grasses can all withstand being nibbled almost to the ground. On chalk downland, it is not just grasses that have been promoted by the relentless grazing of livestock and wild herbivores. Many wild flowers thrive because their growing points are protected in buds which are close to the soil, or even beneath its surface. Such plants can rapidly replace parts grazed by animals, an ability not shared by woody vegetation that grows and branches from points higher up the stem. The beneficiaries of grazing are often spectacularly beautiful. Vetches and trefoils, chickweeds and saxifrages all produce colourful flowers in early summer – a signal to the insects that will unwittingly assist in their pollination. Enticed by scent or colour, or by both, butterflies and other flying insects alight to sip nectar, picking up pollen which is brushed off on the next flower they visit.

None of these plants is as beguiling to insects – or to us – as the orchid. It is on downland, in June, that many of Britain's most handsome orchid species reach their prime. Fragrant, bee and man orchids, for example, are widespread across much of southern Britain. The much rarer monkey orchid is confined to Kent, as is the larger, very showy lady orchid with its frilly spotted skirt and upper petals shaped like a Victorian bonnet, though this is a plant more of chalky woodland edge. The names given them over the years allude, of course, to their often extraordinary floral forms. Other orchids with such exotic names include the spider orchid, fly orchid, butterfly orchid and the stately military orchid with its flowers like soldiers in pale pink tunics and crested, pink helmets. Of them all, the bee orchid is the one that impresses and intrigues most naturalists. Each flower seems to have a bee resting on its outer rim. Even its brown body is furry to the touch. Not only does each flower look like a female of the 'solitary bee' species, the orchids emit a scent that apparently smells like her. This deception is presumed to attract male bees to 'mate' with them and, in so doing, helps transfer pollen to another similar flower. The deception is perfectly evolved, but in Britain it seems that the flowers of the bee orchid are self-pollinating and seldom have a chance to benefit from their beguiling form. On summer winds, their copious lightweight seeds are carried great distances to colonize any patch of newly exposed chalk soil – often like exotic rampant weeds.

Above Some orchids are very scarce nationally, but flower in profusion in a few localities. The burnt orchid – named for the 'scorched' tip of its flower-spike – flourishes on some chalk downlands of Wiltshire.

Right The bee orchid is much more widespread – and can spring up in great numbers on chalk soils. The flower's likeness to a feeding bee is remarkable, and evolved to assist with the orchid's pollination.

One magical place where flowers bloom extravagantly in June is the Outer Hebrides. Here is a coastal grassland without parallel in Europe. Its natural beauty at this time of year is outstanding. Lying between 50 and 80 kilometres (30 and 50 miles) off the west coast of mainland Scotland, the chain of islands runs roughly north to south for almost 200 kilometres (130 miles). There are over 100 islands in all, the largest being Lewis and Harris in the north and North Uist, Benbecula, South Uist and Barra reaching to the south. About 30,000 people live there, in an essentially treeless landscape exposed to everything that the Atlantic ocean can throw at it. The rollers break constantly along the western seaboard of the islands, creating white beaches of sand and broken shells of sea life. This forms the basis of the soil, rich in calcium carbonate, and gives the coastal strip many of the characteristics

of chalk grassland. The special nature of this place derives not just from its chemistry and the prevailing westerly wind and rain, but from the way the land has been nurtured by Hebridean people since the islands were first populated, around 7000 years ago. It seems very likely that people farmed here a full millennium before an agricultural way of life was established on mainland Britain. Perhaps the reason for their settlement here on the extreme western outposts of Europe was the combined richness of the sea and the natural productivity of the land. Whilst the east side of the islands has much in common with the moorland across on the mainland, the west-facing coastal strip is characterized by a natural grassland which is locally called 'machair'. The word is Gaelic and still features in the place-names of the other Western Isles as well as along the western coast of mainland Scotland, and in parts of Ireland. It describes a large, low-lying and fertile grassland that became the basis of people's existence – a place to grow their crops and graze their livestock.

Today, the Hebridean machair is one of the rarest habitats in Europe. Climate and patterns of land use have changed over the centuries, and very little of this coastal grassland survives. Where it does, such as in the Outer Hebrides, it is cherished as one of Britain's most outstanding natural wonders. The intrinsic fertility of the sandy, calcareous soil, combined with many generations of cultivation, established a patchwork of hedgeless fields which are still rotated to achieve optimum

Left From the air, the hedgeless field-strips of the Hebridean machair are clearly visible. This peninsula forms part of the RSPB reserve at Balranald on North Uist.

Right Clover, with flower heads the size of golf balls, blooms where field-strips have been left fallow to rejuvenate their fertility.

cereal crops and grazing. The beneficial effects on wildlife are astonishing. Regular rotation of the strip-fields provides opportunities for the annual plants of the machair to seed and re-establish themselves. This creates the spectacular displays of flowers for which the islands are justly famous. Spring comes late to the Outer Hebrides; cold easterly winds counteract the sunshine. But in a good year, by June the pastures have been transformed into an ever-changing carpet of wild flowers. First come the daisies and other white flowers such as eyebrights. Then the scene changes to yellow with swathes of buttercups, vetches and bird's-foot-trefoil. On the 'wet-machair' there are expanses of yellow iris, marsh marigold and yellow rattle. Intermingled with the rows of cereal crops bloom dazzling rows of corn marigolds. No wonder the machair has inspired generations of Gaelic bards.

The western seaboard of these Hebridean islands is also famous for its breeding waders. A total of 25,000 pairs – including lapwings and ringed plover, redshank, dunlin and oystercatchers – use the machair and the adjacent dunes, marshes and ploughed land to rear their young. In the breeding season, which builds up from the end of April, there can be higher densities of these familiar wading birds here than anywhere else in the world. But it is not just waders for which the machair is famous. Here on the Atlantic rim of the Western Isles is a haven for several species of bird that are rarities elsewhere. Corn buntings still thrive on the machair of the Uists and Tiree, but are almost extinct on

mainland farms. Twites are more common here than the more familiar linnets they resemble. But the most famous Hebridean bird is the corncrake. Rarely seen, but frequently cursed for its rasping calls at night, this rare member of the rail family arrives from Africa in May and sets about the business of raising offspring in the brief Hebridean summer. It is the survival of the crofting regime, with its traditional rhythm of hay and crop cutting, that has made the iris beds and hayfields of the Hebrides the corncrake's last stronghold in Britain.

As the spring progresses and the birds complete their hectic breeding schedule, a succession of wild flowers blooms in the machair. Each cultivated strip has its distinctive character, depending on the crops which have been grown in the past, and how long it has been left fallow to regenerate its fertility. In those strips which are carrying crops such as oats or the local wind-resistant cereal called 'beer barley', brilliantly yellow buttercups, yellow rattle and corn marigolds spring up in regimental rows which ripple in unison in the constant sea breeze. By the end of June, poppies add another vivid splash of colour to this already astonishingly colourful scene. Where field strips are fallow, clover of every conceivable red, white and purple hues richly carpets the machair. The sometimes golf ball-sized heads of the heavily scented clover flower, laden with nectar and

Above Seldom seen but frequently heard, the corncrake is a summer breeding visitor to the meadows of Scotland's Western Isles. The male bird utters its rasping call with its head pointed up and its body held taut. **Right** Marsh marigolds on the 'wet' machair of the Outer Hebrides.

A PRICKLY PROBLEM

Very few land mammals have made their way naturally to the Western Isles of Scotland. Before becoming habitable after the last Ice Age retreated, the islands were cut off by the rising sea level. For some species, this became a great blessing. Waders such as dunlin and redshank, ringed plover and snipe all nest on the ground – easy targets for predators such as stoats and weasels, foxes, badgers and wildcats. But none of these creatures has made the crossing from mainland Britain, and the ground-nesting birds have flourished. Today, the machair and neighbouring 'blacklands' of the islands of North and South Uist and Benbecula are amongst the most important wader breeding grounds in Europe. A survey in 1983 counted 17,000 pairs of the principal six species. The breeding densities of dunlin and ringed plover in particular were the greatest in the world. All that changed with the arrival of one unwelcome visitor – the hedgehog.

The hedgehog is a welcome guest for most people, especially keen gardeners. But for ground-nesting birds and the bird-lovers of the Uists in the Outer Hebrides, these introduced 'aliens' are now troublesome pests.

Back in 1974, it is recorded that seven hedgehogs were introduced to the southern end of South Uist, to help control garden slugs, supposedly their favourite delicacy. These founder animals flourished and soon spread to the machair where, inevitably, they encountered waders' eggs – which they found to their liking. As the hedgehogs multiplied and spread north through the islands, reaching almost every part, the populations of dunlin and other ground-nesting species began to suffer. The total hedgehog population of the Uists and Benbecula is now estimated to be between 5000 and 10,000 – with a density on the machair of 50 per square kilometre (120 per square mile). Snuffling and bumbling their way across the machair at night, they flush incubating birds from their nests and devour the eggs. They break the eggs in a distinctive way – leaving telltale signs that convince the biologists next morning that a hedgehog was the culprit, and not another predator such as a crow or gull. The impact of hedgehogs – especially on dunlin – is now so significant that not enough eggs hatch to offset the annual mortality from other causes, natural or otherwise. Whereas before the arrival of hedgehogs, about 70 per cent of all waders' eggs hatched successfully, now only 15 per cent of them become wader chicks. For the waders this spells disaster – but for the hedgehogs, the birds' eggs are a relatively unimportant source of food, providing only 1 per cent of their diet in spring.

For the conservationists, the problem is how to cope with the successful interlopers. For many people, particularly those for whom the hedgehog is a welcome, native neighbour, the thought of killing them to protect the birds would be a last resort. Until the biologists and conservationists develop a cost-effective and humane method of control, the birds and bird-lovers on the Uists are left with a very prickly problem.

pollen, attract all manner of bees, some of which are special to the machair. Clover is indeed a precious plant – nourishing the windblown soil with much-needed nitrogen, offering sugar for honeybees and providing sweet-tasting fodder for livestock. That it is so beautiful in its June flowering is a real bonus for the summer visitors who come to the Hebrides at this time of botanical splendour.

The west coast of the Isle of Lewis, the most northerly of these Hebridean Isles, is rich in prehistory. Chambered cairns and stone circles are frequent features of its bleak landscape. Most famous – and most inspiring – are the Standing Stones of Callanish. Also known as 'Calanais', this ancient site stands 30 metres (100 feet) or so above sea level on a promontory that reaches into Loch Roag. From here there is a commanding view of the surrounding treeless terrain. Intriguingly, the stones stand in the configuration of a Celtic cross, although the Celts themselves did not appear on this scene until much later. The four rows of standing stones are orientated almost exactly north and south, east and west. At their intersection is a chambered cairn which was used as a burial chamber for many centuries after the stones were raised into their impressive form. Archaeologists think the first stones of Callanish were laboriously transported across the island to this place at least 4000 years ago. It makes them the equal of Stonehenge. To many visitors who have seen both, these stones on remote Lewis have an enigmatic, magical quality which is unrivalled.

Their full significance is not known, but undoubtedly they represent a massive expenditure of time and energy by a people for whom life, here on the very margin of Britain, has never been easy. But there were times in the past when the climate was more benign, with summers much like those of southern England today. Away from the wind, the islands were extensively wooded with birch, elm, hazel and oak, and along the western coastline, there was a naturally fertile plain. It was on this fertility that the first farmers built their prosperity. But in the centuries after Callanish was erected, the North Atlantic climate deteriorated and Britain became wetter and cooler. In the Hebrides, woodlands disappeared and blanket bog spread in its place, in time swamping the sacred standing stones in damp moorland and driving settlements to the coastal fringe. For centuries Callanish languished until, in the twentieth century, the surrounding peat was removed and the magnificence of the ancient stones revealed. Today they stand as a reminder of a time when these windswept islands were a very different place – and as evidence of the long-standing partnership between man and nature throughout Britain.

Above The standing stones of Callanish, on the north coast of the Isle of Lewis, were built at a time when the islands were covered in trees and enjoyed a warmer climate. They stand as celebration of a former natural wealth – and as a reminder of the ever-changing nature of Britain.

'the dog days

of summer'

July

Above This month sees Britain's blue butterflies –
such as these common blues – on the wing and mating.
Left Poppies – one of the world's most successful weeds –
blaze a red trail of defiance across the land.

With the flush of June and the longest day behind us, July can be a disappointment. It seems that summer has barely started but already the days are shortening and there is a sultry feel to the air. The Roman soldiers who, almost two millennia ago, occupied much of England and Wales, knew that this could be a time of fetid heat and flies. In the centuries of their occupation, British summers became much hotter as the world's climate generally warmed. The legions stationed here for some four centuries must have longed for the clear blue skies and sunshine of their Mediterranean home. Perhaps their only compensation was that the red grape vines imported from their homeland now flourished on the chalk downland of southern Britain. They noted that at these latitudes Sirius the Dog Star rose at dawn in July, adding, they supposed, to the uncomfortable effect of the sun's heat. These 'dog days' of summer were reckoned to set in on July 3rd and last until August 14th. When the Roman legions eventually withdrew in the fifth century, in the face of a deteriorating climate in Britain and a degenerating civilization back in Rome, July retained its reputation as the 'dog' month of thunderstorms and showers.

From nature's point of view, July is certainly an in-between time of year. Trees take on a deep green colour as the chlorophyll changes in their leaves. In towns, the common lime tree becomes festooned with drooping heads of blossom. Its sweet, heady perfume is designed to attract the bees and hoverflies needed for its pollination. So intoxicating is the nectar, that bumblebees can fall helpless to the ground. A favourite tree of urban streets and parks, the limes become infested with aphids which exude a mist of sticky honeydew onto cars parked below.

The hazy days of July are due to prevailing westerly winds bringing moisture in from the Atlantic. The weather is more unsettled than June, but snap storms can clear the air. The combination of warmth and occasional rain is ideal for ripening cereal crops. Traditionally, halfway between haymaking and harvesting, July is a quiet month for farmers, except for growers of soft fruits whose harvests need picking. The heads of winter barley sown the previous autumn are now drooping under the weight of their ripe ears, fringed with those distinctive beard-like hairs, which make the fields glisten in the metallic July sunshine. This month, some farmers take a second crop of silage off their ley fields, especially if it has already been a good growing year. The chopped green grass-cuttings are preserved in an improvised 'clamp' which is covered with plastic sheeting weighed down with discarded vehicle tyres to exclude the light. Here the grass ferments into ripe silage. Shiny silos and plastic-covered silage dumps are now a familiar feature of the countryside, signs that agriculture is simply an industrial process where economics, not aesthetics, prevail.

Above A ripening field of barley, heads blowing in the July breeze. Usually sown in spring and harvested in July, barley is Britain's largest cereal crop and is grown chiefly for animal feed, but the best grain is used to make malt for brewing beer. Unlike wheat, its straw is palatable and nutritious for livestock.

THE UNDERGROUND WORLD OF THE MOLE

Despite their apparent liking for lawns and cricket pitches, moles are essentially forest animals. As the ground thawed in the wake of the last Ice Age, moles spread northwards to recolonize the land that the species had almost certainly occupied before that long freeze. Ireland and the major Scottish islands were cut off by rising sea levels before the permafrost melted – which no doubt explains why the mole failed to burrow far from mainland Britain. As the woodlands were felled for cultivation, the mole became just as much at home excavating the soil beneath the new terrain of open grassland, arable land and even heathland.

The mole's principal food, by far, is earthworms, for which it has a rapacious appetite. Its catching technique is to excavate a system of tunnels into which the worms and other invertebrates fall when going about their own subterranean business. The mole simply patrols its network of corridors, harvesting the live prey that drops in on its dark world. In deciduous woodland and farmland where the soil is rich, earthworms are especially plentiful and even a modest burrow system is highly productive. In impoverished soils such as heathland and downland, the tunnels need to be more extensive and the frequent molehill activity indicates a busy mole. Its narrow, naked snout is very sensitive to smell and to movements in the soil, but its eyesight is almost non-existent. Some species of earthworms, such as the so-called 'night crawlers', emerge on the surface at night where they are pursued by moles. This is when moles, in turn, become prey for night patrols above. Barn owls and tawny owls are particularly partial to moles, despite the glands in their skin which apparently make them distasteful to carnivorous mammals such as foxes and weasels.

Below ground, the mole leads a very solitary life. Unaware of daylight, its daily cycle is roughly split into alternating four-hour periods of sleeping and chasing earthworms. In times of plenty, it bites the heads off its prey, immobilizing but not killing them. Rolling several worms into a ball, the mole will push its juicy package with its powerful front paws into a specially constructed store – to be consumed when it wakes from its next siesta. The only time that moles become sociable is in early spring when the male's ardour sends him in search of a receptive female. More often than not, he is repulsed from her tunnel system – but if the signals work, their mutual aggression is subdued and they mate. The male soon makes his way back to his own dark labyrinth, leaving the sow to rear her offspring in the breeding nest she prepares beneath one extra-large molehill. That is perhaps all we ever see of the very private world of the mole.

Life for a mole is a continuous round of digging and patrolling its tunnels, collecting earthworms and sleeping. Except for a brief encounter to mate once a year, they are solitary creatures.

July is also the time when commercial grass crops, allowed to go to seed, are harvested for seeding next year's hay and silage leys. Amongst the waving seed heads of the uncut field, you might spot the blooms of wild flowers that, despite careful grain selection and spraying by the farmer, have germinated and grown to maturity under cover of his crop. What the farmer calls a 'weed' is more often than not a tenacious pioneering plant that, despite all odds, manages to flourish where it is not wanted. Field scabious and greater knapweed look very much alike. Their lilac-blue flower heads sometimes spring up in grassland and arable fields, often towering above the growing crop. Scabious, also known as lady's pin-cushion, is readily eaten by sheep and goats but avoided by cattle. The plant was thought to be helpful in curing scabies and other ailments of the human skin. Greater knapweed, like its lesser relative, is a tough perennial of all kinds of grasslands and appears particularly on chalky soils where it is a favourite of downland butterflies. It too was valued for its medicinal effects, particularly on the skin. The famous seventeenth-century herbalist, Nicholas Culpeper, recommended its use for any bruise or wound, and even for sore throats and ruptures. Common groundsel, the bane of suburban gardeners, persistently blooms and seeds in any cultivated or waste ground. Its name derives from the Anglo-Saxon word 'grondeswyle', meaning 'ground glutton', because of its capacity to spread rapidly and monopolize the soil. But even this unpopular summer bloom was prized highly by herbalists who used it as a poultice for skin sores and for curing the 'staggers' in horses. To discard some of these once common British wayside plants as mere 'weeds' might well be as rash as dismissing the medical potential of the prestigious plants of tropical rainforests.

Left Field scabious and cow parsley cluster to the margins of a 'prairie' cereal field in Wiltshire. Much of the countryside is an agricultural workplace where wildlife is subdued.

Above Poppies, corn marigolds and scentless mayweed run riot in a Norfolk meadow that has not been fertilized or sprayed. The field is not productive for livestock or growing food, but through the summer it supports myriads of insects and other invertebrates banished from intensively farmed land. Its other value is aesthetic – and has no price.

Right Although related to the small and large white butterflies whose caterpillars feed on cabbages, the green-veined white (seen here on corn cockle) is blameless. Its caterpillars feed only on wild relatives of the cabbage, such as charlock.

Admittedly, some wild plants are harmful to livestock or seriously spoil cereals. Corncockles, for example, were once a familiar sight in ripening cornfields. Related to garden pinks and to hedgerow flowers such as campions and ragged robin, their purple-red flowers furled like flags, opened in July and were regarded as the most troublesome of arable weeds. If their large seeds were harvested and milled with the wheat, the resulting flour made bread which was bitter-tasting, even poisonous. Modern herbicides have eradicated these and many other wild plants from our fields and relegated them to the sanctuary of wild-flower gardens. As a result, many relatively harmless field flowers have also gone – species such as cornflowers and corn marigolds. Today it is only in such places as the machair of the Outer Hebrides that you will still see the dazzling beauty of traditional cornfield flowers. By July, the waving strips of barley, oats and rye are illuminated by these brightly coloured jewels that are now branded 'weeds'.

Most tenacious of all is the poppy. It is one of the world's most successful 'weeds', as old as agriculture itself. Wherever corn was grown, these blood-red flowers bloomed. They must have reached Britain with the first pioneer Neolithic farmers who came with their sacks of cereal seeds mixed up inevitably with the tiny black seeds of poppies. They can lie dormant in the ground for years. Once disturbed, they erupt in a blaze of colour. When the Romans came with their Mediterranean strains of wheat, more poppies were sown across Britain. They became an accepted part of the cornfield. Even Ceres, the Roman goddess of corn, was depicted wearing a wreath of common field poppies.

Across rural Britain, weedkillers have largely eradicated this scarlet flower from arable fields. It is along the verges and embankments of new roads that poppies have made a great comeback. A single plant may produce more than 400 flowers in a summer season and each flower forms a pod containing countless minute seeds. Seemingly eliminated from one field, they spring up along the edge of another. Some fields go a decade without the appearance of a single poppy. Then one year, perhaps when spared the herbicidal spray, they reappear with a vengeance. From June through to the end of September, they blaze a trail of defiance through our countryside – a riot of colour in a landscape tamed by the plough and subdued by chemicals.

BRITAIN'S BLUE BUTTERFLIES

Summer is a time when blue butterflies grace heathlands, chalky downland and other grasslands of Britain – especially in the warmer south. Their delicate appearance matches the subtlety of their relationship with their grassland habitat and their dependence on specific plants and insects for sustenance and successful breeding. There are nine different resident species of 'blues' – a family group distinguished by the wing colour of the males (except for the two species of brown argus which have no blue pigmentation in either sex). The others – the small blue, the silver-studded blue, the common blue, the chalkhill blue, the adonis blue, the holly blue and the large blue – all have iridescent, powder-blue scales on their delicately-marked wings – and are emblems of a south-country summer.

The brightest-coloured of all Britain's blue butterflies is the adonis blue – named after the classical god of masculine allure. All the 'blues' have great appeal, and a fascinating partnership with ants.

On the close-cropped turf of chalk and limestone downland, it is the horseshoe and kidney vetches which attract three of the 'blues' – the adonis, the chalkhill and the small blue. Both vetch species have bright yellow flowers and July is their prime flowering month. The horseshoe vetch, named from the resemblance of its seed pods to a row of interlocking horseshoes, flowers first. By late May most small blues and adonis blues have metamorphosed from their caterpillars and are on the wing, followed in late July by the chalkhill blues. The caterpillars of the small blue feed in the flower heads and developing seed heads

of kidney vetches; those of the adonis and chalkhill blue feed on the leaves of the horseshoe vetch. However, because their development is out of synchronization, the different species of butterfly avoid ecological competition with each other. The chalkhill blue produces only one generation of butterflies which fly from late July to early September, whereas the adonis blue and small blue both have two generations – one in late spring and the second in late summer. When the caterpillars of the adonis and the chalkhill blue species pupate, their chrysalises are tended by ants which often bury them in special chambers in their ant hills or very near by. The reward for the ants is the sugary secretion produced by the chrysalis which they 'milk' to feed to their own offspring. In return, the helpless chrysalis is guarded from predators during the time when it is transforming into an adult butterfly.

But it is the large blue butterfly which has the most remarkable relationship with ants. After hatching from its egg, which is also blue, the larva feeds on wild thyme flowers. After moulting three times, it descends the stem of its foodplant and wanders over the summer turf where, if fortunate, it is 'discovered' by a particular species of ant, *Myrmica sabuleti*. With its antennae, the

ant strokes a gland on the back of the butterfly caterpillar and sups the sweet droplet it exudes. Then, as if mimicking an ant larva, the caterpillar arches its back and rears up on its foremost legs, its hind segments swelling like a balloon. This 'programmed behaviour' prompts its attendant ants to carry the caterpillar back to their nest. There it remains through the winter, feeding on ant larvae and rewarding its guardians with rations of sugar. In late spring, the white, grub-like larva eventually pupates and emerges as an adult butterfly. Clambering from the ants' nest, it expands and dries its wings – and flies into the downland sky.

So specific and demanding are the ecological needs of the large blue butterfly that in 1979 it became extinct in Britain – a reflection of the fragility of its lifestyle, the wholesale changes to the way downland is managed, and the fact that, even in southern England, it had long been on the edge of its climatic range. Attempts have been made by dedicated conservationists to re-establish continental stock into specially prepared sites in Devon and Somerset – with some limited but promising success. Maybe global warming will also come to the rescue of the 'British Blues'.

It is now in July that chalk downland comes into its own. Across the short-cropped turf of southern England, the air is filled with the scent of herbs such as marjoram, thyme and basil – all reminiscent of the smell of Mediterranean summers. Harebells bloom in delicate clusters and blue butterflies flit between the vetches and thistles that bring colour to the sward. High above, the skylark patrols his domain, while his partner rears her second brood. Their nest is a simple scrape hollowed by the hen bird or set in a footprint left by a cow. Lined with fine grass, it is hard to spot. When the hen bird returns to the nest, she alights on the ground several metres away, then runs swiftly through the grass by a devious track intended to deflect attention from her brood. When she rises, her white outer tail feathers flash, perhaps as a recognition signal to her partner.

In winter, skylarks feed on seeds, but now in July there are plenty of downland insects to support them and their offspring. It is the impact of pesticides on the insect life of modern farmland that has been responsible for the recent dramatic loss of skylarks from our countryside. Once the most widespread of our songbirds, skylark populations plummeted during the closing two decades of the twentieth century. An official report to the government revealed an overall decline of 58 per cent on farmland. On downland pasture, where the use of herbicides is less severe, the birds still sing their evocative summer song. Elsewhere they are being silenced.

Beyond the open agricultural landscape, summer is moving on. By mid-July the roe deer have embarked on their annual rut. This graceful mammal, the smallest and prettiest of our native deer, is also the most shy. It is found in most wooded areas of Britain, from the hazel thickets of the south to the conifer plantations of the northern uplands. In spring, the time when the females give birth, roe deer are almost impossible to see. The only telltale signs are the tracks left in drying mud by their small cloven hooves. In summer, you might find a concentration of these tracks at the base of a single tree. Known as 'roe rings', these patterns are made during their courtship.

Roe deer seldom congregate in large herds, but stay in small family groups. They are good swimmers and move about the countryside with quiet stealth, often feeding at night. The bucks claim their territories in spring, marking the boundaries by scraping bark at the foot of trees and fraying stems to make the 'stocks' which they mark with scent from glands at the base of their antlers. The new season's antlers mature in May, when the does are giving birth. By the time the females emerge from their confinement, the bucks are ready to court them. Defending his patch with aggressive displays of fraying and scraping the forest floor with his forefeet, accompanied by his rasping bark, the suitor takes on other males who invade his space in a form of pushing match. Their antlers are not

Left Young roe deer. Born in spring, roe deer fawns are becoming self-sufficient when woodland vegetation is most productive. The family groups feed on tree shoots and shrubs of the understorey. Roe and red deer are the only truly native British deer.

grand affairs, but the intruder is prodded repeatedly by the defending buck, even when lying submissively on the ground. Inevitably, the territory holder wins, and the vanquished victim scampers away. The victor then turns his attentions to the doe, chasing her in circles round a tree, leaving the telltale circle of 'roe-rings' before she defers to his ardour. From July, it will be ten months before she produces her one or two offspring, a biological process of delayed implantation of the fertilized egg which ensures that roe deer fawns are born at the peak of woodland productivity.

July can be a wonderful time for woodland butterflies. Although often large and vividly coloured, they can be difficult to spot as they flit through the glades and high in the canopy. The best chance to see these most summery of insects is when they come down to feed on flowers and rotting fruits, and to drink at pools. The perfect butterfly wood has both mature trees and open sunlit glades and rides – a combination that is attractive to these sun-loving insects as well as to us. Although young conifer plantations have some of these qualities, when they mature and cut out the light, most woodland butterflies disappear. The comma particularly delights in sunshine and will bask for hours with its ragged-looking, spotted wings giving effective disguise from sharp-eyed birds. Even its caterpillars have evolved to look like bird droppings. Though essentially a woodland species, the comma visits gardens, especially those with buddleia and Michaelmas daisies. It is one butterfly that we can confidently say is doing well in Britain. Similarly russet-coloured and spotted but larger and with an even outline to its wings, the silver-washed fritillary has the distinction of being the only British butterfly which lays its eggs on the trunks of trees. The foodplant of its caterpillars, like that of other fritillary species, are violets, but unlike its relatives, the silver-washed female lays her eggs on tree bark a few metres away from a clump of violets. The caterpillars that hatch in late July have to hibernate for nine months until the following spring when they make the long march down the tree and across the woodland floor to find their first sustenance.

It is from mid-July to the end of August that you might catch sight of a butterfly that many people consider to be Britain's most spectacular – though nowadays one of the least common. Once known as the Emperor of Morocco and eulogized by poets, the purple emperor is more successful in central southern England, including parts of the New Forest, but is still

Top left The comma butterfly – well camouflaged in its woodland home.
Middle left Male silver-washed fritillary, showing distinctive bars on fore-wings.
Left Purple emperor – spectacular butterfly of oak woods.

found in a few woodlands elsewhere, such as the Forest of Dean, and is conserved on one well-guarded site owned by the Ministry of Defence. The wings of the male have a rich purple-blue sheen which glints when sunlight catches it from certain angles. The females, although larger, are even more difficult to see, because they are dull-coloured and spend their time feeding in the canopy of trees, usually oaks. They only come down to lay their eggs on the leaves of sallow, the foodplant of their caterpillars. The males fly along the woodland rides and glades, feeding on the nectar of flowers and supping moisture from the dung and corpses of woodland mammals, a habit never celebrated by poets. As noon approaches and temperatures rise, they ascend to the canopy, where they chase off rival

males from their treetop territories. The small, green caterpillars remain well camouflaged on the sallow leaves where they hibernate through the winter.

More common, more widespread and almost as handsome are white admirals. In the eighteenth century these large, dark, woodland butterflies with the distinctive white band across their wings were a rarity. The warmer summers of the mid-twentieth century and the neglect of coppices, where trees were once trimmed and undergrowth kept tidy, led to a population explosion. In July, they fly with powerful grace through the glades

Above Elephant hawk moth feeding on honeysuckle.

of oakwoods of southern England, feeding on bramble blossom and honeysuckle where the female lays her eggs. The scent of honeysuckle is the sweetest and most recognizable of any British wild flower. On summer evenings, its perfume is carried on the air, attracting moths from afar. Various hawk moths, such as the exotic-looking elephant hawk moth, come to feed on its nectar, and leave with pollen which they carry to another honeysuckle bloom.

Also on the wing in some of the woodlands of southern England are the country's largest beetles. The flight of the male stag beetle on a warm July night is an awesome and alarming spectacle. With its antler-like jaws outstretched, it careers through woodland glades in search of females with which to mate and males to engage in combat. The gigantic jaws turn out to be more ornamental than effective as weapons. When they engage in their head-on, rut-like encounters, rival males seldom do each other any harm.

Travelling north, summer has a different rhythm. The Pennines dominate the life and landscape of the north country – Derbyshire, Yorkshire, Lancashire and Durham. The special character of these counties is shaped by their geology and by their climate. Summer comes late to the gritstone moors and limestone dales, but when it eventually arrives, it bursts on the ancient landscape in a blaze of colour. July is a perfect time to be there, even if the weather can be unpredictable. The Pennines form an imposing north-south barrier to the westerly winds carrying moisture off the Atlantic. Even in summer, cloud and rain can prevail, but when they clear and the sunshine breaks through, this becomes one of Britain's most green and beautiful landscapes, revealing peat bogs swathed in nodding heads of cotton grass and spangled with Pennine specialities such as bog asphodel.

If you visit the Upper Teesdale National Nature Reserve on such a day, you will discover one of the most colourful and fascinating plant communities in Britain. It has survived almost intact for 10,000 years, ever since final remnants of the last Ice Age retreated from the Pennines. Much of the area is made up of 'sugar limestone' which, because of its unstable, granulated texture, has prevented colonization by woodland. Instead, the ground is carpeted in late spring by colourful alpine plants such as the brilliant, deep blue spring gentian and by mountain avens, with their distinctive eight-petalled white flowers that rise on tall, slender stems from evergreen clusters of hairy leaves. Now in summer, their place is taken by the flowers of lady's mantle and alpine bartsia, and sometimes by the rare alpine meadow-rue. Another notable speciality is the Teesdale sandwort. In all, there are some 75 rare and beautiful plant species surviving in the higher parts of the Pennines. They are a relic flora from past millennia when the demanding climate of these uplands dominated much more of Britain. Now in July they are in their prime.

Top left Dragonflies that dart at their prey or rivals are termed 'darters'. They tend to be sturdier-bodied than the 'hawkers' which restlessly patrol their territory – such as this elegant southern hawker dragonfly with a wingspan of 10 centimetres (4 inches).
Left Sundews can grow in impoverished terrain such as heathland and moorland because they absorb the nutrients from insects caught in their sticky leaves, which curl over and trap the struggling prey. This is the oblong-leaved sundew.

THE BARN OWL – FARMERS' ALLY IN RETREAT

Of all Britain's six species of owl, it is the barn owl that, for some time, has given conservationists the greatest concern. With the wheezy cry that builds into the classic eerie shriek, the adult bird has white underparts and a white, heart-shaped face with bold staring eyes which add to its ghostly appearance in flight. Though not the most numerous of British owls, it was often the most familiar because it used to frequent buildings, even in populated suburbs. In the dusk and at night it hunts over grassland and scrub for its prey of mice, voles, shrews and small rats. Its soft wing pinions make no sound as it flaps and glides as a silent shadow, conspicuous only in moonlight or caught briefly in the beams of vehicle headlamps.

To the farmer and the horticulturist, the barn owl has been a useful ally – controlling rodent pests – but it is the change in the agricultural scene which has contributed most to its demise. Rough meadows harbouring field voles, over which barn owls used to quarter, play no commercial part in modern farming. Yards and haystacks that once attracted rodents have been replaced by covered silos, and derelict or ramshackle farm buildings have been modernized or converted to fashionable dwellings. There are very few traditional barns left for barn owls. This preoccupation with sanitizing the countryside extends to the fields themselves. Field margins have been eliminated by more efficient machines, scrubland cleared and old trees cut down. Hollow elms were once a favourite roosting and breeding site for barn owls and other species, but, plagued by Dutch elm disease, these have fast disappeared as features of the hedgerow.

Although its wings are silent in flight, the barn owl often utters a long, eerie shriek while flying through the darkness. Dubbed 'the prophet of woe', it is now feared that this handsome bird is in decline.

Other owls seem to have escaped the barn owl's fate. The short-eared owl has fared better because of the spread of conifer forestry on the margins of moorland where it hunts for its prey, and because it also favours saltmarsh. The long-eared owl is also benefiting from mature stands of conifers – and the tawny and little owls seem to have held their numbers until recently, despite the changing woodland and agricultural scene. A census of barn owls in the mid-1980s showed that there had been a dramatic drop of 70 per cent since the 1930s, when traditional farming patterns were still the rule and the barn owl population in England and Wales alone exceeded 12,000 pairs. Severe winter weather in the 1960s took its toll by depleting prey – as has poisoning by pesticides. Insect and fungal sprays also enter the food-chain via field voles and mice, and toxins are passed to the owls that eat them. The latest survey in the late 1990s showed that although the overall number of barn owls in Britain had stabilized at 4000 breeding pairs, the species is very patchy in its distribution. The lowlands of south-west Scotland remain a real barn owl stronghold, as do parts of East Anglia, but this attractive and useful species has a precarious future in much of Britain – unless conservation measures, such as providing special owl-friendly nestboxes, can be targeted in places where small mammals still thrive.

Down in the dales of Yorkshire and other valleys of the Pennines, you can still discover traditional hay meadows. Heavily grazed in spring, they are at their floral best in June and July. It is the underlying limestone which gives them their special character and because they lie at altitudes of 200–300 metres (700–1000 feet), these upland meadows are not ready for haymaking until late July. By then, most of the meadow grasses and other plants that flourish on the limestone soil have completed their cycle of flowering and setting seed. Such ancient hay meadows often feature a great variety of grass species – sheep's fescue, cock's-foot, common quaking-grass, false brome, meadow foxtail and the scented vernal grass which gives the distinctive sweet smell to new-mown hay. Intermingled with the grasses are the familiar flowers found in many lowland meadows – species such as buttercups and daisies, dandelions and clover. But these northern meadows boast many local specialities such as the beautifully upright wood crane's-bill with its bluish-violet flowers and the brilliant magenta geranium called bloody crane's-bill, the flowers of which are often as large as a 50 pence coin. Equally striking is the globeflower – a large, luscious yellow buttercup which adorns wetter meadows and the edges of streams in these northern dales. By the end of July each species, in turn, has flowered, set seed and begun to fade. One of the last to complete its flowering is the yellow rattle. When its seeds ripen, they are released into the seed-capsule which rattles in the summer breeze – the traditional signal to the dalesman that the time is ripe for making hay.

Throughout July, the long hours of daylight work their magic. In Scotland the sun rises early and sets much later than in the south of England. Because of its often cloud-free days, Tiree in the Inner Hebrides has the most hours of sunshine anywhere in Britain. In Orkney and Shetland, the most northerly isles, nights are so brief that you can often read at midnight in the perpetual twilight. Plants and animals which started their reproductive processes late in the spring can now catch up with their counterparts in the south. For some birds of moorland such as meadow pipits, lapwing and golden plover, the long hours of daylight give them a second chance to rear a family. Long-legged waders such as curlews use their probing bills to extract insect larvae and worms from the soil beneath the sward. Their chicks grow rapidly and are soon ready to leave for the journey to their wintering grounds. Most curlews stay in Britain for winter, moving to the coastal mudflats and saltmarshes where their long bills and legs will help them find food of a different kind.

The moors and highlands are left to a few bird species that have yet to complete their breeding. The hangers-on include several smaller moorland birds such as ring ouzels, wheatears and whinchats, all of which run the gauntlet each time they go out in search of food for the chicks waiting in their nests. Britain's smallest falcon, the merlin, inhabits open country above the tree-line. The slate-grey male is no larger than a thrush. It flies fast and level in search of prey, darting erratically and expending much energy in its hunting. Its prey include beetles and other insects, lizards and mice, but mainly the smaller birds of the moors – particularly meadow pipits which make up 80–90 per cent of its prey. An individual merlin may take two or three a day to satiate its hunger and fuel its energetic flight.

Merlins nest late in the spring. When the clutch of four or five eggs hatch, there is a surplus of newly fledged young birds of other moorland species for the male to pursue as food for his growing family. After fledging, the young birds sometimes stay together in a family group for the remainder of the summer, before dispersing to spend winter in warmer places such as the western seaboard of France. Here in Britain, the merlin is a rare bird compared to earlier this century. In winter, its haunts include the coast and low-lying marshes of England and Wales. Its beautifully marked, reddish eggs were prized by collectors before the trade was outlawed. Now the merlin's only enemies are intolerant gamekeepers who fear for the chicks of their precious grouse, and the general pressure on wilderness to which we all contribute one way or another. Shy creatures such as the merlin still have mixed fortunes even in today's enlightened Britain.

Right Female merlin on 'plucking post' with dead meadow pipit which she will deliver, ready-plucked, to her fledglings waiting in the heather.

'sandy heaths

and moors of

glorious purple'

August

Above and left
If the month of August has a natural colour, it is purple.
The fragmented heaths of southern England and the great expanses
of northern moor are swathed in heather.

Britain has the General Education Acts of Victorian times to thank for selecting August as the customary month for the annual family holiday. It was traditionally the time for gathering the grain harvest, and almost everyone in the countryside was required to lend a hand. Even children were useful in turning sheaves or scaring crows from the gleanings. So when primary education became obligatory for every boy and girl up to the age of ten, a summer break was established for the month of August and everyone took to the fields. Now less than 1 per cent of the population work on the land, and very few of those have anything to do with harvesting. Massive machines and a handful of specialists is all it takes to crop and process the vast expanses of wheat and barley that now make Britain more than self-sufficient in grain. Gone are the wavy lines left by the reaper and the rows of stooks left to dry in the late summer sun. In a few rural counties where there are thatched cottages, wheat with long straw is specially grown from old-fashioned hybrid stock and cut with a pre-war binder to conserve the length and strength of the reed. Only there might you catch the smell and flavour of the bygone harvest field and the general urgency to gather in the bounty of the land.

Today's commercial harvesting takes place in July, sometimes earlier. Winter-resistant hybrids, artificial fertilizers and pesticides all hasten modern wheat and barley to immaculate perfection long before schools end their summer term. Nowadays, by the time most British families set off for the seaside or the hills, the arable countryside is a featureless sward of close-cropped stubble ready to be ploughed and drilled with next year's grain. Disappointingly, August often has less sunshine than either July or September. It is the annual lament of many holiday-makers that the month can be wet, especially inland.

In the hedgerows, the first elderberries and blackberries are ripening and trees such as rowan and yew already carry red fruits. The leggy stems of cow parsley, the first umbellifer to flower, are now a withered tangle topped by long, black fruits. Its close relative, rough chervil, which also carries large umbrella-shaped flower heads, now has purple seeds which are ridged and tapered towards their tips. Alongside, you might find hedge parsley still flowering and another related species, wild carrot, which favours chalky soils. Soon even these late-flowering umbellifers will turn to seed and add to the jumble of dry stalks that signal the end of summer.

Above The agricultural revolution during the latter half of the twentieth century has transformed the look and the rhythm of the British countryside. The ancient grasslands of Salisbury Plain are now cereal crops, which have been harvested by August.

FORBIDDEN FRUIT

Why so many late-summer and autumn berries should have such deadly properties is an intriguing riddle. The poisons certainly deter many creatures, including us, from eating them, safeguarding the fruits to be devoured by others that might more effectively distribute their seeds. Pheasants, for example, eat deadly nightshade berries with impunity. The flesh of the fruit is absorbed by the gut, while the seeds pass right through to be deposited on another hedge bank, the start of a new generation of this sinister plant.

Along hedgerows and woodland edges, the conspicuous fruiting spikes of the arum lily, or cuckoo pint, lure wildlife to their brilliant, orange-red berries. They contain a nauseous-smelling juice with an acrid taste which is poisonous to people, sometimes fatally. Slugs and snails, however, devour the ripe berries and blackbirds remain unscathed – and thrushes, pigeons and pheasants also seem immune to the toxins. Equally poisonous to us are the berries of the various nightshades, members of the very wide-ranging Solanaceae plant family, which includes tomatoes, aubergines, bell peppers and the humble potato. Interestingly, some parts of these familiar plants can be mildly poisonous such as the tomato-like berries of the potato. Their wild relatives, the nightshades, contain alkaloid poisons which become concentrated in the berries and are especially harmful when unripe. Woody nightshade, or bittersweet, scrambles over hedgerows producing a succession of flowers which,

Black bryony berries are poisonous to people, yet hedgerow creatures such as the common, or hazel, dormouse seem immune to their toxins. If such berries were harmful to all wildlife, their seeds would never be distributed.

through the summer and early autumn, produce berries that turn from green, through orange to bright red. A necklace of woody nightshade berries was found in the tomb of Tutankhamen.

From August, the 'fruit' of the yew tree – technically termed an 'aril' – turns red and becomes attractive to many hedgerow birds, particularly mistle thrushes and blackbirds, which unwittingly help distribute its seeds. Most of the principal parts of this evergreen are poisonous – especially the bark, its leaves and its seeds. The young 'fruit' looks like a small, greenish acorn and is set in a paler-coloured, cup-like base which swells and envelops the poisonous seed in a fleshy, berry-like aril. This is the part which turns bright red – and is not at all poisonous. The arils are not only harmless to autumn birds but are sweet-tasting as they contain natural sugars. The birds devour them greedily, digesting the fleshy aril, but the poisonous seeds pass through their bodies intact. The toxic constituent of the seeds and the other parts of the yew is a cocktail of several alkaloid chemicals which are unique to the yew. Clearly they give the tree protection against browsing animals such as deer and domestic stock, which either instinctively avoid it or learn from bitter experience. The yew trees growing in churchyards are protected from horses and cattle – but that does not account for the ancient relationship between the tree and places of worship.

On open chalkland, most downland flowers are past their best, but harebells hang on often until September. Nodding in the summer breezes, their paper-thin, sky-blue flowers borne on delicate stems give them numerous other folksy names, such as witches thimbles, fairy bells and blue bonnets. Easily overlooked in the same downland turf is the curious downland orchid called autumn lady's tresses. This flowers in August, the buds sprouting in a near-perfect spiral around the stem. The small spikes of white flowers can form dense patches on short turf, especially in Sussex and Wiltshire and other chalky southern counties. The plants can survive mowing, which explains why in some years, they appear in profusion on some lawns, filling the evening air with their orchid fragrance. Their erratic appearance is also probably due to the irregular activity of the fungus which supplies the roots of the orchid with the vital nutrients that allow it to thrive in impoverished soils.

Picnickers spreading their rugs on downland turf are often irritated by the unseen presence of the dwarf or stemless thistle. This low-growing plant produces up to four flower heads from the centre of a very prickly rosette of leaves so hidden by the grass that they have earned the nickname 'picnicker's peril'. Its flowers attract butterflies, especially the rare silver-spotted skipper. Other more conspicuous thistles also flower in August and become rich in nectar. The large, drooping, cup-shaped flowers of nodding thistles, also called 'musk thistles' because of their fragrant scent, are favourite foodplants of several species of bees and butterflies, and of the distinctive six-spot burnet moth. Their caterpillars fed earlier in the season on downland trefoil and vetch. Now adults are on the wing, flashing their brilliantly red-spotted front wings before landing on the thistles to feed, often leaving their wings open, revealing a vivid, red warning to would-be predators. The trefoils and vetches on which their caterpillars fed, contain cyanide derivatives which are passed on to the adults. These moths are indeed poisonous to birds.

Above The spear thistle, the tall, very spiny thistle of cultivated land throughout Britain, is a contender for the honour of being the original 'Scotch thistle' of coins and heraldry.

In Scotland, the thistle is king. It was probably first adopted as the national emblem by the Stuarts – borrowed from their French allies – who since the fourteenth century had depicted it on their heraldry. To the rebellious Scots, the thistle represented everything that was fearless and durable, and its tufted flower and spines graphically celebrated their preferred method of defence – an impenetrable barrier of spears. The most likely candidate for the design used in Scottish heraldry and coinage is the cotton thistle with the tightly splayed components of its flower – despite the botanical fact that this species seldom grows north of the border. More appropriate perhaps is the spear thistle, a close relative of the creeping thistle, so unpopular with farmers and gardeners in the south. This noble-looking thistle is not only larger, but it has spear-like tips to its leaves which savage anyone who dares to pick it.

By mid-August, many deciduous trees have a conspicuous flush of new leaf growth. You might notice it particularly with oaks as they recover from the ravages of caterpillars which, through late spring and early summer, stripped much of their foliage. From the trees' perspective, this respite comes at a period in the annual cycle when they need to make their own preparations for autumn, when leaf-fall greatly slows photosynthesis until the following spring. Through the long days of summer, the energy absorbed from sunlight not only revitalizes the chemical processes within the infrastructure of the tree, but also materializes as the fruit and seeds that will fall and be dispersed at the end of the summer. This timely flush of new activity used to be known as 'Lammas growth' because it coincided with Lammas, a religious festival which celebrated the first harvest of the year and the baking of loaves from the new season's grain. The name had its origins in the Norse word 'hlafmasse', meaning 'loaf-mass'. Once these principal crops were harvested, cattle could be returned to the land for common grazing through the winter. These 'Lammas Lands' were vital to the commoners who had no pastures of their own. Churches and other benevolent landowners opened their gates to the local community until the fields were needed for ploughing or to promote the growth of grass for hay. Today the National Nature Reserve at North Meadow, Cricklade, in Wiltshire, famous for its spring flowering of snake's-head fritillaries, is still acknowledged as Lammas Land. From February 13th each year until the end of haymaking, this 18-hectare (44-acre) field is shut up to protect the growth of these rare and spectacular plants. Then from Old Lammas Day on August 12th, it becomes common pasture and, technically, any resident of the Borough of Cricklade can come along with 10 head of horses or cattle and graze them on this famous meadow. If they all took up their ancient rights, the sacred fritillaries would surely be trampled beyond recognition!

Many insects capitalize on the Lammas flush of new oak leaves, notably the purple hairstreak butterfly. Unlike some of the other hairstreak species, this is not a rare butterfly but is especially admired by lepidopterists. Old oakwoods are the best places to search for adults on the wing, but these are butterflies to be watched through binoculars and not by folk who suffer stiff necks. On sunny days in July and August these dark iridescent butterflies can be seen high in the oak canopy, dancing in groups around the growing tips of branches. It is here, on new twigs, that the females lay their eggs. The flight of both sexes is energetic as they weave around the new leaves in search of partners and egg-laying sites – and feed on the sticky honeydew deposited by aphids. They are very pugnacious butterflies, attacking other insects moving in their oak-leaf territory, including wasps. Even when not in flight, the purple hairstreak is a restless creature. When it lands on an oak leaf, it parades in a circle, flaunting its rear end where there is a bright eye-spot at the base of each hind wing, adjacent to a short 'tail', which together form a false head with the wing-tails resembling antennae. This arrangement is common to all hairstreaks and no doubt deceives would-be predators into attacking less critical parts of the butterfly's body, allowing it to escape with minor harm. The purple hairstreak is a true woodland butterfly and almost everything about it is associated with the oak tree.

Above The purple colouring of the hairstreak butterfly changes as the light strikes its wings from different angles. Their scientific name 'Quercusia quercus' doubly reflects their association with the oak tree whose Latin name is 'Quercus'.

THE BUTTERFLY BUSH

Little more than a century ago, no gardener in Britain had ever heard of the buddleia bush. Now it is one of the commonest sights of summer, attracting many species of butterfly to its impressive lilac and purple blooms. Justly known as the 'butterfly bush', it was first introduced to Britain in the late nineteenth century from China, where it is known as summer lilac. In their more natural form, the flowers are pale blue, but garden varieties range from white, through lilac to dark purple. Butterflies seem to prefer the white-flowered and very widespread lilac forms. The large compact spikes of buddleia blooms not only enhance the shrub's visual attraction to the butterflies but also intensify the powerful scent of its miniature flowers. Butterflies such as peacocks and red admirals, small tortoiseshells, rare silver-washed fritillaries and the common and garden large whites all flock to the bush to feed on its nectar. Other insects, such as hoverflies, and moths such as the 'silver Y', come for the same purpose, and several species of moths and at least two species of weevils lay their eggs on its leaves which the larvae then devour. For a plant introduced so recently from such a distant land to be accepted and integrated into the lives of so many native British insect species is a biological wonder, and encourages the thought that not all alien introductions need be a bad idea. The buddleia bush is now very much part of the British scene and has tenaciously colonized the most unlikely places, beautifying disused quarries and city wasteland, railway sidings and embankments with its vivid blooms.

Peacock and small tortoiseshell butterflies feeding on the nectar of buddleia – the alien shrub that has become the 'butterfly-bush' of suburbia.

August can be sultry. On average it is the fourth wettest month of the year. The combination of warmth and moisture makes some days almost tropical. This often humid time can be made even more uncomfortable by plagues of insects which take to the wing in vast hordes. In some years there is a population explosion of ladybirds. Aphids, the staple food-source of adult ladybirds and their grub-like larvae, can become scarce in late summer, and the adults fly great distances in search of them. Swarms are reported in towns and on the beaches, plaguing holiday-makers in their search for food and moisture. Some people have even been bitten by them.

Another familiar insect, almost equally dependent on aphids, is the black garden ant. These ants can certainly bite and also exude drops of formic acid which irritate our skin and deter other insects and some birds from eating them. They diligently defend aphid colonies from competitors such as ladybirds, and frequently 'farm' aphids in their nests where the aphids feed on roots while providing the ant colony with a convenient source of honeydew. On sultry days in August, it is common to see the mating flight of the black garden ant. Males and queens emerge from the nest in great numbers, usually at midday. They take to the air in black swarms, and mating happens in flight. Many fall victim to insect-eating birds such as starlings, swallows and martins. The fertilized queens fall to the ground and tear off their wings before returning to their ancestral nest or selecting a sheltered place in which to overwinter. The males, their task completed, are either consumed in the air by birds or fall to the ground and die. This swarming of ants often presages a summer thunderstorm, which clears the air and washes away the millions of spent corpses.

On sandy heathland, these August rains bring replenishment at a crucial time. Across the country, this is when many heathland flowers bloom and for several typical heathland creatures it is the peak of their breeding season. The rain brings out the exciting smell of the common gorse which has flowered through spring and early summer and is now heavy with clusters of ripe seed pods. When the sun reappears and dries them, the dark pods burst with a distinctive, sharp report. On heaths such as Purbeck in east Dorset, Britain's other gorse species, dwarf gorse and western gorse, are now coming into bloom, providing heathland insects with a late summer bonus. The yellow of these gorses, combined with the purple of the heather just coming into flower, is an image of August in southern England that few summer visitors forget.

Right A cluster of seven-spot ladybirds – the most familiar of 40 or more species of these little red beetles found in Britain. Their bright and boldly marked bodies warn predators such as birds that they are distasteful. The ladybirds – and their larvae – are themselves voracious predators, devouring countless aphids – to the relief of gardeners.

These fragments of heathland marooned by housing and road development are precious reservoirs of native wildlife. In particular, they harbour the handful of reptile species that endure the British climate. The sand lizard, for example, flourishes in Studland and neighbouring sandy heaths where it is dependent on a plentiful supply of insects. The female lizard lays her eggs in sandy soil where they are incubated by the sun and hatch in late summer. On the same heaths in August, the slow-worm gives birth. Like the common lizard, the female retains her eggs until they are fully developed and produces a litter of animated, thread-like offspring. The slow-worm, as every keen schoolchild will remind you, is really a legless lizard and not a snake. Studied closely, it has vestiges of limbs and distinctive eyelids which, together with its notched and not forked tongue, distinguish it from snakes. Despite its name, it can move very fast, slipping through your fingers if handled. The sensation is that this reptile has no scales, because they are so polished and neatly overlapping. Due to its close evolutionary affinity with lizards, the lower jaw of the slow-worm is fused in one piece and cannot stretch to accommodate large prey. Instead, it voraciously pursues small creatures such as slugs which it consumes in great quantities. For gardeners fortunate enough to have resident slow-worms, this is another good reason for protecting this remarkable reptile.

Above As heathland is developed for housing or agriculture and sand dunes become less remote from people, the sand lizard has become scarce. This pressured reptile is now protected by law – but not its habitat.

Left The slow-worm is another lizard in need of encouragement. Sometimes mistaken for a snake, the species has been treated with suspicion, but is the gardener's friend, with an apparently insatiable appetite for slugs.

SNAKES ALIVE!

All British snakes produce their young in late summer. The grass snake, the country's largest species, is commonly found in many different habitats especially damp meadows, ditches and the banks of ponds and slow-moving streams. It is at home in rural and some suburban gardens and is, of course, completely harmless to people. In early summer, the female lays hundreds of eggs in places where they can be left unattended to incubate. Garden compost heaps are much sought after, and a female grass snake will travel great distances in search of them. In August, when the young usually hatch, gardens can be alive with miniature snakes which disperse to grow and fatten up for the long winter sleep.

The smooth snake is not so cosmopolitan. Its sole habitat is the heathland of southern England. In August, females give birth to 15 or so fully formed offspring which, once free of their enveloping birth membrane, are self sufficient. Given a chance, smooth snakes can live for up to 20 years but with the continuing demise of heathland, precious few of these rare and handsome reptiles reach breeding maturity. They are protected by law, but many starve in the aftermath of heathland fires or succumb to the pressures of the rapidly changing face of southern Britain. The other native snake, the adder or viper, seems much more adaptable. It too prefers open places such as moors and heathland but also flourishes along woodland edges and on scrub-covered terrain throughout Britain. It is very catholic in its eating habits, preying on a variety of small mammals, birds, amphibians and other reptiles as well as slugs, worms and insects. It is our only poisonous reptile, but will only bite if accidentally trodden on or handled. Their young are usually born in August, and, like the other native snakes, they come into the world as miniature adults – each enveloped in a membranous 'birth sac', which is torn open almost immediately by the 'snakeling'. To encounter these newborn adders making their way across dew-covered heathland is a magical experience. Other than us, they will have few enemies in their long adult lives.

Female grass snakes often lay their eggs in a garden compost heap where the heat of fermentation helps with incubation. This, Britain's largest snake, is harmless to humans but is a skilful predator of frogs.

If the month of August in Britain has a natural colour, it is purple. It is the time of year when heathland and the great expanses of moorland are swathed in flowering heather. On dry southern heaths, such as Studland, the dominant heather is known as 'ling', a name which derives from the Anglo-Saxon word 'lig', meaning 'fire'. For country people, heather was a valuable fuel and, when dried, its brushwood made bedding for themselves and their livestock, whereas in towns it was used as packing material for the pottery and brick industries. In Scotland, they even managed to make ale from heather, a practice that started in Stone Age times, long before the advent of whisky. In Scotland the word 'ling' is not confined to heather and can refer to any coarse grass and rush that grows on heaths and moorland. Its association with fire reflects the way that so many heathlands were born as a result of tree clearance and the effects of burning. Without regular grazing and burning, most heathland areas revert to scrub and eventually to woodland. The same is true of moorland. Originally forested, these upland areas of Britain were cleared of their trees over the centuries for fuel and timber, and to create grazing land. They are all landscapes initiated and maintained by fire. If traditional management ceases, they are invaded by a different regime. In the case of populous areas such as the south coast, the usual fate of neglected heathland has been commercial development.

Left Arne Heath in Dorset is one of the few remaining refuges for sand lizards and smooth snakes. In August, the heath is a blaze of purple – but dry summers spark blazes of a different kind which further threaten these rare reptiles.

Right The adder, or viper, has a distinct zigzag line down its back and a 'V' marking on its head.

There is an area of broken heathland in the heart of East Anglia which in summer has the feel of central, continental Europe, rather than temperate, maritime Britain. For those who know it, Breckland is a place of haunting beauty, rich wildlife and with a long and fascinating relationship with people. With its centre considered to be the town of Thetford, this mosaic of undulating landscape, covering almost 1000 square kilometres (385 square miles), consists of sandy heaths interspersed with pockets of chalky grassland. It was one of the first parts of Britain to be colonized by the people who came from the European mainland as the climate warmed. Five thousand years ago, this was probably the most populated part of Britain, which had then been an island for some 2000 years. The famous archaeological site called Grimes Graves is the largest network of Neolithic flint mines found in Britain and could be considered its first industrial landscape.

Not all of Breckland is heath. Some parts have been planted with commercial conifers and others are farmed for wheat and arable crops. The mix has added to its wildlife diversity. Native red, fallow and roe deer are plentiful, as are the diminutive muntjac deer introduced from Asia to Woburn

Abbey about 1900 from where they escaped and spread rapidly over much of southern England. Unlike the native deer, they breed at any time of year and the females can conceive again a few days after giving birth. Though small, they are now considered to be potential pests on some farmland and in young forestry plantations, and are included in the annual programme of culling – if they can be tracked down. The older bucks of fallow deer re-grow their antlers in August, in readiness for the autumn rut. They can be seen rubbing them against trees to make their surfaces clean and hard, ready for combat. August is the start of the selective culling season of male fallow deer, but any culling of the females is left until the end of their autumn season.

Above The diminutive muntjac deer are most often seen at dusk, feeding on grass and shrubs, and even poisonous ivy and yew to which they seem resilient. The buck has short antlers and prominent fang-like upper canine teeth.

Above The Pinnacles of Staple Island at the Farnes, Northumberland are best viewed from the sea. In August, they are covered in auks and kittewakes, feeding their young until they are ready to take the plunge and start their independent lives as seabirds.

As August progresses, the seabird colonies around Britain become quieter as, day by day, the new generations leave the security of their breeding ledges and take to the air and the sea. At Yorkshire's Bempton Cliffs, most of the fledgling seabirds have left the crowded colonies and only gannets remain on the ledges until September. The juvenile guillemots and puffins are rafting on the sea, learning to fish by diving and swimming underwater. The young kittiwakes and gannets soon develop their graceful aerial skills which enable them to cruise effortlessly out to sea, and the gulls soon learn that scavenging from others is a rewarding way of life. Further north, off the Northumbrian coast, the same has been happening all summer at the Farne Islands. Free from foxes and most other predators and protected from the unrestrained disturbance often experienced on the mainland, these offshore sanctuaries are the final bastions for seabirds dependent on British waters for their food and nesting sites. Anyone who has seen the Farnes in July or August, when these rocky islands overflow with life, will appreciate their importance. As the visitors disembark at the jetty on Inner Farne and make their

Left Puffins – perhaps Britain's most appealing seabirds. They rear their young underground on grassy clifftops. When ready to leave, the fledglings emerge at night and by dawn they have taken to the water and started fishing for sand eels.

way past St Cuthbert's chapel, they are bombarded by noisy arctic terns that peck the heads of the unwary, sending them ignominiously for the modest cover of the information centre. But here on this closely managed refuge, away from the maelstrom of mainland Britain, most of the birds seem at ease with the presence of people – so long as we do not stray from our designated routes across the island. To watch the puffins emerge from their burrows just before sunset and stand in gregarious lines in the warm evening light, it is difficult not to imagine that they, too, take some satisfaction from the security and wildness of the place. The narrow but turbulent stretch of coastal water dividing the Farnes from the mainland is a graphic reminder of how nearly all of Britain's natural history – as well as much of its human history – has been shaped by its insularity.

On the west coast, this maritime influence is even more apparent. The warm waters of the Gulf Stream, known now as the North Atlantic Drift, not only bring a mild climate to the land, but occasionally in summer attract tropical sea creatures close to the shore. Basking sharks surprise the shrimp fishermen who trawl the Irish Sea and the Minches between the Scottish mainland and the Outer Hebrides. In recent years, holiday-makers setting off to cross the road bridge to the Isle of Skye first wonder at the palm trees flourishing at Plockton and are then amazed by the sight of bottle-nosed whales leaping from the narrow strait that leads into the Kyle of Loch Alsh. These previously rare visitors to northern waters now also reach the Moray Firth on the north-east coast of Scotland, and global warming may make their appearance a regular feature of the Scottish summer.

Summer in Scotland is a brief but glorious affair. On the moors, the purple heather almost glows. The first flush of red grouse have been routed from the tracts of land set aside for their summer breeding. The new generation of golden eagles are on the wing, patrolling the glens and making their own kills. In more wooded areas, wildcats are out on hunting forays with their growing kittens, the juveniles learning the field crafts that will enable each to survive alone in the autumn. For Scotland's other rare mammal, the pine marten, summer is the season when they mate. Resembling an overgrown stoat, but with longer legs, pronounced triangular head and longer, bushy tail, this adaptable but shy member of the mustelid family feeds on the bilberries and blackberries now ripening as well as preying on small mammals such as mice and voles and larger ones such as rabbits and hares. It will also take ground-nesting birds, including, of course, red grouse. This reputation has, for a century or more, put a price on the pine marten's head and been responsible for its demise in most other areas of Britain where private estates are managed by gamekeepers. Mainly nocturnal, these cat-sized mammals can sometimes be spotted in the headlamps of cars as they move swiftly between conifer plantations and moorland in search of their next meal. They are agile and graceful, equally at home on the ground and in trees, where they are one of the few predators swift enough to catch a squirrel. Their courtship and mating is said to be a passionate but somewhat violent affair. Like the wildcat, there is a delay before the fertilized egg is implanted in the wall of the uterus, a process which ensures that the young are not born until the following spring when food for the new family will be more plentiful.

Right The pine marten is not restricted to pine forests, although with the spread of conifer plantations, there is hope that it will expand its range from the remote pockets of woodland and rocky moorland to which it is now confined.

Left Red-throated divers spend the summer breeding season on secluded lochans throughout much of northern Scotland and its islands. Elegantly streamlined, they are graceful both in flight and when swimming underwater to catch fish. Their legs, set at the rear of their body, make the birds front-heavy and awkward on land, but they can almost 'run' on water when courting, by vigorously beating their wings. Both sexes have the distinctive red throat. Larger Scottish lochs are also breeding grounds for black-throated divers.

Below right At sunset, after a day spent foraging in the seaside town, starlings return to roost at Brighton's West Pier.

By the end of August, the highlands of Scotland are already showing signs of autumn. Soon the birches will turn to their classic, golden brown. Further south, in the lowlands, the last hay cut is long since complete. There will still be walkers in the hills throughout September and beyond, but there is now a chill in the air which sends them back to their lodgings well before dark. South of the border, the Lake District will host families until the beginning of the new school term. Then the fells and lakes will become the quiet retreat of walkers and boating people who escape from Manchester and the other northern towns for a late summer break. South of Lake Windermere are Morecambe Bay and Blackpool, summer playgrounds for families from Yorkshire and Lancashire in search of seaside fun. The hotels and boarding houses do good business well into September, by which time the tidal flats of Morecambe host the annual bird invasion from the north – the vast flocks of waders and wildfowl that spend winter on its ice-free mud.

At Birmingham, the M6 motorway becomes the M5, continuing its arterial course down the west of England. The traditional August Bank Holiday weekend turns this highway into the final traffic jam of summer. Cars, coaches and caravans ply in both directions as the Lakes in the north and the sunny resorts of the West Country tempt people out for the last official break before Christmas. All too soon, the holiday season is over and the long trek home begins. Glimpsed from the cocoon of the motor vehicle, the countryside rolls by, surreal and out of reach. Its sounds and smells remain cut off by glass and tarmac, but its images fleetingly draw the eye. Driving northwards from Devon and Cornwall, heading for Bristol and the M4 junction to London, the wagon-train of returning holiday-makers snakes over the Somerset Levels. To the right, the distinctive landmark of Glastonbury Tor rises like a beacon from a timeless agricultural landscape of meadowland, reedbeds and waterways. When people first came to Britain, this flat land was hidden beneath the sea. At a glance, you are transported from the fast lane to one of the country's most ancient and vibrant landscapes.

Today the Somerset Levels rank among the most productive dairy lands in Britain. They are also one of the country's most cherished wild places. In summer the pastureland is ablaze with meadow flowers that hum with a myriad of insects. It is a vital place for breeding waders such as lapwing, snipe, redshank and curlew. In winter the same Levels can be hauntingly bleak, as floodwater rises in its man-made network of ditches and canals, and reclaims the fragile nature of the land. Now at the beginning of autumn, the lapwings are massing in great flocks that weave across big skies. As dusk falls on the last day of summer and the motorway becomes a liquid trail of lights, a million starlings explode into the air in oscillating clouds to perform their twilight roosting ritual. It is an event which signals the change of season over the Somerset Levels. Throughout the country, the generous days of summer are making way for the uncertainties of winter.

'the fruits

of summer

gathered in'

September

Above The red kite – once the scavenging denizen of medieval
England – has become the conservation success of Wales.
Left Autumn colours are revealed first in the northern uplands.
Silver birch and bracken turning gold in the Peak District.

The very name of the month captures its temperament. Eulogized in poetry and song, the sound of the word evokes the bittersweet character of this time of year. We hang on to the memory of summer, knowing all too well that the mellow days ahead are but a prelude to damp and darkness. In the capital, the Albert Hall is packed for the last night of 'The Proms' – that stirring blend of nostalgia and patriotism which marks the end of 'the season'. As the promenaders leave the hallowed hall and mingle with the crowds in Hyde Park, there is an unspoken melancholy, a lament for the brevity of summer. But statistically, September is sunnier than August, and October can bring an 'Indian summer'. Autumn in Britain can be its finest season.

In Glen Affric and the other patches of ancient Caledonian forest, the birches begin to turn gold towards the end of this month, but further south the spectacle of autumn colours is sometimes not apparent until the end of October. Just as spring unfolded northwards at walking pace, autumn sweeps down the country in a measured way. Ramblers on the moors of the Scottish Highlands may notice the well-worn tracks of the mountain hare among the fading heather. Through the summer, the hares have feasted on bilberries, which ripened in August, and on the shoots of flowering cottongrass. Now they revert to their staple diet of heather shoots and wiry moorland grasses. The last of their litters were born in August, and these leverets still have their light-coloured juvenile coats. Soon the adults will begin to moult, shedding their brown summer disguise and taking on the white of winter. The process is triggered by the decreasing hours of daylight, but can be prolonged over several weeks, leaving the hares conspicuous and even more vulnerable to predators such as foxes, wildcats and golden eagles. Their defence is to feed mainly at night, using their long ears and good all-round vision to remain alert. Like all rabbits and hares, their breeding rate makes up for the losses to their overall populations, and ensures that sufficient numbers survive the deprivations of winter.

Where they occur, red squirrels are very evident in September, scurrying across the forest floor in search of autumn fruits to eat immediately and nuts to store. Beech mast and hazel nuts are their favourites and, like their grey cousins, they go to great lengths to hide them. So intent are they on burying their cache, that they can be easily approached and watched for minutes on end. In early

Right Unlike the mountain hare, the brown hare has little need to change colour with the seasons. It is a shy but very alert mammal favouring open, lowland country where it can shelter in a ploughed furrow or in 'forms' scraped in the bare soil. Its main defences are its eyes and ears – sharp and mobile. If threatened, it can take to its ample heels and outrun most predators. The arable counties of eastern England now hold almost two-thirds of Britain's hares – but there is a nationwide campaign to double the population by 2010.

Above Compared with their grey cousins, red squirrels are more susceptible to fluctuations in their food supply. A poor autumn harvest of pine cones will severely dent their numbers and many will die from starvation in the winter.

autumn, their ear tufts develop and they become more bushy-tailed. These agile, russet-coated creatures perfectly complement the amber-coloured woodland of the Scottish glens.

Rain brings a vibrant clarity to the colours of the Highlands, making it a favourite time for walkers. The quality of September sunshine is unmistakable. Shirtsleeves can be the order of the day, but by late afternoon the mist begins to form. At night, temperatures drop dramatically and ground frost is common. The air clears to reveal breathtaking star-scapes that reach right down to meet the sharp outlines of the hills, punctuated by familiar silhouettes of the Scots pine. Far from the light pollution of any town, Glen Affric and the other vestiges of the prehistoric Caledonian forest seem on a grander scale at night. You could be forgiven for thinking that they go on for ever.

In the lowlands of Scotland, cereal crops sometimes stand until September, but such late harvests have become exceptional. As with agricultural areas further south in Britain, modern hybrids usually ripen in July and August, and the grain and straw is 'safely gathered in' long before the season of harvest festivals. On many farms throughout Britain, as soon as the combines have returned to their yards, the ploughs are turning the stubble. This greatly reduces the autumn and winter food for birds such as skylarks, linnets and corn buntings – another reason why their populations have plummeted. Some farmers also save time and trouble by drilling seed directly into the freshly harvested fields. Early planting gives the seedlings a head start before falling ground temperatures slow the growth and frost deprives the roots of moisture. Other farmers wait for spring, the more traditional time for sowing. They all share the same problem of how to dispose of the stubble and straw. There was a time when September in cereal country was characterized by palls of dark smoke that rose from fields crackling with fire. Undeniably, the brief, intense heat cleansed the ground, helping to rid it of weeds and the larvae and eggs of insect pests. But the impact on field margins and hedges could be devastating to harmless wildlife.

Since 1990, the practice of stubble and straw burning has been outlawed in England and Wales by legislation and common consent. Instead, the countryside is strewn with an ever-increasing number of giant, cylindrical bales, waiting for a cost-effective scheme for their recycling or disposal. Turning in the stubble with the plough adds very little nutrient to the soil, although in the long term it can add to its texture. What it does is to bury and destroy most weeds and begin the process of breaking up the compacted top soil of the field. Worms and all manner of beetle larvae and other grubs are brought to the surface – a bonanza for the waiting rooks and gulls that follow every movement of the farmer and his plough. Today's tractors are powerful and the ploughs they wield are massive. Although the basic design has changed little since the plough was invented in prehistoric times, the mechanism has become so sophisticated that, in one pass, the driver can carve four or five furrows. The reversible system can turn the sod to either side, allowing the ploughman to work from either end of the field and to plough every part of it without leaving traditional headlands. From a wildlife conservation perspective, this advance is double-edged. It reduces the rough grass – an essential habitat for insects and other invertebrates needed by many birds and mammals – but it does away with the need to grub up more hedgerows to make turning space for these giant machines.

Left The wood mouse – also known as the long-tailed field mouse – does not resort to full hibernation, although it can cut down its energy consumption by adopting a state of torpor. To prepare for winter, it must fatten up on the fruits of autumn, and blackberries are especially sweet at this time of year.

Best known of the hedgerow's autumn fruits is the blackberry. For generations, 'brambling' has been a British countryside pursuit in August and September. Delicious in jams and jellies, with apples in pies, or simply fresh from the hedge, blackberries are one of the enduring symbols of the country way of life. The name 'bramble' embraces many different forms. Some expert students of the bramble consider that Britain has 400 micro-species, each one slightly different in its flowering and fruiting schedule and in the size, shape, texture and flavour of its berries. In all its forms, the flowers at the tips of the mature, thorny stems are the first to set and usually produce the sweetest fruits. As they ripen, the multi-seeded berries turn from green through red to a deep, glossy black, as the transformation process works its way back up the bramble. For six weeks or more, these stalwarts of the hedgerow provide a feast for wildlife, all of which raid the brambles for the sweet, energy-rich flesh of the berries. The benefit to the bramble bush is that its seeds pass undigested through the wildlife diners and are shed elsewhere in ready-manured seed packets. Tits are not as effective at this distribution because they strip out the seeds before consuming the pulp. Song thrushes, blackbirds and bullfinches, being larger birds, are not as fussy and devour the whole berry. So do small mammals such as wood mice, dormice and squirrels. Blackberry picking is also a favourite autumn pursuit of foxes, badgers and deer which can be seen foraging in broad daylight for these tempting shiny fruits.

EXILES FROM THE HARVEST FIELD

The harvest mouse is so diminutive that it can balance on a wheat stalk. Holding on with its hind feet and prehensile tail, it uses its delicate but manipulative front feet and incisor teeth to cut off the ripe ear of wheat. Sliding head-first down the stem, with its pliant tail acting as a brake, it carries the complete cereal head to the ground where it picks out the seeds. During the summer, the diet of harvest mice also includes grass shoots and hedgerow autumn fruits as well as insects and weevils which they catch with great agility. Although they breed from May onwards, harvest mice synchronize their main production of offspring to the time when grass and cereal fields are most lucrative for them. August and September are the months when most litters are born in the intricate breeding nests they construct above ground level, suspended on long grass or cereal stalks. Using tail and hind feet for support, the female shreds green leaves into strips which are left attached to the stems and are woven to form the framework of the characteristic, ball-shaped nest, 5 to 10 centimetres (2 to 4 inches) in diameter. Working from the inside, she packs the interior with chewed vegetation and finally gives birth to her litter of several blind and naked offspring.

Traditionally the harvest was gathered in late summer. Today, wheat crops fall to the combine several weeks earlier, and, to survive, harvest mice have had to move away from cereal crops to breed in field margins, hedgerows and places such as rough ground set aside from mainstream, arable farming. They thrive in the warmer south, but are absent from much of Wales, northern England and almost all of Scotland. Optimistically, warmer summers may herald a return of this charming, acrobatic rodent to the grassy embankments of motorways which remain relatively undisturbed through the spring and summer. Active by day, the harvest mouse is prey to the keen-eyed kestrels which are a feature of our highways. In late summer, when we pass beneath the hovering bird, we can reflect on the agricultural changes which have made these marginalized corridors of grass stalks so vital as havens for wildlife.

The harvest mouse is one of the smallest rodents in the world, weighing less than a 2 pence coin. August and September are their peak breeding months – but, by then, their traditional home has been harvested.

Elderberries have also been ripening since August. In early summer their heavily scented, flat-topped clusters of creamy-white flowers attract battalions of small flies and sometimes bees and hoverflies which come to sip the nectar. The cut heads of elder flowers, steeped in water, make delicious cordial drinks and tea. In autumn another wave of raiders flock in to strip the elder bushes of their berries. Hanging in dense, heavy heads on their claret-coloured stems, they festoon the countryside. Elder grows well in any place rich in nitrogen, which is why it is so familiar on wasteland and near abandoned houses, in churchyards and rubbish tips – all places where the soil has been enriched by organic matter and refuse. For a similar reason, elder often springs up on rabbit warrens and on the latrine pits of badger setts. Elderberries are particularly rich in vitamin C and make dark wines, jams and jellies – healthy antidotes against winter chills. Well into autumn, the bushes are a larder for blackbirds and thrushes, pigeons and rooks, robins and blackcaps, all of which equally relish their rich, succulent berries.

Another highlight of the September hedgerow is the guelder rose or dogberry whose shiny, red berries are poisonous to us. The wayfaring tree, which is a relative of the guelder rose, has oval berries that also change from deep crimson to shiny black as they ripen. Although very astringent to human taste, they are not poisonous and are gorged by a great variety of birds. Through September, sloes –

the fruits of the blackthorn – ripen; they are the largest and most exotic of hedgerow fruits, revered by enthusiasts of sloe gin. Pricked with a skewer, sprinkled with sugar and steeped in gin, this traditional country liqueur is ready for drinking at Christmas.

In contrast, the hawthorn produces oval berries, known as haws, which are initially as hard as stone and seldom fully ripen before October. These haws, together with the equally resilient hips of the dog rose, help sustain many birds such as thrushes right through the winter. They are also favourites with small mammals whose teeth can penetrate the hard case that protects the pith. Similar skills are required to

Left The 'haws' of hawthorn – together with the 'hips' of the wild rose – are the hardest berries of the autumn hedgerow. They remain intact for much of the winter, providing food for seed-eating birds and mammals.

tackle the wild nuts of autumn. To watch a grey squirrel deftly incise its way into a hazelnut is a lesson in mechanics. After nibbling a hole in one end, it inserts its lower incisors and splits the shell in half. These nuts are so plentiful in late summer that squirrels only open those that have large kernels. You can watch them weighing up the nuts and discarding the lighter ones that they decide are not worth their time and trouble. Like all rodents, squirrels have teeth which grow throughout their lives and must be constantly worn down by gnawing. They nibble incessantly, including the bark of trees.

During autumn, grey squirrels methodically prepare for leaner times, burying or hiding caches of surplus hazelnuts and oak acorns near their winter dreys. Weeks or months later they can smell out these larders, even when the ground is cold and hard. Those that remain undiscovered or uneaten may sprout into a seedling in the spring. For the oak tree, this is its reward for all that autumn productivity. A mature oak can produce as many as 50,000 acorns in a good season. The warmer the summer, the larger the acorns grow. In September and October they fall to create a dense carpet in woodland, most of which is quickly consumed by squirrels and other woodland mammals, and by birds such as magpies, jays and pheasants. By November, most acorns have been cleared but a few are carried away from the parent tree and left where they might germinate. The jay, like the grey squirrel, is a fastidious hoarder of acorns. The bird can carry several at once in its specially enlarged oesophagus. Jays fly considerable distances to their favoured hiding places where they bury each acorn individually in the ground, often first creating a new hole with their beak before inserting the nut. Jays must have good memories. In winter, even when the ground is covered with snow, they can retrieve their hidden treasure. It is thought that if an acorn remains unearthed until spring and then sprouts, the emergent seedling acts like a flag and reminds the jay about its secret cache. But some acorns survive, albeit a precious few. In its long lifetime, an oak tree produces an astronomical number of acorns. Only one is needed to replicate its mighty parent.

Above Jays depend on nut-bearing trees, especially oaks, for much of their diet. Acorns and beechmast are greedily devoured when they are first ripe – and then hidden in underground stores as a cache for winter and beyond – if they can find them again.

PREPARING FOR THE RUT

In the New Forest, and in many other woodlands and parklands of Britain, autumn is the time when fallow deer engage in their annual rut. During summer when food is plentiful, the bucks build up their reserves of fat which will help them through the winter and also stand them in good stead during their battles for male supremacy. The massive development of their neck muscles dramatically changes their appearance. The mating rituals start in September when their palmate antlers are fully formed and they rejoin the herd of does and their fawns. The bucks parade round their territories uttering threatening groans and thrashing trees and bushes with their massive head-gear. They will strip the bark from trees and anoint the smooth, bare timber with a musky oil secreted from glands at the corners of their eyes. They scuff the ground with their front hooves and spray pungent urine on the bare soil. This very masculine business reaches its frenetic peak in the third week of October, when from parks and woodlands throughout Britain, you may hear their deep, belching cries as the dominant bucks fend off lesser males. Seldom pausing to eat, these driven males exhaust much of the fat of summer as they constantly herd the does and guard them from interlopers. When confronted by a buck of equal stature, the two will strut shoulder-to-shoulder, sizing up their respective strengths and resolve. This ritual 'parallel walking' probably serves to avoid escalation to actual physical conflict.

Red deer are also preparing for their rut. These handsome animals are the largest of Britain's land mammals. The mature stags can stand 125 centimetres (4 feet) at the shoulder and weigh, on average, 85 kilograms (187 pounds). Their antlers are quite different from those of fallow bucks. As they grow, the antlers branch to produce several distinct tines. Interestingly, red deer stags that frequent woodland and grasslands in the south of England usually produce heavier antlers with more points than those that feed on the poorer vegetation of northern uplands. It is only the exceptional 'Monarch of the Glen' that can boast a set of antlers with more than six points on each side. But the number of tines is not necessarily an indication of age; young healthy male red deer that have fed well through the summer can develop impressive antlers by autumn. Contrary to expectations, large antlers do not impede their running, even in forests.

Woodland is their natural home, but in Scotland much of that has disappeared, through felling or by overgrazing by the deer themselves, preventing regrowth of the forests. The stags spend summer alone feeding on high, open moorland. By the end of September, they begin to re-join the herds of hinds and young deer which move together down to their ancestral rutting grounds. By the first week of October, the larger, older stags find their voices and the rut begins in earnest.

Autumn is made more dramatic by the rutting of red and fallow deer. The palmate antlers of the fallow bucks (above) and the branched antlers of the red deer stags are specially grown for this annual event.

When the autumn equinox approaches, there are as many hours of daylight as in early April and some wildlife responds as if it were spring. The dawn chorus is revived and the familiar songs of chiffchaffs, robins and song thrushes return to the countryside and gardens. In hedgerows and in woodland glades some flowers bloom again. Violets which first appeared early in the year will sometimes produce a second flush of heart-shaped flowers in September. Interestingly, in early spring they rely for pollination on insects attracted by their mauve colour and, in the case of the sweet violet, their heady perfume. Now with few insects still on the wing, their seeds are set by self-pollination.

Some butterflies emerge late in the year and are still flying. Commas, for example, find nourishment by sipping nectar from autumn-flowering plants such as ivy whose globular flower heads open from now until the end of November. These flowers also attract the last of the summer's bees and wasps, and the autumnal moths which help in pollination. Rotting fruit offers butterflies and other insects a final summer fling. Fallen apples attract red admirals, painted ladies and tortoiseshells as well as the seasonal plague of wasps. The warm days of September bring out the last wasps of the year. Attracted by the colours of clothes or by the smell of sweet drinks and food, they harass picnickers and people in pub gardens. Unlike the bee, the wasp has an unbarbed sting which can be repeatedly used to kill other insects for food or as a defensive weapon. When fruit is plentiful and begins fermenting on the tree or ground, wasps literally become intoxicated and behave in an apparently angry, irrational way. It will not be long before the drones and the workers all die, leaving the fertilized queen to hibernate through the winter.

One effective strategy for escaping the worst of the British winter is, of course, to leave the country for a few months. September is the key month for bird migration. The migrants that came to Britain to spend summer and to breed are now gathering to move south. Chiffchaffs are frequently seen in gardens, singing as if it were spring, but gleaning the last of the summer insects from fruit trees and rose bushes before setting off across the Channel for warmer, insect-ridden climes. Some chiffchaffs may, however, overwinter in southern England, particularly in the mild south-west. Redstarts and whinchats stop to feed in hedgerows and yellow wagtails rest around reservoirs and in riverside meadows. Swallows and house martins, having raised their broods, gather on telegraph wires, waiting for the collective signal to leave. A burst of late September sunshine brings out swarms of gnats and other insects that provide the migrant birds with a last-minute opportunity to fuel for the long journey.

The hanging sessile oak woods of central Wales which resounded to the songs of the continental visitors in early summer, fall almost silent. A few resident songsters remain for the winter. Juvenile robins, now in red-breast plumage, proclaim their adulthood. The autumn song of robins is more wistful than their territorial and courtship routines of spring. Now that their moult is complete, many other birds resume singing, including starlings and blackbirds. Flocks of goldfinches, appropriately called 'charms', dance between patches of thistles and teasels feeding on their ripe seeds. Their tinkling, bell-like calls carry through the woodland, now burnished with the first real autumn colours.

Left Goldfinch on teasel head. At the end of the harvest, goldfinches and other finches flock to the fields to feast on the seeds of arable weeds. In the hedgerows and woodland clearings, thistles and teasels have formed their seed-heads which attract the noisy 'charms' of goldfinches.

BATS IN THE BELFRY – AND THE ATTIC

After the last Ice Age, bats were among the first mammals to re-colonize the British Isles. They first lived in caves, as many still do. Then, as the forests developed, roosts were established in hollow trees and the bats took to woodland clearings at dusk and at night to hunt for flying insects. As the forests were felled by people, some bats moved into man-made habitation, taking advantage of the protection afforded by roof spaces and other cavities in permanent buildings and capitalizing on the profusion of insect-life often associated with people and their livestock. For their part, people accepted bats as part of their lives – a mystique and folklore grew from their nocturnal habits and predilection for sharing our buildings. Medieval castles and abbeys became notorious for large bat roosts, and in later years church belfries and country mansions attracted their own colonies.

Today buildings of all kinds can be adopted by bats, and play an increasingly important role in their survival. In summer, 14 of Britain's 15 resident bat species commonly establish their nurseries in houses – giving birth to their young in attics, wall cavities and even beneath suspended floors. Pipistrelles, the smallest British bats, weigh just 3 to 8 grams and can easily roost in the narrow gap under roof tiles. In winter, many stay in their breeding venues and use them as roosting sites in which to hibernate. For this reason, when, in 1981, all bat species became officially protected in Britain, it was not just the bats that were given legal safeguards but also the buildings in which they breed and roost, even when the bats are seasonally absent.

One of the major threats to bats is the chemical treatment of roof and floor timbers. Fungicides and insecticides, principally sprayed to prevent or cure infestation by mould and wood-boring beetles, can be absorbed by bats through their skin, their lungs and their intestines. Because of their extensive wings which consist of thin membranes of skin stretched between their limbs, the surface area of a bat is about 25 times greater than that of a rodent of the same weight. Bats hanging on treated wood readily pick up the toxins on their fur and skin – and, being so meticulous in their grooming, they ingest whatever chemicals are not absorbed directly by their warm skin. The chemicals gradually accumulate in their body tissue, particularly the fat stored for winter hibernation. As this fat is metabolized, the toxins become more concentrated – and finally the bats succumb to poisoning. There are pesticides which are less harmful to mammals – including people – and which leave less residues for the bats to breathe or ingest. Used at the right time of year when the bats are away from the roost, such treatments can spare untold carnage in the bat world. The law requires home-owners and timber-treatment companies to seek official advice – for everybody's benefit. Healthy bats in the belfries and attics of Britain are a good omen.

The greater mouse-eared bat, last seen in Sussex in 1985, was the first mammal to be declared officially extinct in Britain since the wolf. The future of the other 16 species of British bat is in the balance.

The great British September migration is two-way. For as many birds that move south, there are probably just as many which arrive from the north to spend winter in the British Isles. It is the influence of the Atlantic Ocean which gives Britain and Ireland their temperate climates. Compared with Iceland, central Europe and the tundra of Siberia, winter in Britain is a mild affair. In September, flocks of fieldfares and redwings begin to cross the North Sea from their northern breeding grounds to feast on the hedgerow berries and fruits of a British autumn. Lapwings, golden plover and skylarks arrive from middle Europe and settle on the arable land of eastern England. On the Wash, the first waves of waders arrive. By October, countless knot and sanderling, dunlin, bar-tailed godwits and oystercatchers will be wheeling between the tides. From Chichester Harbour on the south coast to the Dovey estuary in Wales, Morecambe Bay and the Dee estuary in the west, up to the Solway Firth and the other great river mouths of Scotland, Britain is a winter Mecca for waders and wildfowl. Now in September these impressive flocks begin to gather.

Top and below For resident and visiting members of the thrush family, the British hedgerow in autumn is a bonanza. Hawthorn berries are particularly appetizing to redwings (top), fieldfares (below left) and blackbirds (below right – a female). Visitors mingle in great flocks with the resident population to 'raid' newly ripened bushes, often stripping them of their entire complement of fruit.

Left Hoverflies have bands of yellow and black which convincingly mimic honey bees and wasps. Many appear in late summer and autumn when they feed on Michaelmas daisies and other late-flowering plants. By then, the new generation of birds have learned from experience that black-and-yellow stripes warn of danger.

It is a month in flux. Migrant birds coming and going, foliage on the turn, the weather increasingly unsettled. The equinox brings storms and high tides that beat against the coastline, piling sand and shingle higher on the beach. On the dunes and shingle beaches of the south and east, there are still colours of summer. Bright yellow-horned poppy is in flower, soon to produce its extraordinarily long seed pods. The large and spiky sea holly is sporting its showy display of powder-blue spherical flower heads. On saltmarshes, the purple sea lavender has just faded but the sea aster is still in flower. Its attractive small florets of purple and yellow made them popular as garden plants in Elizabethan times when they became known as 'Michaelmas daisies' because the flowers were at their best around September 29th, St Michael's Day. At this end of the month, vast areas of estuaries and salt-marsh take on the purple hue of these salt-tolerant daisies. In the eighteenth century, from the former British colonies on the other side of the Atlantic, a more showy American aster was found to grow well in Britain. By Victorian times, these 'New World' Michaelmas daisies, together with that other North American import, golden rod, had taken over in Britain as the most popular cultivated plants of September. Some plant-watchers consider them unworthy escapees, taking over roadside verges and waste ground. Their saving grace is that they, like buddleia in summer, are alien plants that attract native British butterflies and other insects. Michaelmas daisies have a special value in autumn, when other foodplants have ebbed away.

Michaelmas was traditionally an important date in the farming calendar. Many farm tenancies ran from this date and in parts of Britain it is still a time of great livestock fairs, particularly for the sale and exchange of sheep. In some regions, geese that had been fattened on pickings in the stubble fields were sold at special goose fairs. All these get-togethers offered a chance for hiring farm workers for the coming agricultural year. Ploughing and sowing marked the beginning of the arable season and each employer would work out his finances and labour needs at Michaelmas, and take on farmhands accordingly. Hired for a year, the deal was sealed with a shilling coin which the new employee could immediately spend on 'all the fun of the Michaelmas fair'.

By the end of September, the autumnal pattern of weather has become established and in upland areas, such as the Welsh hills, farmers start to bring down their livestock to lower grazing where the grass will continue to grow. Red kites gather in small flocks to scavenge for carrion. In central Wales conservation of these dramatic raptors has been a local success story. They were once very common, especially in the towns of medieval England where they thrived on refuse. The kites did a very useful job and their boldness was proverbial. They even ventured into butchers' booths to filch meat and into the slaughter houses at London's Smithfield market. With the introduction of sanitation and formalized refuse collections, red kites disappeared from cities and took to the countryside where they

became familiar sights hovering or gliding gracefully over livestock land in search of carcasses and carrion, and sometimes raiding poultry pens. For the sheep farmer, these scavenging birds continued to be refuse collectors, clearing up the afterbirth and casualties of the lambing season. With the rising popularity of game shooting in the nineteenth century and the introduction of professional gamekeepers charged with protecting pheasants, partridges and grouse, fortunes turned again for the red kite. Wrongly believing that these birds were predatory on their precious charges, gamekeepers trapped, shot and poisoned the kites almost to extinction. The last English pair nested in Lincolnshire in 1870. Once they became a rarity, egg collectors finished them off – except in central Wales where a handful of pairs managed to escape the wholesale persecution. With admirable tenacity this small nucleus has survived through the twentieth century as one of Wales' best-kept conservation secrets. Without protection and feeding, they would have certainly perished. Today, a remarkable kite community flourishes in a valley fringed with remnants of hanging oak woods where the kites nest, and damp meadows where they can hunt for rabbits and young crows and rooks, and forage for tasty morsels such as lizards and frogs, snails and worms. Their catholic diet has been part of their

success, but for half the year they compete with ravens and buzzards for sheep carrion. This supply is crucial if red kites are to survive through the Welsh winter and from late autumn they are provided with extra food in the form of waste offal and abattoir trimmings. The lifestyle of this handsome raptor has come full circle. To watch them lifting and tumbling above the feeding station in the Welsh hills on a late September afternoon is one of the spectacles of autumn. It is especially reassuring to know that the untutored and irrational attitudes that were once the reason for the kite's demise have been replaced by an overwhelming affection and support for these birds that has its roots right in the heart of Wales. This innovative plan has also been adopted on Black Isle in north-east Scotland and is being copied in suitable places in England where the red kite can be reintroduced and encouraged. For Cardiff, Westminster or Brussels to issue protection laws and guidelines is not enough; matters of wildlife and countryside conservation need the commitment and involvement of local people who can make a real difference. Throughout Britain, nature has found new champions.

Above As September advances, the colours of autumn move further south. By the end of the month, places such as the Brecon Beacons in south Wales have succumbed to the new rhythm. Here, at Sgwd yr Eira waterfall in the Brecon Beacons National Park, the visitor is left in no doubt that autumn can be Britain's finest season.

'first frosts

and

ever-shortening

days'

October

Above Now is the time for hedgehogs to fatten up in
preparation for winter. Slugs and snails are still in abundance.
Left Horse chestnut leaves turning gold. October sees most
of Britain's deciduous trees change to autumn colours.

Nearly two millennia after it was so laboriously built by the Roman legions, Emperor Hadrian's wall still stretches, in sizeable fragments, 130 kilometres (about 80 miles) westwards from Wallsend at the head of the Tyne estuary across fine border country to the Solway Firth. Here, at Bowness, it meets an even more formidable frontier land – one of the largest expanses of mudflat and saltmarsh in Britain. Over those centuries the contours of the estuary have shifted and been shaped by the restless daily tides and by the fall and rise of sea levels. But its essential character and atmosphere have hardly changed at all. Even in recent times, the Solway Firth has escaped the reclamation and major commercial development suffered by the Firth of Forth, the Thames and the Severn estuaries. It is still a wet and salty, wildly beautiful place that ebbs and flows beneath the biggest skies in Britain.

On the north shore – the Scottish side – is Caerlaverock, the largest wetland nature reserve in Britain, covering almost 5700 hectares (14,000 acres). Much of this is saltmarsh, known locally as 'merse'. Here, from May to September, farmers graze their cattle on the vegetation which consists mainly of nutrient-rich saltmarsh grasses including red fescue, the grass much favoured for lawns. The close cropping through the summer turns the merse into a smooth sward, pleasing to walk on. Only the highest spring tides inundate this turf, but the salt water soon drains back into the labyrinth of muddy creeks and channels that break up the brilliant green. In winter, this lawn becomes the feeding ground for thousands of wild geese. With predictable regularity, in the first week of October, the serenity of the saltmarsh is broken by the yelping cries of barnacle geese as they wing in from the Norwegian-administered arctic island of Spitsbergen, 2900 kilometres (1800 miles) to the north, where they spend the summer rearing young on the tundra. Winter sends them south to Britain's more benign climate, and most of them return faithfully to Caerlaverock. By the end of October, when all 20,000 barnacle geese have taken up their winter residence, the spectacle of their dawn flight is breathtaking. As the easterly light hits this northern shore of the Solway, the roosting flock begins to stir and then, in ripples, lifts into the morning air with excited dog-like yelps. In a matter of minutes, the entire noisy rabble is heading towards its chosen feeding ground in the pastures and fields of barley stubble set aside for the birds' winter grazing. In flight, with their necks extended, the white faces of the adult birds contrast starkly with their black napes and necks and the light plumage of their underbellies, making the handsome form of the barnacle goose unmistakable. The more subtly-coloured juveniles stay with their parents until the next breeding season. Families spend their time together through the winter and, in the spring, fly as a party back to Spitsbergen.

WILD GOOSE STORY

Barnacle geese won their unusual name in the days before the Arctic was explored and the secret of their summer breeding grounds discovered. How and where these big birds raised their young was a mystery. Each April they flew north, returning each October with well-grown offspring. It was believed that the conical shells of barnacles seen attached to floating timbers contained the embryos of the birds – and the name stuck.

The Solway Firth barnacle goose saga is a conservation success story of immense proportions. For two centuries, possibly much longer, they have wintered at Caerlaverock, and at the beginning of the twentieth century the saltmarsh supported more than 10,000 of these noisy, sociable birds. By the early 1930s, their number was down to about 5000 and in the winter of 1948, when an official survey was made, no more than 400 could be counted. Three things were blamed: a run of bad summers in their arctic breeding grounds, the rise of wildfowling as a popular winter sport, and the fact that the Caerlaverock foreshore had been used as a practice bombing range during the recent war. Within ten years, barnacle geese were given legal protection in Britain and Spitsbergen, and in 1970 Peter Scott's Wildfowl Trust (now the Wildfowl and Wetland Trust), created a new refuge area adjacent to the existing National Nature Reserve, on grazing land made available by the Caerlaverock Estates. This, together with the tidal area known as Blackshaw Bank and similarly leased from the Crown Estate Commissioners, combined to create a very extensive winter sanctuary for the geese. Numbers bounced back dramatically, aided by a complete ban on shooting in Norway where the geese stop over in the spring during their return journey to Spitsbergen. There, on their breeding grounds, nature also helped by delivering a succession of fine summers through the 1970s. By the winter of 1982-83, the flock of barnacle geese over-wintering at Caerlaverock was estimated to be 8500 strong. By the mid-1990s, that number had reached 20,000. The spectacle of this immense flock taking off from their roosting sites at dawn, to feed on the nearby saltmarsh and fields, is a living tribute to one of the most successful international conservation stories of the twentieth century.

The white face and black crown, neck and breast make the barnacle goose very distinguished. The story of its conservation is a remarkable international achievement.

Barnacles are not the only geese that spend some of the winter at Caerlaverock. Pink-footed and greylag geese also roost on the foreshore at night and graze inland by day.

The shift from September to October usually brings a marked drop in general temperatures, as well as ever-shortening days. The first frosts kill off many adult insects and the birds dependent on them for food have to move south. Their destinations in tropical and southern Africa will provide them with an ample supply of insects before they head back to northern Europe six months later. Many of the birds that stay behind in Britain are fruit and seed eaters. Blackbirds and other thrushes, together with linnets and other finches, make great capital of the autumn harvest of berries and seeds that will also help them through winter. With chattering calls, they descend on bushes in large flocks, stripping them of their colourful fruits and moving north-east to south-west down the country as winter progresses. Later, flocks of migratory finches such as bramblings, siskins and redpolls move in from continental Europe to feed on beech mast or the seeds of other native British trees. Many of our resident birds now travel further afield in search of the best autumn pickings.

Left The wood pigeon is the largest of Britain's wild pigeons and doves, distinguished by the white patches on its neck and wings. It is undeniably the country's most destructive avian pest, wreaking havoc in crop fields and gardens. But viewed simply as a bird, they are immensely successful – and their plumage is handsome.

Wood pigeons, which gorged on the commercial harvests of rape seed and pea crops during the summer, are now joined by large numbers which have bred elsewhere in Britain. Together they maraud the countryside in huge flocks, raiding kale and clover fields and glutting on the wild harvest of acorns, hedgerow berries and the seeds of weeds and grasses. Their capacity to eat almost any seed has made them understandably unpopular with growers and farmers. Its relative, the collared dove,

Left Differentiated from the wood pigeon by its distinct black half-collar on its nape, the collared dove has invaded Britain at an alarming speed and with great success. There are now few corners of the country where its monotonous call cannot be heard. It is clearly here to stay.

was virtually unknown in Britain until the second half of the twentieth century. The species made its way through Europe from the Balkans, spreading at unprecedented speed. It crossed the Channel in the early 1950s and by 1955 had begun to breed in Britain. In its first decade of occupation it increased its numbers 100 per cent each year. Its formidable success was largely due to its ability to exploit commercially grown grain of any kind and in any place. Seemingly fearless, collared doves boldly enter corn mills and warehouses, maltings and livestock feeding sheds to eat corn – but in autumn they join the throng of other birds to raid nature's larder of its fruits and seeds. Like many other pigeons and doves, they breed at any season and can rear as many as six broods in a year, adding to their unbridled success. For many people, the most alienating feature of the collared dove is its monotonous tri-syllabic call, an irritating, mournful 'coo-cooo-ook' that it transmits in the early hours of the morning from telephone wires and television aerials, within earshot of open bedroom windows. Were its song more like that of the turtle dove, there might be fewer grievances. This visitor to Britain has a gentle purring call that blends with the feeling of summer. Essentially a bird of the countryside, the turtle dove breeds in the lowlands of southern England, feeding on the weeds that spring up on disturbed ground, plants such as fumitory and chickweed. In recent years, its success has been greatly affected by pesticides and numbers of this attractive bird have been drastically reduced. By October, the turtle doves' foodplants dwindle and, like the other summer visitors from Europe, they move back south.

Throughout the summer, fox families have, for the most part, stayed together near their dens. The cubs have grown fast and by autumn are almost indistinguishable in size from the vixen who still tends to them, bringing food, grooming and playing with them. The dog fox appears now and again but his interests lie more with the vixen than with his offspring. He may well have another family elsewhere, and as winter approaches, the capacity of his home range to support so many mouths will become stretched. As they have grown up, the cubs have become increasingly self-reliant. From August they have been exploring the countryside around the den, venturing further each day with their mother. In late summer, you might see a vixen with a large cub running at her side, purposefully copying its parent's every move as she seeks for signs of food. By autumn the cubs spend time on their own and on warm September days it is common to see small groups of cubs – probably sisters – lazing in the sun, alert to danger but relaxed with their new-found independence. The dog cubs become even more self-sufficient and soon break away from the family group, setting up on their own in good time for the testing winter ahead.

In the October hedgerows, there is now a damp inevitability that winter will come. Along the parapets of the hedges, the fluffy seed heads of wild clematis soften the stark, leafless outline. Known commonly as 'old man's beard' this straggling climber of chalky soils is a woody member of the buttercup family. In appreciation of its vanilla-scented summer flowers, it was called 'traveller's joy' in the days when people moved across the country following dirt tracks that hugged hedgerows. The sap in its fresh stems contains an irritant, apparently used by beggars in quest of sympathy, to create ulcers on their legs. In late autumn the plant is made very apparent by its profusion of shaggy heads, each consisting of numerous plumed seeds. With the onset of the first storms of autumn, the old man's beard is torn from the hedgerows and cast into the wind.

In the hedge banks, families of hedgehogs rummage for autumn pickings. It is the time of year when they are most numerous – and most conspicuous. The last of the summer litters has left the nest and the young hedgehogs are intent on fattening up before the cold forces them to hibernate. A cold snap may send well-grown individuals to their winter hide-outs by the end of the month, but with the tendency to milder autumns across Britain, many now stay on the move almost until Christmas. The youngest still need to fatten up and reach a body weight of at least a pound before they can successfully hibernate. These 'autumn orphans' can often be seen in broad daylight frantically foraging for beetles and worms and the slugs that seem so numerous on damp autumn days. There are

Above The red fox. At the end of summer, the adults look ragged and spent. Now, as winter approaches, they regain their splendid thick red coats.

23 species of slug native to Britain. All of these molluscs have voracious appetites and can rasp their way through almost any organic matter. In autumn there is a plentiful supply of discarded root crops, fungi and rotting vegetation. Even carrion is consumed, making the slug one of the countryside's most efficient food processors. The beneficiaries include not only hedgehogs but a multitude of birds – converting the rot of autumn into life that may well see another year.

It is now that orb-web spiders also reach their full size and maturity. In September and October their large circular webs seem to appear overnight. In the heavy dew of morning, their creations inspire admiration. No matter how many times we might see the process speeded up by modern techniques of film and television, their accomplishment is a determined feat of engineering that is simply amazing. The webs built by young spiders are just as elaborate, albeit in miniature. Spangled with morning dew, their design is very effective in ensnaring flying insects such as crane flies whose low, blundering flight carries them into the gossamer trap. The spider, lurking near the side of the web, remains in constant contact by a single thread of silk which it holds with its foremost legs. Alert to every vibration, it senses when an insect has stumbled on its trap. Sprinting across the strands of the web, to which it cannot stick because of special oil exuded on its feet, the spider grasps its prey and paralyses it with venom. Deftly, it cocoons its captor in silk, subduing its death throes and packaging it for storage. The venom injected in the prey also contains an enzyme which pre-digests the tissues of the corpse into a convenient liquid lunch for a future rainy day.

Left A hedgerow or garden early in an autumn morning can shimmer with dew-laden webs. Britain has 40 species of orb-web spiders – including the familiar garden spider.

Right After the insect is snared by the sticky web, the spider spins a silken cage around its victim – here a small tortoiseshell butterfly.

As gardeners will endorse, October is a time for clearing up. Lawns and grassy areas need their last cut before the frosts and lack of daylight halt their growth. The spent heads and stalks of Michaelmas daisies and sunflowers are sinking back into their beds and the last leaves have fallen from the apple trees. In well-established country gardens, the small, hard apples of the crab apple tree have fallen to form a durable carpet of fruit. This will eventually be consumed or carried away by slugs and rodents such as wood mice. This valuable native tree, now scarce in the wild, was the principle ancestor of the 6000 named varieties of cultivated apple. Its name derives from the Norse word 'skrab', meaning 'scrubby', which well describes this gnarled tree. On sunnier days a few butterflies still flutter, supping sweetness from decaying fruit and searching for a place to hibernate. The peacocks and small tortoiseshells that fed on the Michaelmas daisies of late September need sugar in their blood if they are to survive the cold of winter. Converted into glycol, it acts like an antifreeze while they are torpid. Some hide in fallen leaves, others seek out dry places in garden sheds and attics. If disturbed, the hibernating peacock has a reflex response which suddenly reveals the startling eye-spots on the upper surface of all four wings. Accompanied by an audible hiss created by the rubbing together of the front and hind wings, this is usually enough to deter winter predators such as house mice in attics and birds probing through the leaf-litter.

Visits to the compost heap might reveal amphibians and reptiles settling down for winter. During the summer, grass snakes and slow-worms feed on slugs, beetles and lice attracted by the warmth and decaying vegetation. In late autumn these reptiles lay up until spring. The compost heap is also a favourite hibernating place for frogs and toads – making it one of the most conservation-friendly of the gardener's activities.

In the woodlands, it is fungus time. October is the prime month for the appearance of their spore-bearing fruiting bodies – mushrooms and toadstools. These often bizarre and colourful growths erupt from the ground or emerge from the damp bark and rotting timber that now litters the woodland floor.

Through spring and summer, their mycelial threads have been insidiously 'eating' their way through the soil, 'digesting' dead micro-organisms or penetrating dead and decaying wood, and converting the organic matter into the basic ingredients that make up their own cells. Unlike true plants, the fungus has no chlorophyll and must absorb its energy and nutrients from other lifeforms. Many fungi depend solely on dead plant or animal matter, but some are parasitic, attacking living plants. The familiar bracket fungus that emerges from the trunks of beech and other trees, is the fruiting body of a mycelium that invades living tissue beneath the bark and may eventually kill its host. The honey fungus is feared by gardeners and foresters because of the way its black, 'boot-lace' threads reach out to ravage the roots of healthy trees. In autumn, its honey-coloured, strong-smelling caps erupt from the base of living trees and from the rotting stumps of dead trees. But most fungi are greatly beneficial. Without them, woods and gardens, fields and hedgerows would be overwhelmed with dead material. Constantly consuming discarded organic matter, fungi recycle the vital ingredients of life. As the fungus itself dies, as eventually it must, it releases precious nutrients back into the soil, ready to be reprocessed by a new generation of plants and animals. In autumn, from these unseen mycelia, weird and wonderful fruiting bodies emerge to cast their myriad spores into the damp, musty air – a tangible and colourful celebration of their inestimable worth.

Above Fly agaric toadstools. One of the most beautiful sights in an autumn conifer or deciduous woodland is to discover a group of these fiery red toadstools, freshly emerged from the soil. Although the fungus attracts flies, it contains a chemical that kills them. This property has been known for centuries and probably gave it its name. Recently, pharmaceutical researchers isolated the toxic substance from which they developed the insecticide, ibotenic acid.

In urban parks and country estates, horse chestnut trees, planted in avenues for their ornamental summer blooms, are now laden with conkers. First introduced to Britain in the late sixteenth century from its native homelands in the Balkans, this handsome tree is impressive at any time of year. Its sticky buds mark the end of winter and open to reveal some of the first leaves of spring. In early summer, its candle-like spikes of white flowers are truly magnificent and in autumn its luxuriant foliage brings burnished gold to city centres and village greens. Its leaves are the largest of any tree in Britain and as they curl and fall, they reveal the spiky green capsules protecting the seeds that swell into the conkers much prized by generations of children. The duelling game first became popular in the nineteenth century when the most durable horse chestnuts were known as 'conquerors'. As conquering children become adults, the sight of these glossy, brown nuts gleaming from within the splitting seed case, lined with soft white pith, remains irresistible.

Of the native British trees, the common beech ranks as one of the most beautiful, especially now in autumn. Pollen studies show that the species arrived here before Britain became an island, and advanced northwards through the maturing wildwood. Beech was valued by Bronze Age people for its timber, which made excellent firewood and for its autumn harvest of beech mast that fed pigs and other livestock. The beech trees of that time were probably more like the stocky, sprawling giants of today's New Forest than the elegant, upright stands now familiar in places such as the Chiltern Hills. Here, in the eighteenth century, the beech found fame with furniture makers who valued the colour, grain and malleability of its wood. Vast areas of the Home Counties were set aside as beech plantations and coppices, many of which have been allowed to mature into spectacular pollarded woods such as Burnham Beeches in Buckinghamshire. Such places are tame in comparison with the original forests of Britain, but they have a beauty which is quintessentially British.

AUTUMN GOLD

For many people – especially visitors from abroad – the most memorable season in Britain is autumn. This is still essentially a wooded country and although the great tracts of forest disappeared long ago, in nearly every corner of the realm there are substantial woodlands or small copses, splendid avenues and small stands or simply individual trees, all of which contribute to the nation's autumn spectacle. Most of Britain's native trees are deciduous and it is their dramatic change of colour just before leaf-fall that gives the months of October and November their special character. The leaves are the power-houses of the tree. In spring and summer the sunlight they absorb, with the catalytic help of the green-coloured chlorophyll in their cells, helps fix carbon dioxide from the air, combining it with water in the leaves to make simple sugars. This process of photosynthesis manufactures the building-blocks for the tree, providing the energy and basic organic molecules that will drive its metabolic systems and create growth.

The chemistry of 'the fall' is one of nature's triumphs. Whether in an ornamental setting such as this avenue of horse chestnut trees or in the depths of a beech wood, the transformation of deciduous woodland both delights and intrigues.

The green pigment of chlorophyll dominates the colour of the leaves of trees and most other plants including grasses. It is this rich, verdant vegetation that gives Britain its well-deserved reputation as a 'green and pleasant land'. But the leaves of deciduous trees contain other, complex, chemical compounds which add different coloured pigments to their cells. Most abundant are the various flavonoids (which are yellow) and carotenoids (which are orange-red like carrots). These pigments have evolved to help protect the chlorophyll from excessive sunlight radiation which breaks the catalyst down and impedes photosynthesis. During the spring and summer, the chlorophyll masks these other pigments and the leaves are predominantly coloured green. As the days shorten and the intensity of the sunlight wanes, the valuable chlorophyll is broken down and its constituents re-absorbed into the main body of the tree, to be stored until the following spring. As this green pigment drains away from the leaves, the other colours are revealed – and the glorious yellows, browns, reds and golds of autumn shine through.

The prevailing westerly winds and the ever-present influence of the Atlantic Ocean restricts the intensity of the sunlight through the British summer. Across the other side of the Atlantic in the north-eastern states of the USA and south-eastern Canada, there is less cloud in summer and the intensity of the sunlight can be more

harmful to the chlorophyll in leaves. In defence against
the intensity of light radiation, deciduous trees over there
generate more riboflavins and carotenoids – and, in
consequence, the autumn colours can be more saturated
than the damp, muted beauty of British woodlands. The
North American term 'fall' aptly and picturesquely
describes this season of golden colour and leaf-drop. The
reason why the leaves have to fall in these temperate
regions of the world is principally the coldness of winter.
Water becomes locked-up as the ground freezes. To
retain a dense foliage requiring constant replenishment of
water would be a taxing strain on the metabolism of the
tree. With the processes of photosynthesis slowed right
down due to shortage of sunlight, shedding their leaves
for winter is the expedient solution that has evolved for
deciduous trees.

The key trigger for casting off their leaves is not the
falling temperatures of autumn but the shortening days.
In response to the reduction of daylight, the cells at the
base of each leaf change their texture, creating a corky
abscission layer which seals off the sap channels that
serve the leaf, eventually separating it from the body of
the tree. Before the fate of the leaf is sealed, tannins and
other by-products of summer pass into the leaves, adding
to the brown autumn hues of trees such as oaks and
elms. As they fall, the leaves carry many surplus
compounds to the ground where, in the course of time,
they decompose with the leaves, to be recycled into new
plant life. By late November, most trees are bare. A few,
like young beeches, hang on to the vestiges of summer
right through the winter months or perhaps until a violent
storm strips them of their withered leaves and prepares
them for the renewal that comes with spring.

There is no mistaking a rutting red deer stag. The antlers of a mature stag are darker and thicker than those of a younger male, and he is further distinguished by the shaggy mane that clads his neck and shoulders, making him look ungainly and front-heavy. His fine red summer coat becomes darkened by the mud and peat in which he wallows and it also absorbs the rank odour of the urine which he sprays liberally over the heather and other vegetation in which he energetically rolls. Roaring guttural threats, he struts stiff-legged through his chosen group of hinds, banishing all other contending males with his bellicose posturing. Seldom pausing to eat or sleep, he must be vigilant for three weeks as each mature female comes into season. Each hind is receptive for only 24 hours or so, and he must mate with her to ensure that the next generation carries his genes alone. A large stag will hold together as many as 30 hinds in his herd, defending them against all rival males. As the end of October

approaches, although his ardour remains fervent, his weight and vigour begin to decline. He is now most vulnerable to competition, and younger males, sensing their opportunity, attempt to break up the herd. Demonically, he races through his harem uttering staccato coughs as he routs the interloper. Those that stand their ground take part in a ritual confrontation in which the two contending stags pace side-by-side in their stiff-legged gait around the contested group of hinds. The defending stag keeps to the inside of the circle with his head just in front. If the challenger bows out, he often vents his frustration by scything a

Above Red deer stags in combat. If posturing fails to deter the intruder, actual physical contact takes place – a trial of strength in which the antlers become more than a status symbol. Some battles are to the death as one stag is gored or expires from the combined exhaustion of the rut when he seldom stops to feed, and the physical conflict with rival males.

patch of heather with his antlers. Rarely, the sparring may end in actual combat. The two pacing stags suddenly wheel round and bring their heavy antlers together with great momentum. After the initial, noisy clash, there is an awesome silence as the two beasts perform a duel of strength and strategy. Each tries to gain the higher ground to force their opponent backwards in a rush. Battles seldom last more than a few minutes before one of the suitors senses defeat and takes to his heels. The victor returns to the herd, bellowing in triumph. As evening falls over the late October glens, the raucous music of the red deer rut reaches its crescendo. Soon the fever will subside and the herd will placidly move to its winter feeding grounds, alert only for the hunter and his gun.

In the fourth week of October, the clocks go back – a rude reminder of the impending season. In the north of England and in Scotland, winter rolls down from the mountains and hills and sends a shiver through the land. Wildlife and people hasten to prepare for the less propitious months that lie ahead. Traditionally it was a time for finalizing the winter larder, laying in provisions and stocking up with fuel. Legs of wild boar and domestic pig were salted or smoked and wild fruits were made into pickles and preserves to add extra zest to the dried meat that lost its flavour as winter advanced. Leaves and twigs of the juniper were burnt with beechwood to give an aromatic flavour to smoked hams and their berries used in pork and venison stews – and, of course, to impart their distinctive flavour to gin. Juniper, a native, evergreen shrub, grows naturally in colonies on moorland such as in the Lake District and Upper Teesdale, in Scotland and on chalk downland in the south. Through September the berries of the rowan have deepened in colour, and those that escape the attentions of fieldfares and other thrushes still hang in brilliant bunches when the leaves turn to their scorched autumn colours. Also called the mountain ash, the rowan is a hardy tree, growing with birches at high altitudes. Its more ancient name probably derives from the Norse word 'runa' which means 'a charm' and in Scotland, especially, its magical powers have long been revered. Planted near homes, it was believed to ward off witches because of the protective powers of its berries.

The end of October traditionally brings witches and goblins. In pagan times, it was a brief season when the divide between this world and the next became less secure and the dead returned from the grave to haunt the living. Ritual fires were kindled at dusk on hilltops and open spaces – to purify the land and defeat the powers of evil. Boisterous games were played and horns and other raucous instruments blown to counteract the fear of darkness. In AD 835, in an attempt to distract its congregation from these pagan practices, the Church moved Hallowmas, the feast of All Hallows or All Saints, from mid-May to the first day of November. Undaunted, the populace focused their ghost-busting rituals on the night before All Hallows – and 'Hallowe'en' became a folklore fixture in the calendar which spread around the world.

'morning mists

drain colour

from the land'

November

Above The nuthatch was previously known as the 'nut-hack' because of its ability to wedge nuts in crevices in tree bark and hack them open with its bill.
Left Mist lingers over farmland, often until noon.

November nights can be foggy. The mixture of bonfire smoke and spent cordite hangs on the damp, autumn air. As we return from the local Guy Fawkes party, figures loom from the mist like an Edwardian melodrama. In towns, disembodied street lamps barely light the ground. Other November nights can be crystal clear and the sky as high as the moon. In the country, the star constellations are bitingly real and the air carries the first taste of frost. Mornings can be magical, the frost and fog combining to cast a spell across valleys. There is a transparency that drains all colour from the land. Then, almost reluctantly, the flagging sun burns off the remnants of the night, and returns the richness of autumn foliage to the lanes and hedgerows.

In the field margins, a few late flowers are still in evidence. Mayweeds, despite their name, hold on to their daisy-like blooms, and even wild pansies and speedwells make a gallant show – a last fuelling station for bees still on the wing in search of nectar. These late-foraging insects move on to the large, generous-mouthed flowers of white deadnettle, a plant which will continue to bloom beyond Christmas. Of all the wayside plants, it is the flowers of ivy which seem the

Above Ivy flowers attract the last of autumn's adult flying insects, including the greenbottle fly which lays its eggs on dead animals or uncovered meat – and the ichneumen 'fly', a species of solitary wasp which parasitizes butterfly caterpillars.

most durable. From mid-summer onwards this tenacious climbing plant with its copious, dark green foliage produces knobbly flower buds which eventually begin to open in September. Their globe-shaped clusters of yellow-green flowers are laden with nectar which sustains many different insects throughout autumn and beyond. The nectaries of the flowers are easily probed by short-tongued insects such as bees and wasps, hoverflies, bluebottles and blowflies. For some, such as worker wasps, it is the last supper of their lives. For others, like honey bees that will hibernate, ivy flowers are their last stop before the long sleep. By the end of November, the frosts will rob the hedgerows of their colour and perfume, and the buzz of insects will finally fall silent.

Above As temperatures drop and the days shorten, life in the countryside slows down.

Many insects and numerous other kinds of invertebrates do manage to keep going through the winter season. From November onwards, you may come across a huddle of hibernating ladybirds, gathered together near the base of a fence post or in the corner of a window frame, relying on their bright red colour and black spots to warn hungry birds of their unpleasant taste. In the garden and woodland they pack tightly under loose bark, and in hedgerows they seek out the hollow stems of umbellifer plants such as cow parsley and giant hogweed. Numerous other beetles and weevils creep beneath logs and stones or bury in the leaf-litter. Others leave eggs and larvae in rotting timber or buried in the soil.

Woodlice, Britain's only land-based crustaceans, are also great survivors. They remain active all year round, keeping out of bright light and hiding beneath stones and fallen branches where they feed on dead plant material and animal carrion. Though they may seem unattractive and certainly primitive, they perform a vital function in the garden and wider countryside, particularly during late autumn and winter. Despite sticky fluids produced from glands along their sides, woodlice make winter meals for other active 'creepy-crawlies', such as centipedes, beetles and spiders. Toads and shrews also seem to relish them and ants scavenge their remains. Those that escape detection will mate, and the females store the fertilized eggs in a liquid-filled brood pouch on their undersides, from which the young eventually emerge as perfectly formed, miniature woodlice.

Above The woodlouse is a close relative of crabs and lobsters, but lives exclusively on land. Their crustacean body-covering is not waterproof, and they must constantly keep out of sunshine to avoid dehydrating.

As the summer seeds and autumn fruits are consumed and invertebrate food becomes scarce, many birds and small mammals perish. Young and inexperienced wild animals suffer a high mortality, especially those that were born or hatched late in the breeding season. Three-quarters of the young robins that fledge one year will not survive to the next, and the percentage is even greater with smaller garden birds such as blue tits and great tits. Their very name derives from the old Nordic word 'tittr' which describes anything tiny. In proportion to their weight, they must consume large quantities of food, especially in cold weather. Only the fittest and most artful survive – or the luckiest. The same is true of voles and shrews and other smaller mammals such as wood mice. If not taken by predators, most adults simply perish from cold and lack of food. With so much winter mortality, it seems surprising that our gardens and countryside are not littered with their corpses. One creature's misfortune is another's salvation. Scavenging birds such as carrion crows, magpies, red kites and mammals such as rats and foxes, all help clear up the debris – as well as the hordes of carrion-consuming invertebrates.

THE BODY-SNATCHERS

Most infamous of all of nature's undertakers is the sexton beetle. It is claimed that these rather large, black and orange flying beetles can smell a corpse from 1.5 kilometres (1 mile) away downwind. Several may be attracted to the same dead body – often a mouse or vole, but sometimes that of a larger mammal such as a weasel or hedgehog. They work together in pairs, using their powerful legs and jaws to scrape away the soil beneath the carcass, creating a chamber into which it can be dragged and buried. Their task complete, the industrious pair of beetles mate, and the female, having driven the male away, lays her eggs in the chamber where she protects them, along with the precious corpse, from maggots and other subterranean competitors. When the larvae hatch, the female sexton beetle feeds her offspring with partially digested morsels of a small, fleshy piece of the carcass which she has specially set aside for the benefit of the emerging grubs. When they are large enough to feed for themselves, they progress to the corpse itself, which by now is ripe for consumption.

Also known as 'burying' or 'grave-digging' beetles, sexton beetles of various kinds are found all over Britain. Their scientific name 'Necrophorus' aptly describes their habits.

Together, mother and offspring spend a week or two feasting in their private pantry, until, replete, the larvae burrow deeper into the soil and pupate. The female beetle, her maternal duties discharged, also spends the winter under ground.

As the winter sets in, slugs and snails join the ranks of invertebrates that line rotten timber and crevices in walls. Slugs bunch their bodies to reduce their surface area, and snails clamp tightly to tree trunks and posts above the reach of ground frost. They weatherproof the openings to their shells by secreting a mucus that dries to make a protective seal. Garden spiders favour upturned flowerpots and the gaps between slatted fences and in trellises. Long-legged harvestmen, distinguished from spiders by their one-piece bodies, may overwinter as adults by creeping under logs or simply as eggs. Crane flies, those familiar flying 'daddy-longlegs' of autumn evenings, leave the next generation to overwinter, buried in the soil. Their maggot-like larvae, known as 'leather jackets', eat the roots of grass and other plants and make tasty morsels for many garden and farmland birds. On parkland and playing fields in winter, armies of rooks and crows probe the turf in search of them.

It is insect larvae of all kinds that form the basis of survival for so many birds through the colder months. Woodpeckers and others with strong bills have the ability to penetrate into rotting timber where many species of beetles, sawflies and wood wasps lay their eggs. Treecreepers and nuthatches pick over the rough surfaces of trees and probe behind loose bark for dormant adult insects and their grubs. Blackbirds, thrushes and robins rummage through the leaf-litter for centipedes and millipedes and, of course, hunt for the earthworms which are active throughout the year and provide observant early birds with nutritious winter sustenance.

As November advances, temperatures begin to drop. Even by day, there is a distinct chill in the air. Grey squirrels now sport their winter coats – a dense, silvery-grey fur tinged with yellowish-brown that spreads forwards from their rump during autumn. Their winter shelter will be their windproof dreys built of twigs and other vegetation which they weave together into a football-sized den, high in a tree. Other smaller mammals, such as voles, shrews and mice, also grow thicker, warmer fur. Harvest mice weave winter nests of dry grass near to the ground or beneath a hedge. This species is one of the world's smallest rodents and has to keep active day and night to find enough food. Few get through the winter and the surviving population has to compensate by prolific breeding the following year. It seems an omission of nature that none of these small mammals hibernates.

Right As autumn turns to winter, deciduous woodland takes on a subdued character. Birdsong almost ceases and there is a gloom in the air. But for many creatures, life goes on – albeit in a less conspicuous way.

TO SLEEP OR NOT TO SLEEP

In the temperate climate of Britain, full hibernation is unusual. Mammals, such as squirrels and badgers, are simply sleeping during cold weather and emerge on warmer days to replenish their bodies. Hedgehogs, however, feed on earthworms, slugs and beetles for which they forage at night. In cold weather they can use more energy searching for food that they gain from their meals. The solution is to save energy by seeking a safe refuge and allowing their body temperature to drop to that of their surroundings. They fall into a deep torpor in which many metabolic processes shut down almost completely. This true hibernation is also the way that some species of bats survive the British winter. Being insect eaters, there is very little accessible food supply for them during the colder months so they find somewhere safe such as a cave or deserted building or a hollow in a tree. Here they hang upside down, often communally in roosts, and switch off for winter. Their body temperature drops from their normal 36 degrees centigrade to 8 degrees, and the breathing rate becomes ten times slower – frequently ceasing completely for long periods. But a sudden noise or rapid increase in the air temperature can reactivate their breathing, quicken their heartbeat and cause them to shiver. In milder spells bats such as the pipistrelle will fully wake from hibernation and fly out in search of insects that have been aroused by the same spell of warmth.

The dormouse is the only other British mammal to hibernate through winter. In the autumn each builds its own nest in which to bed down, often among tree roots just above or just below the ground. From October onwards, when the temperature falls below 15 degrees centigrade, its metabolic processes slow down and it falls asleep – waking only during spells of warmer weather or when spring arrives in April. This is the time when hedgehogs usually emerge from their long sleep and scurry about replenishing the weight they have lost during the winter months. Cold-blooded creatures such as frogs and toads, snakes and lizards have less of a problem fuelling up their bodies. Their winter torpor is an almost total shut-down and consumes minimal energy. Frogs can survive in frozen ponds and thaw out apparently unharmed – as can many overwintering invertebrates.

The common dormouse – also called the 'hazel dormouse' because of its predilection for hazel coppices – is the only British mammal, other than bats, to hibernate throughout winter, usually from October until April.

It is warm-blooded birds and mammals that face the greatest challenge when the temperature drops – and, here in temperate Britain, most find ways of staying awake through even the coldest weather. They keep warm by flocking together or by moving to a warmer place such as human habitation. This seems preferable to switching off their systems and submitting to the privations and predations of a British winter when many other creatures are still out and about, and when unseasonally mild weather can return unpredictably.

Above Starlings roosting for the night. Gregarious and noisy, starlings are seen as successful opportunists in modern Britain. But recently numbers have seriously declined, especially on arable land where, like song thrushes, blackbirds and dunnocks, the birds have been affected by agricultural chemicals and changing farming practices.

Many species of birds that have spent spring and summer in breeding pairs now flock together in large numbers. Starlings do so most of the year – their noisy squabbling is a feature of town and country – and many other birds find communal roosting of great mutual benefit. There is clearly safety in numbers, particularly when roaming far afield in search of winter food. Predators are also hungry, and faced with a flock of a thousand or so wheeling birds, a bird of prey such as a sparrowhawk can be disorientated and visually confused. Even small birds such as finches will turn as one in bouncing flight and confront their pursuer which frequently diverts from its intended course. Even if a sparrowhawk strikes a fleeing flock, the chances of an individual being the victim are minimal if they stick together in a group. Buzzards are frequently mobbed by birds much smaller than themselves and tawny owls and barn owls abroad in daylight are invariably accompanied by a twittering rabble.

The other real advantage of flocking is the sharing of the search for food. Linnets, chaffinches, greenfinches and goldfinches flit in groups along field margins and hedgerows, alighting wherever they find seeds and berries. Many eyes make lighter work in finding a rich source of food in which all can share, and a flock, working the fields as a group, will be far more successful. When it moves on, the flock spreads out to cover more ground. Now that winter is setting in, this collective strategy is very effective. In more open country such as downland, yellowhammers and skylarks behave in a similar way, and lapwings and gulls wheel in unison as they move across arable land in search of the best pickings.

Rooks have vacated their breeding rookeries and now spend the daylight hours moving between the most productive feeding sites. They are highly intelligent birds and when working together for mutual benefit their success rate at finding food is extremely high. Their staple diet of earthworms and leatherjackets is supplemented in late autumn and early winter by

Below Intelligent and adaptable, the rook looks like a bird that will continue to flourish in the next millennium, but some rookeries have fallen silent.

the grains of late-sown cereals. An arable farmer is not so bothered by the sight of a troop of rooks following his plough, but the prospect of them returning to his field after sowing sends him running for his shotgun. Modern 'scarecrows' that let off detonators at intervals are fairly effective at deterring the marauding flocks of crows, rooks and jackdaws and many farmers direct-drill the seeds deeper into the unploughed soil. Through the twentieth century, rook numbers steadily declined in Britain, and also across much of the farmland of mainland Europe. Although many young rooks are shot in late spring while still in the rookeries, it is thought that the natural deaths in summer, when the fields yield little for them, is the season when rook mortality is highest. There are signs that the British rook population is recovering. Certainly, on a November evening when rooks in flocks of a hundred or so commute noisily in straggling lines back to their favoured roost, you could be forgiven for thinking that they are making a comeback. For most people, a British countryside without these bold and boisterous birds would be a sad and silent place.

Throughout the country, and on the other side of the Channel and the North Sea, all kinds of birds are on the move. The summer visitors have long since gone to their tropical wintering grounds, but in northern Europe there are localized migrations as birds respond to the onset of winter. Just like the redwings and fieldfares, some of the blackbirds we see in British suburban gardens from November onwards might have raised their summer broods as far away as Finland. They now join resident blackbirds and thrushes to forage on the wealth of seeds and berries to be found in the gardens and hedgerows of lowland Britain – before moving on to 'pillage' the countryside of France and Spain. British chaffinches are extraordinarily loyal to their place of birth. Ringing records show that in their lifetimes, which can be up to 12 years, few ever move their nesting territories more than a few hundred metres from where they themselves were hatched. In winter these home-loving chaffinches are joined by international travellers from Scandinavia. Forced south by the cold, these migrant chaffinches join the British residents as they flock with other finch species such as bramblings and greenfinches.

In winter a much rarer visitor from Scandinavia is the great grey shrike. About the same size as a blackbird, this handsome bird with black, grey and white plumage and a distinctive black eye-band on each side of its head, shares a remarkable habit with its close relative, the red-backed shrike. They are both known as 'butcher birds' because of their skilled technique of storing their prey in an outside 'larder'. Shrikes are predatory and hunt rather like hawks. In winter they perch on fences or overhead wires, watching for small-sized prey such as finches, pipits and mammals such as voles and mice. The red-backed shrike, although scarce, is a summer visitor to Britain and still tries to breed in East Anglia and one or two other southern localities. In addition to preying on small birds, it also swoops on frogs, lizards and large insects such as beetles and grasshoppers. Normally hunting singly, the shrike snatches its victim and carries it off to a favourite hawthorn or similar bush where it is either eaten straight away or impaled on a thorn or similar spike, to be saved for another hungry time. The fact that the red-backed species is still declining in Britain is a reflection of the cold springs and wet summers experienced in the 1990s. The tendency of a few of the grey species to stay in summer and try to breed is no doubt also due to climate change and the generally increasing warmth of British summers.

Due to the increasing mildness of our winters, in recent years we have been seeing blackcaps in winter gardens, often feeding at bird tables alongside robins and great tits, especially if they discover bits of fat. These warblers are more familiar as summer visitors from the Mediterranean to which they return in September or October. As these blackcaps move south, others move in to Britain from central Europe where winters can be particularly severe. It is estimated that more than 10,000 come to share in the harvest of wild fruits and berries, and the insect larvae and pupae overwintering in the vegetation. When the countryside hedgerows are depleted, the hungry flocks of foreign visitors and residents move into the well-stocked parks and gardens which are a feature of the British way of life.

Right Great grey shrike with prey impaled on thorn. This 'butcher-bird' has been a winter visitor to Britain, taking advantage of mild winters. With warmer summers forecast, it may well stay to breed.

GREY SEALS – BRITAIN'S LARGEST WILD MAMMALS

Hauled up on sandflats or secluded, rocky shores around Britain are half of the world's population of grey seals, also known as Atlantic seals. Along many parts of the British coastline, November is the peak of their breeding season – when the females produce their pups and then mate again before resuming their lives at sea. Most of the 85,000 or so grey seals in British waters live around Scotland, particularly the offshore islands of the Outer Hebrides and Orkney – but places such as the Farne Islands off Northumberland and the rocky coasts of Cornwall and Wales also have thriving breeding colonies. Females are at least five years old before they produce their first pup, usually at the colony site where they were born. The bulls are first to come ashore to establish the male hierarchy. Weighing perhaps 275 kilograms (600 pounds), the mature males are Britain's largest mammals, unless you count visiting whales. Their rivalry for space and females is a powerful and noisy affair and by the time the females arrive, the strongest have taken prime positions in the breeding grounds.

Grey seal bull emerging from the sea. Between September and December, according to the locality, mature females come on land to give birth and immediately to be mated. It is a noisy and sometimes brutal business.

Each successful bull has between 5 and 10 cow seals on his patch where they give birth to a single pup within a day or two of arriving. As with all marine mammals, the birth is extremely quick, often only seconds. The cows suckle their offspring on the rocks and sandbanks, often suffering the bullish bad manners of the males as they rampage around defending their harem and engaging in bloody battles with rival bulls. The cows defend their pups from this mayhem in which they can be savaged or crushed by a bull – even if the offspring is his own.

For three weeks, the pup is suckled three or four times a day by its mother who continues to respond defensively to its whelping cries. When weaned, it is left to fend for itself. The female immediately comes into heat and mates with the dominant bull. Although the gestation period for grey seals is five months, the implantation of the fertilized embryo is delayed so that the birth coincides with the seals' annual gathering next winter. While at sea, where they can spend weeks at a time, the seals travel great distances in search of fish shoals. They also eat crustaceans such as crabs and lobsters, and are very partial to squid for which they can dive to great depths for up to half an hour without the need to take a breath. Much to the consternation of some fishermen, they are known to congregate at the mouths of rivers when salmon are running and are also very adept at 'rescuing' lobsters from lobster pots. Grey seals are protected by Acts of Parliament and, although officially sanctioned culls are carried out now and again to control numbers, their future in British waters is reasonably assured.

For many of these winter migrants, the east coast of Britain is a first landfall after crossing the North Sea. Although, in the right conditions, the journey may take hours rather than days, this early-winter passage is demanding for small birds. From late autumn onwards, large straggling flocks of snow buntings can be seen scavenging the dunes and beaches in search of a 'breakfast' of insects and other small invertebrates. Around 15,000 of these dainty finches are thought to spend winter in Britain. In their less striking winter plumage they are hardly visible against the sand and shingle – until, like dandelion clocks, they are carried across the dunes, dancing in the wind.

For bird-watchers in Britain, one of the compensations for the onset of winter is the return of millions of waders to the numerous tidal estuaries that make up a large part of the nation's extensive coastline. These long-legged, long-billed birds – such as redshank and dunlin, bar-tailed and black-tailed godwits – all seem perfectly suited to life probing the endless mud of this watery world between the tides.

Above The long legs of the dunlin, like those of all 'waders', enable it to feed and roost in shallow water. Its long bill is ideal for probing the sand and mud – and also for finding insects on the damp moors of the Pennines and Scotland where many breed in summer.

Although, at the end of winter, many redshank and some dunlin stay to breed in Britain, most waders from Britain's estuaries migrate north to the vast tundra of the Arctic where, for a brief few months, they lead a very different way of life and change to a very different diet. In place of worms, crustaceans and molluscs hidden beneath the surface of tidal mud, the waders turn to the insect hordes that are a feature of that northern summer. Here their striding legs and long narrow bills are equally effective in searching and probing the arctic grassland and pools for the adults and larvae of crane flies and midges to feed to their young. As the days shorten dramatically in those latitudes, the family groups hasten to complete their breeding season before the returning cold kills the adult insects and forces the birds back south.

Through these winter months, the estuaries of the British Isles – more than 300 in all – play host to more than half the total number of wading birds in Europe. Three places are the most significant – the Wash on the east coast, the Solway Firth on the west-coast Scottish border and the vast mudflats that link Morecambe Bay with the estuaries of the Ribble and Dee. Tens of thousands of birds flock to these wild, bleak, beautiful places. They can only feed when the tide goes out and reveals the gloriously rich mud. Being where it is on the rim of the Atlantic Ocean, Britain experiences some of the most extreme tidal ranges in the world. Twice a day, vast areas of mudflat are exposed, especially at the 'spring tides' that correspond with the full and new moons. Because of the complexities of the tidal currents that surge around the British Isles, different parts of the coastline experience different rhythms. On the east coast, in places such as the Wash, the highest spring tides occur in the early morning and evening, offering the flocks the best of daylight for feeding and the night-time to roost. On the other coast, in Morecambe Bay for example, life for the waders is not as straightforward. The spring high tides tend to occur either in the middle of the day or around midnight. The flocks are forced to spend much of the brief, winter daylight roosting above the tideline, waiting for their muddy feeding grounds to be revealed. At this point in the month, west-coast estuaries become a paradise for bird-watchers who are able to observe the flocks crowded together in immense congregations – and at a time of day when the low, winter light is most perfect for binoculars and cameras. One such place revered by bird photographers is Hilbre Island lying right at the mouth of the River Dee – a long walk off West Kirby on the west side of the Wirral. With sturdy tripod and long lenses, each stakes out a pitch beyond the reach of the spring tide as it races back across the sand and mudflats. By midday the water will be lapping in front of the line of photographers that brave the biting wind.

As the tide advances, at walking pace, and the flats become submerged, each flock lifts off as one and wheels above the tideline, searching for another, drier place to resume their endless probing. Most visible and audible are the flocks of piebald oystercatchers. As they rise into the air, their piping calls carry across the estuary, announcing their approach to the silent watchers looking down their lenses. There are perhaps 20,000 oystercatchers in the Dee estuary at this time of year and the spectacle of their flocks leap-frogging from sandbank to sandbank ahead of the advancing tide is one

Right A vast flock of dunlin – Britain's most abundant wintering wader – wheels against the evening sky. It is the scale and richness of the mudflats and tidal reaches around Britain that makes the coastline so valuable for winter wildlife.

of the most memorable visions of a British winter. They and the other larger waders such as godwits, curlews, redshanks, knots and grey plovers soon succumb to the inevitable – and settle on a dry roosting place, to sleep out the high tide, their heads tucked under their wings. The much smaller waders such as dunlin, sanderling and ringed plover must all work harder to keep their miniature bodies fuelled. Darting like clockwork toys, they work the water's edge. They are the last to rest and the first to leave the roosts, chasing the receding water as it uncovers the rich, invertebrate prizes on the surface of the sand and mud. As the winter afternoon heads towards twilight, the larger species wake and disperse across the rapidly growing flats. There will be another precious hour of daylight in which to feast on the generous cornucopia of the Dee.

Packing up their cameras and binoculars, the army of silent watchers heads for the safe haven of West Kirby. The return trek seems much longer and the sea breeze stiffens with every stride. Behind them, as evening clouds draw in from the Atlantic, the flocks of feeding waders lift and fall like smoke until they merge into the night.

'wistful nostalgia

and new

resolutions'

December

Above The robin – this much-loved garden bird, noted for its tameness
especially in winter – has become a symbol of Christmas.
The male defends his territory throughout the year – mainly by singing.
Left The bleakness of winter can have a dramatic appeal.

The headlong rush towards the shortest day is cheered by the prospect of Christmas. It is surely no coincidence of social and natural history that the festive season in Britain and much of the temperate northern hemisphere comes when the natural world is at its lowest ebb, waiting for the year to turn. The bare trees and the dearth of birdsong signal that nature is marking time. With the old year nearly spent and a new cycle just ahead, this period is traditionally one for taking stock and for reflecting on the past as well as planning for the future. It is a time for good old-fashioned nostalgia and for brand-new resolutions.

The winter solstice, when the nights are longest and the sun appears above the horizon for the shortest time, usually falls on December 22nd and is followed by Christmas Day three days later. But it has not always been that way. When the change from the old 'Julian' to the new 'Gregorian' calendar

was eventually adopted in protestant Britain in 1752, a total of eleven days were lost. Prior to this swingeing date-shift, Christmas was celebrated almost two weeks later in the winter. A bemused proletariat, still irate at the imposition from Rome, waited to see if nature would adjust. People flocked to Glastonbury Hill, that rises above the Somerset Levels, to see if the famed thorn tree would oblige by advancing its unique mid-winter flowering to the new date of Christmas Day. Believed to have taken root from a staff thrust into the summit of the hill by Joseph of Arimathea, this legendary landmark of early Christendom in Britain is botanically a genetic variant of the familiar hawthorn tree, quite possibly imported at some time from the Middle East where it would indeed flower in their mild mid-winter.

Over here it still produces some blossom and foliage at its customary flowering season – and again in late April, the more familiar time for Britain. For many years after the national change of calendar, crowds gathered at Glastonbury, wanting the thorn tree to give them a sign. Disappointingly, it seldom produced flowers before January 5th – exactly eleven days late.

Above The famed thorn tree at Glastonbury flowers in mid-winter – and again in spring – adding some credence to the legend that it was brought from the Holy Land.

Above The floods of spring 1998 inundated most of the Somerset Levels. Such scenes will become more frequent as global warming continues to change Britain's climate.

Since then, the seasons in Britain seem to have shifted further. Although past the shortest day, Christmas comes too early for those who look forward to a white yuletide. True mid-winter, when snow and ice grip the countryside, now comes in late January or February – if it arrives at all. December these days is more often a wet and stormy month, marked by high winds and flooding. The change in weather patterns, we are told, is all part of the tendency towards milder, wetter winters in Britain, followed by wet springs and hotter, drier summers. It seems convincing that this is directly attributable to 'global warming', but whether that trend is entirely driven by our own modern activities or is part of a long-term natural cycle is still not clear. But there is no doubt that the world's climate is getting warmer. On average, global temperatures in the 1990s were higher than at any time in the century – and in Britain the five warmest years since records began back in 1659 were all in the closing 25 years. Since the last Ice Age, world temperatures have risen on average 1 degree centigrade every three millennia. That increase has turned Britain from an ice-bound wilderness into the green, temperate land it is today. The same rise in temperature elevated global sea levels by more than 100 metres (325 feet), creating the British Isles and drowning the land that is now beneath the English Channel and the North Sea. During the twenty-first century, average global temperatures are predicted to rise by as much as a degree or two centigrade – perhaps more. If this happens, the effects on climate and sea levels are potentially very dramatic, and the balance and distribution of vegetation and animal life will be radically altered. The reality of global warming comes at a time when conservationists and ecologists are already concerned about the welfare of many threatened habitats and species. As the prospect of a 'white Christmas' recedes even further, it is worth considering – albeit briefly and somewhat speculatively – what kind of Living Britain the next two or three generations of British people might inherit.

Some parts of the world might experience lower temperatures than in recent times, but because of its position on the globe, Britain's air and sea temperatures will increase by more than the global average. Winters will become milder with less snow and ice. Heatwaves will become a regular feature of summer, but there will be a general increase of rainfall, particularly in northern and western parts. The south-east of England will receive more rain in winter but summers there will become drier and more like those on continental Europe. Sea storms and gales over land will be more frequent, and coastal erosion and flooding will increase, especially on the eastern side of Britain. If this forecast is true, the long-standing image of Britain as a 'green and pleasant land' will be replaced by one in which the winters are characterized by rain and floods and the hot summers, particularly in the south and east, give rise to a parched, almost desert-like countryside.

Around Britain's coasts, the sea level could rise by as much as 1 metre (approx. 3 feet) by the end of the twenty-first century – but the more likely scenario is that there will be a rapid increase of half a metre by 2030 and then a levelling out. The impact on the estuaries and coastal saltmarshes will be far-reaching. Places such as the Wash and the Solway Firth will lose vast areas of tidal mudflat and marshland which will become permanently flooded by salt water. Birds are considered useful indicators of the shift in weather patterns. Their mobility allows them to respond as the climate and food sources change. The millions of overwintering waders and wildfowl that now invade Britain's coastal wetlands would be forced to seek other feeding grounds – perhaps further north in areas

Right Much of the east coast of England is being eroded by the sea. Geologically it is sinking, whereas the west coast is rising. But the effects of this very slow process are being accelerated by the rising sea level and more frequent winter storms. At Happisburgh on the north Norfolk coast, the cliff is being eroded at a rate of 20 metres (65 feet) a year and houses are falling into the sea.

Below Little egrets which have been rare summer visitors to estuaries on the south and east coasts of England are already showing signs of staying all year round.

which are now too cold during the peak of winter. The wild geese and swans and the great flocks of knot and dunlin which, for thousands of years, have annually migrated long distances between their breeding grounds on the high Arctic tundra and the temperate ice-free mud of Britain, may no longer need to travel so far south. In their place, Britain may see more immigrants from southern Europe. Already Cetti's warbler and the Mediterranean gull have been added to the British list of breeding birds. Little egrets are now resident all year round, nesting in several estuaries of south-west England and south-west Wales. The blackcaps overwintering in gardens and woodlands of southern Britain are a sure sign

Left Bee-eaters occasionally bring a dash of exotic colour to Britain's summers, and will become more common-place – if there are enough bees and other similar insects to support them.

Right Gulls are opportunists 'par excellence'. Already, many black-headed gulls have moved inland to take up a new lifestyle away from the sea, roosting on reservoirs and ornamental lakes. They find ample supplies of food in places such as this landfill site in Essex – which is also home to foxes.

that winters there are becoming milder. In future, we might also expect to see more Mediterranean visitors in summer. Already several pairs of golden orioles have bred annually in East Anglia. Southern and eastern Britain may soon be playing host to breeding hoopoes and bee-eaters, cattle egrets, black kites and a bevy of warmth-loving, insect-eating warblers which would find the new British summer scene perfect for raising their young.

In the short term, conditions might favour many of Europe's commoner breeding species, but as the effects of global warming create more extreme and testing conditions, birds and other wildlife will polarize into two categories – those that flourish and those that will decline. Blackbirds, chaffinches and wrens all seem set for success. Other familiar birds such as house sparrows and starlings which have declined in recent years may make a comeback in the new climate of Britain. Tenacious and adaptable birds such as gulls, wood pigeons, magpies and carrion crows will also fare well. Birds such as kingfishers, which now suffer high mortalities in winter, may well make advances – if their habitats remain intact.

The losses will include those species that are already on the southern edge of their range – arctic birds such as the snow bunting, dotterel and ptarmigan, red-necked phalarope and greenshank. Other species which are dependent on very specialized and limited habitats will also be at risk – corn buntings and grey partridges in traditional arable land, and bitterns and bearded tits in reedbeds. With wetter springs, warmer summers and milder winters, Britain's farmers will be able to grow a new range of crops including maize and vineyards of red grapes. Land such as dry heaths will become economically viable and may be ploughed for profit. Upland moors and grassland will be able to support cereal crops or be planted with trees. Some of these changes will benefit some wildlife and they will flourish – but many species will be obliged to shift or adapt to the new-look landscapes of twenty-first century Britain.

From the wildlife point of view, these changes will be gradual and, for the individual animal and plant, imperceptible. On our human scale, the predicted changes are rapid – they will happen in the course of a lifetime. As the science of monitoring and prediction becomes more precise, we can take stock of what can and should be done to compensate for the losses of habitat that Britain will experience – and to put them in a European and a global context. If here in Britain there is a decline in some kinds of habitat and their attendant species, other neighbouring parts of Europe may experience an increase of a similar mix of vegetation and climatic conditions. Of all the challenges ever faced around the world, global warming is an international issue that needs to be viewed in the overall scheme of things. Britain's response probably depends on having confidence that in other parts of the world there will be the same or even a more enlightened attitude to wildlife conservation. And there is always a matter of national pride. To lose such species as bitterns and ptarmigan from Britain, and the multitudes of wildfowl and waders that grace our estuaries in winter, would reduce the natural richness of our country, and thereby the richness of our own lives. For a nation that prides itself as one of the most conservation-conscious in the world, that would be an unwarranted loss.

Like all such issues, it comes down to the value we place on the wildlife and the wildness of Britain. There is, perhaps, little we can do to ameliorate the rising temperatures, except to press more urgently and convincingly for a reduction of those human activities that contribute to global warming. But, at a local and national level, there are ways of compensating for the physical changes that will take place. The saltmarshes of Britain, particularly those on the east coast of England, are among the finest in Europe and harbour a great diversity of wildlife in all seasons. Crucial wildlife sites such as Spurn Point in Humberside, Gibraltar Point in Lincolnshire, Holme, Titchwell and Scolt Head in Norfolk will be threatened by rising sea levels. Predictions put the maximum rate of rise at

Left Petrochemical plant at sunset – Grimsby, Lincolnshire. Global warming is certainly exacerbated by our modern lifestyle, but there are other, more natural factors to take into account.

Right above If global warming is inevitable, there are positive preparations that can be made. These wildfowl overwintering at Welney on the Ouse Washes are there by design, not default.

about 1 centimetre (less than half an inch) a year. That is more or less the rate at which a saltmarsh grows naturally. With skilful management and space to expand inland, such places could keep pace with the inundation of the sea. The same could apply to many of our estuaries and coastal mudflats. If there is space for them to advance landwards, free of industry and urban development, there could be a viable solution – but only if there is a will to do it.

One important prehistoric event is in Britain's favour. Between five and seven millennia ago, the whole world experienced a previous 'global warming' – one that could certainly not be blamed on the population of that time. A relatively sudden surge of temperatures melted the remaining ice sheets and glaciers that had lingered since the close of the last Ice Age. The ice sheets, which in some places such as the northern latitudes of North America had been almost 2 kilometres deep (more than a mile), now released their locked-up water which ran into the oceans of the world. The expansion of the oceans due to the global warming combined with the extra volume of water from the melt raised the mean sea level more than 1 metre (3 or 4 feet), flooding coastal areas around the entire world. It was during that period that the British Isles finally became separated from mainland Europe. Here in Britain, many of the estuaries and fertile flatlands we have today are a legacy of that time. Since then, the sea has receded again as temperatures have subsided by 2 or 3 degrees centigrade. It seems almost as if that prehistoric era was a prelude to the global warming we face today. In many respects, there is an in-built capacity to absorb the inundations once again. Part of the natural history of Britain is being repeated – but this time with an already diminished bio-diversity and much-changed landscape. But nature itself is predisposed to change. The land and its wildlife have done it all before – shifting and responding to the fluctuations of climate and the rise and fall of the sea. The new ingredient is us – and our ability to be flexible and responsive. Our great asset is our ingenuity which, if applied in good time, could really make a difference.

Conservation organizations seem to be agreed that we should be flexible in our attitudes, as well as in the way we respond opportunistically to the changing scene. Low-lying agricultural land near the coast may have to be abandoned rather than defended expensively against the oncoming tide of global warming. Some of this land will be suitable for conversion to marshland and other wetland refuges for wildlife. The cost might be a lot less all round. Some species can be 'helped' by the artificial creation of habitats in places which we know will offer the right climatic and other ecological ingredients. Such 'ecological restoration' has been happening elsewhere around the world, particularly in North America, where some precious and valued habitats have already disappeared for other reasons at an alarming rate. The science of restoration and re-creation of landscapes to meet the specific needs of wildlife and people is a new and constructive solution to our worst conservation fears. It is not a substitute for wilderness – of which we in Britain have precious little – but it is another avenue.

With the return of hotter summers, heathland might be a candidate for expansion in various parts of the country, not just in the south. Birds, such as the Dartford warbler, and heathland reptiles, such as the sand lizard, which are now all struggling to survive, could expand their range northwards if land that is now upland pasture or moorland is made ready to receive them when the climate warms. Already, bush crickets and other insects that thrive on warmth are spreading north through Britain, colonizing at the rate of several kilometres a year. As the British climate changes, wildlife will need to be transported and re-established on new sites – and provided with 'green corridors' along which to move as a community of species. Free of environmental hurdles, such as large tracts of agricultural land, these linear 'nature reserves' should not exclude people. Indeed, there is every indication that the landscapes where people live are far more 'user friendly' to many British species than much of the agricultural landscape that we think of as 'the British countryside'.

Winter brings wildlife and people together. The cold and lack of food and shelter in field and hedgerow, send many species into gardens and parkland, and to the protection afforded by buildings

Left Studland Heath in Dorset is within 20 minutes driving distance of half a million people – but is still one of the finest examples of lowland heath in Europe. Rich in species and owned by English Nature, it is an example of a vital nature reserve in the heart of modern Britain.

and even by industrial sites. There are over a million acres (over 400,000 hectares) of gardens in Britain and, since the great majority of British people live an urban life, their gardens are in towns and cities. Ranging in size from a backyard to a country mansion estate, these manicured patches of landscape number more than 16 million. In London alone, private gardens amount to a total area equal to that of the Isle of Wight. Buckingham Palace, that most famous of London's private homes, has 38 hectares (93 acres) of walled gardens, and London naturalists have counted 61 bird species in the grounds, 21 of which have nested there. Less obvious – but just as crucial – are the 90 beetle species and 343 species of butterflies and moths which frequent the Palace borders and shrubberies, representing almost 10 per cent of the total British species list. Most mature gardens contain 200–300 species of plants, wild and cultivated. These provide food and protection for countless insects and other invertebrate life on which birds and other larger animals depend. Even small gardens contain trees and bushes which give shelter to nesting and roosting birds, and act as a focus for the lives of many different insects and spiders, millipedes and other tiny creatures. We know that exotic plants such as buddleia attract native and migrant butterflies and that many other cultivated plants provide foliage and flowers, fruits, berries and seeds on which many other species thrive. Stinging nettles and other weeds add to the wildness of gardens, offering butterflies and moths foodplants on which their caterpillars will feed. Ornamental ponds and lakes are renowned for their wildlife value. It is thought that more frog tadpoles successfully hatch each year in gardens than in the wider countryside. To have these plants and animals on our doorstep is seen as a real bonus by most British people. In some ways it compensates for what has happened to much of the nation's countryside where modern farming practices are no longer sympathetic to the rhythms and needs of nature.

In winter, reservoirs and other man-made inland waters such as flooded quarries and gravel pits are havens for wildlife, particularly water-birds. Black-headed and other gulls move inland to join cormorants on the open, sheltered water. Here they find secure roosts by night and by day set off for parks and refuse tips where they find easy winter pickings. Winter seems to bring out the best of wildlife concern in British people. Birds are fed at garden bird tables and in parks by enthusiastic carers. Squirrels and pigeons share in the bounty – and even foxes and badgers are left titbits to help them through the winter. In Scotland, shy pine martens have even been coaxed into homes to be fed peanuts and pet food, and in coastal fishing ports, such as Kyle of Lochalsh, crews of returning shrimp-boats leave generous scraps of their catch on board for the local otters to discover under cover of darkness. Scaling the ships' ladders, these shy creatures feast on the leftovers with no apparent fear. For their patrons, the fishermen of Kyle, there is satisfaction in simply knowing they are there.

Throughout the country, one bird epitomizes the British people's affinity with their native wildlife. Particularly in winter, when other species are hidden or silent, the robin strikes a chord. Its wistful song and jaunty red breast endears it to almost everyone. There are probably more than four million pairs resident in Britain and the great majority hold territory all year round, doing almost all their feeding, courtship and breeding within this prescribed patch. However, some British robins do move away in winter, crossing the Channel to find less inclement conditions. There on the Continent, robins are far more retiring and have none of the cocky confidence of their British counterparts. Here in Britain, they have earned their place as the nation's best-loved bird because of their tameness and entertaining habits. In woodlands they pick over soil disturbed by other creatures such as moles and badgers. In gardens they extend this technique of finding food by watching gardeners at work. Perched on the handle of a garden fork, a robin will drop nonchalantly to snatch earthworms and grubs from the freshly turned soil. The robin's association with the Christmas season seems to have started in Victorian times when the livery of the postmen included a bright red jacket. Nicknamed 'robins', their red-breasted namesakes were portrayed on traditional Christmas cards with an envelope in their beak, posting greetings into the letter box, which was invariably covered with snow and a sprig of holly.

Right No bird epitomizes the British people's affection for its native wildlife better than the robin. Everyone likes to think that the robin that shared their garden last autumn is the one that stridently proclaims his territory the following spring. It probably is. They are very loyal to their place of birth, and very tolerant of people.

Today all kinds of wildlife are featured on greetings cards – not only at Christmas. Other birds, such as owls and blue tits, and woodland flowers such as bluebells and wood anemones, are among the most popular subjects – but badgers and foxes, rabbits, squirrels, young deer and otters all have a high profile in the British psyche. Less appealing perhaps are moles and weasels, sparrowhawks and ravens, bats and beetles. But each group of animals and plants has its devoted fans who admire their qualities and would lament their demise. Britain without its present diversity of landscapes and wild plants and animals would be a less enjoyable place in which to live.

The variety of Britain's habitats has come about through a long and eventful partnership between its people and the land. Wildlife was seen as a source of food and raw materials, until agriculture and horticulture provided the nation with all it needed. Some wildlife became competitors to be culled or cut down. Others were seen as pests and weeds to be banished by ploughing and spraying and by persistent persecution. Not until the seventeenth and eighteenth centuries did our native wildlife become elevated to the realms of 'appreciation' and 'fascination'. Pioneering writers such as John Ray and Gilbert White helped popularize the study of 'nature', giving it a respectability and purpose – providing amateurs and professionals alike with endless speculation and debate about the infinite diversity of life. 'Natural history' combined the systematic classification and identification of species with a rational attempt to fit them into a natural scheme. That the term embraced 'history' is more important and relevant today than it has ever been.

To look back on how the landscapes and varied habitats of Britain were changed by time, climate and the day-to-day, century-by-century activities of the British people is to appreciate that it is a process in continuous flux. In the past, as the climate warmed or cooled, ecosystems advanced or retreated, carrying their wildlife with them. There were gains and losses at every stage. The mix we enjoy today is a product of those natural comings and goings – and, of course, a reflection of the way that we and all those earlier generations of Britons managed the land and its wildlife. In the past, habitats such as water meadows and heathland – both created by the activities of people – have been lost by default. They simply went out of fashion or found new commercial value. What we do today is essentially 'by design'. Every hedgerow that is grubbed up to make way for larger fields has an impact on the vitality of the local wildlife and the look of the countryside. Every river bank that is canalized by the local water authority means less vegetation and less freshwater life. Conversely, every buddleia bush that is planted in suburbia means more butterflies, and every carefully managed reedbed could become a home for bitterns.

Above and left Two centuries ago, the bittern was regarded as a delicacy and was so common that special shoots were organized on the fens and broadlands of East Anglia and other marshy parts of Britain. Today it is one of our rarest birds. It needs seclusion but, above all, it needs reedbeds. Such places can be created and managed, like the reedbeds at Cley on the north coast of Norfolk where the Norfolk Wildlife Trust manages the oldest nature reserve in Britain. As that coast is already threatened by flooding from the effects of global warming, there is now a great opportunity to extend the areas of reedbed and saltmarsh in the interests of wildlife — and, indirectly, for our own satisfaction.

Right The traditional New Year's Eve celebrations in London's Trafalgar Square are echoed up and down the nation; each community has its own way of heralding the New Year. It is a time for wistful nostalgia and for brand new resolutions.

The effects of global warming are, as yet, unquantifiable – but the fear of what might happen has galvanized us into reassessing the future of wildlife in Britain. Government and voluntary organizations and centres of research are combining their knowledge and passion to work out what would be best for the country at large. Some regions may have to be prepared to lose some habitats and species; others will have to adopt responsibilities for the nation as a whole. Britain, as part of Europe and the wider community, will continue to play a vital role in providing feeding grounds and refuges for migratory species, and a home for cherished residents. Extinction will continue to be a part of Britain's natural history. Just as we lost the wolf because it no longer fitted in with the British way of life, so we may lose other species – large and small – which no longer have, or can maintain, a natural place in the wider scheme. The essential challenge is that we, as a nation, should *have* a scheme – and not lose more of our wildlife heritage by neglect or default. The concept of 'conservation' is something relatively new in the equation – but to 'conserve' does not imply a static system. Ever since these islands emerged from the ice, 10 to 20 millennia ago, there has been constant change. The last Ice Age left Britain a legacy of wildlife which was relatively impoverished by standards elsewhere in the world. Since then, time and the activities of people have created a unique mosaic of landscapes

which support a great variety of habitats and wildlife. It is this variety that makes Living Britain what it is – a small archipelago populated by an essentially urban people who are becoming increasingly aware of their natural heritage. As the lights go up for Christmas and we look back over another year, we can take stock of the long and eventful natural history of Britain – and celebrate our hopes and aspirations for its future in the new millennium.

Guide to the Nature of Living Britain

Britain has several thousand nature reserves and other sites which have been set aside and designated for their national or local wildlife importance – or simply for their natural beauty. Many organizations are involved in their creation, ownership and management. Together, these special parts of Britain add up to an inestimable resource of habitat, flora and fauna – but their total area is still only a fraction of the land surface of Britain. The entire country is our principal 'nature reserve' – but these special places highlight the wealth of wildlife that can be found in modern Britain. They are the jewels in the nation's conservation crown.

Region by region, this gazetteer lists nearly 300 of them. Some are large and nationally well-known such as Dartmoor National Park; others are more modest, such as Doxey Marshes in Staffordshire or Sydenham Hill Wood close to the heart of London. They have all been selected because they have something special to offer visitors who wish to see for themselves the varied nature of Britain.

The entries have been specially compiled for *Living Britain* by David Tyldesley and Anne Gatti to reflect the range of reserves that are open to the public up and down the country, in both remote and accessible places. Each brief description mentions some of the wildlife highlights and often indicates the best time of year to visit. The organization responsible for managing the reserve is indicated by an abbreviation which is explained in the key on the opposite page. Basic directions are included and there is an Ordnance Survey map reference as well as a simple map of each of the

1 The Highlands and Islands
2 Central Scotland
3 The Borders
4 The Pennines
5 The Lake District
6 East of the Pennines
7 West of the Pennines
8 Cambria
9 The Severn
10 The English Midlands
11 East Anglia
12 South Wales
13 The Chilterns and Cotswolds
14 South-east England
15 Wessex
16 The South-west Peninsula

Right The kingfisher – one of the jewels of Britain's birdlife.

sixteen regions showing the selected reserves. This gazetteer is by no means comprehensive – there are many more places in Britain to explore where visitors are also very welcome. The organizations mentioned below will be happy to give further advice about their reserves. The entries that follow have been compiled with their help and from information that they have supplied for *Living Britain*. Whilst we have endeavoured to make the entries as accurate as possible, there may be minor errors or omissions. Please use the gazetteer simply as a guide.

HOW TO FIND THEM Each regional section of the gazetteer has a map which shows the general location of each site. You can then pinpoint its exact position from the description of the nearest main roads and towns, and from the Ordnance Survey National Grid Reference Number that accompanies the site entry. All OS maps explain how to use the system.

IF YOU WANT TO KNOW MORE about the site and its wildlife or wish to check details of access, you should refer to the organization that manages it; this is not necessarily the owner of the site. There may be seasonal or other restrictions to access which are not detailed in the gazetteer.

THE ORGANIZATIONS ARE:

Abbreviations used in the Gazetteer Regions

AW	Anglian Water
BBONT	Wildlife Trust for Berks. Bucks. and Oxon
C	local Council
CB	local County Borough
CBC	County Borough Council
CC	local County Council
CCW	Countryside Council for Wales
CEC	Crown Estates Commissioners
CWPS	Cotswold Water Park Society
DC	local District Council
DOC	Duchy of Cornwall
DOM	Duke of Marlborough
EN	English Nature
FC	Forestry Commission
FSC	Field Studies Council
HA	Highway Authorities
IOSET	Isles of Scilly Environmental Trust
KAMT	Kenneth Allsop Memorial Trust
LT	Landmark Trust
MBC	Metropolitan Borough Council
MOD	Ministry of Defence
NGC	National Grid Company
NPA	appropriate National Park Authority
NT	National Trust
NTS	National Trust for Scotland
NWWT	North Wales Wildlife Trust
RSPB	Royal Society for the Protection of Birds
SE	Sandringham Estate
SNH	Scottish Natural Heritage
SWT	Scottish Wildlife Trust
WdT	Woodland Trust
WPCC	Wimbledon and Putney Commons Conservators
WT	local Wildlife Trust
WTWW	Wildlife Trust, West Wales
WWT	Wildfowl and Wetlands Trust
YWT	Yorkshire Wildlife Trust

Definitions

NP National Park: an expanse of spectacular countryside in England and Wales, largely owned by farmers and private landowners but with areas managed by a variety of public and voluntary conservation bodies. They range in size from 303 sq km (The Broads) to 2292 sq km (Lake District) and each is administered by its own, independent National Park Authority (NPA).

NNR National Nature Reserve: an important area of wildlife habitat which is carefully managed by English Nature or another conservation body. Most welcome visitors.

MNR Marine Nature Reserve: an area of the sea, within Britain's territorial waters, where the flora and fauna are legally protected and can be studied. There are also a number of voluntary marine reserves around Britain.

1 The Highlands and Islands

One of the last great wilderness areas of Europe, the Scottish Highlands have the most dramatic and distinctive combinations of scenery and wildlife of any region in the British Isles. It is the region most sparsely populated, least affected by man and with the landscapes of the grandest scale and beauty. The Highlands can be intimate and sheltered or wild and exposed. They are far larger, more remote and inaccessible than we imagine. They support many habitats which are unique to the region or are the best examples of their kind. Mountain summits, vast desolate moorlands, extensive bogs, beautiful upland lochs and rivers, and fiord-like sea lochs all provide homes for a range of species distinctly associated with Scotland.

The Islands are an integral part of the Highlands and we cannot fail to be impressed by their remarkable cliffs of seabirds and a wealth of other natural habitats which include the incomparable Hebridean machair.

On the subarctic summit of Cairngorm or at the top of St Kilda's sea cliffs you are looking at some of the best natural history stories in the world.

❶ Argyll Forest Park
Argyll and Bute · FC
Established in 1935, Argyll was the first forest park in Great Britain and demonstrates exceptionally well how commercial forestry can be combined with recreational and tourist uses and nature conservation interests. In fact, only half the park is forested, the remainder being left as valuable moorland, wetlands and montane habitats.

NN272034 at Ardgartan and elsewhere north and west of Loch Long.

❷ Ariundle Wood
Highland · SNH/FC
This Atlantic oakwood, situated in the wildness of Sunart's sea loch scenery, shows how the natural woodlands of the Highlands are more than just pine and birch. In Strontian Glen oak was once coppiced and grows with birch, hazel and rowan. The high humidity and heavy rainfall result in luxuriant growth of mosses, liverworts and lichens.

NM835645 near Strontian on A861, 12 miles west of the Corran ferry.

❸ Beinn Eighe NNR
Highland · SNH
The summit of Torridon's wild landscape is an awe-inspiring mountain of considerable biological importance. There

is a valuable remnant of Caledonian pine forest on the north-eastern slopes, together with fine moorland and bog communities. The higher levels of the mountain have arctic alpines and other unusual species including dwarf cornel

and moonwort. Birds and animals are hard to see but ptarmigan, red deer, mountain hare, golden eagle and merlin are present.

NG952610 immediately west of Kinlochewe.

❹ Ben More Coigach
Highland · SWT
If you want to see the range of moorland and heathland habitats from the edge of cultivation to the mountain tops, this site is ideal. The rolling western moorland is

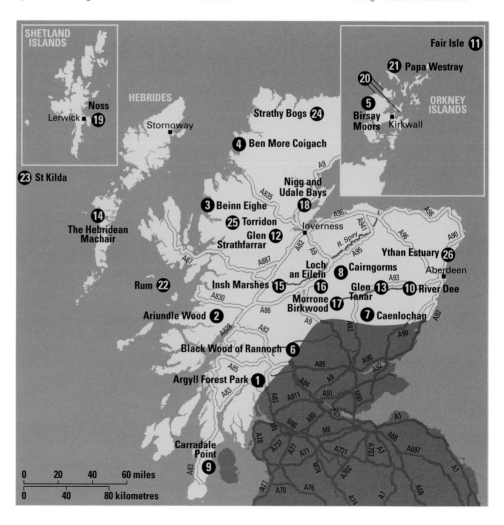

covered in deergrass and cottongrass blanket bog with sundews; the higher slopes are of heather. The sandstone slopes of Beinn an Eoin rise steeply from the heather-grass moorland typical of the Highlands and dramatic in scale. The cultivation of the crofts has ceased and they have reverted to grazing land for stock, and visiting barnacle geese.

NC085040 on Coigach west of A835, 6 miles north of Ullapool, via Achiltibuie.

❺ Birsay Moors
Orkney · RSPB
Both the hen harrier and short-eared owl need extensive areas of moorland heath for hunting, a habitat declining in Orkney as the heather and deergrass are replaced by cultivated grasses and clovers. But here on this moorland nature reserve they are secure with skylark, snipe, redshank and wheatear among other breeding species. The area has lochans, peat banks and shallow valleys to add interest.

HY370194 from lower Cottasgarth.

❻ Black Wood of Rannoch
Perth and Kinross · FC
Despite its gloomy name the Black Wood is one of the finest remnants of Caledonian pine and birch forest with an exciting range of plants and animals of the wildwood. Capercaillie, black grouse, siskin, Scottish crossbill, redstart, spotted flycatcher and tree pipit are all breeding here. The forest and the Camghouran birch woods to the east are of international importance for their species of rare moths and other insects.

NN570550, south of Loch Rannoch off B846, 28 miles west of Pitlochry.

❼ Caenlochan NNR
Angus · SNH
Red deer, fox and blue hare are on the mountains with ptarmigan. Dunlin and golden plover breed on the high moorland. Eagles soar over the glens. The cliff ledges on the corries display a flora of arctic alpines including alpine bistort and northern bedstraw with montane willows. Lichens, sedges and mosses are abundant on the summits.

N0200750 above the Devil's Elbow on A93, 10 miles south of Braemar. From June to October access is restricted.

❽ Cairngorms
Highland/Aberdeenshire · SNH
Stand on the Cairngorm summit and the breathtaking view below covers a hundred square miles of high mountains. This forms the most extensive area of land over 900 metres (3000 feet) high in the British Isles. With an arctic chill even in July, only the toughest plants and animals can survive. This is the land of red deer, wildcat and golden eagles. There are no trees or shrubs. The flowering plants are small, tough, arctic species with ferns, mosses and lichens covered in snow for most of the year. Roseroot, mountain sorrel and other flora shelter in the corries.

NJ010040 take Ski Road via Glen More from Aviemore.

❾ Carradale Point
Argyll and Bute · SWT
From the low cliffs of this grassy peninsula, porpoise, white-beaked and bottle-nosed dolphins and killer whales can be seen in the Kilbrannan Sound. Otters are often seen on shore. Grazing is undertaken by a curious herd of white feral goats.

NR815375 off B842/B879 on east side of Kintyre.

❿ The River Dee
Aberdeenshire
The epitome of Scottish rivers, the Dee is clear, fresh and free of hydroelectric interruptions. Famous for its salmon it also has trout, eels, mink and otter. The middle section of Deeside is clothed with superb woodlands which are the haunt of pine marten, crossbills, buzzard and deer.

From Braemar downstream to Banchory.

⓫ Fair Isle
Shetland · NTS
The natural aggression of great and arctic skuas can be turned on to visitors who walk over their rough hill ground territories on this magnificent bird island. From Siberia and North America windblown rarities find themselves on Fair Isle and the species list is fascinating. The bird ringing station has handled 150,000 birds of 250 species, some of which have reappeared in Greece, Siberia and even Brazil. But the real treasure of the island is its breeding seabird colonies which include 30,000 puffins, 50,000 fulmar, 40,000 guillemots and as many as 100 pairs of the storm petrel which comes ashore only at night.

HZ210720 between north Ronaldsay, Orkneys and Sumburgh Head, Shetland.

⓬ Glen Strathfarrar NNR
Highland · SNH
If you want to see one of the most memorable wildwoods of Britain there can be few more compelling scenes than the native pine forest of Strathfarrar. It clings to the deep gorges and spreads around the alder marshes which persuaded successive generations of fellers to leave it untouched. Fine, mature pines are mixed with birch and open areas of heather and bilberry in a colourful mosaic. The plants and animals of the

once extensive Caledonian Forest are present, including crested tit, roe deer and pine marten.

NH270375 vehicular access is controlled at Leishmore, access via Glen Strathfarrar off A831, 6 miles north of Cannich.

⓭ Glen Tanar NNR
Aberdeenshire · SNH
The native Scots pine are naturally regenerating in this eastern section of the Caledonian Forest, even spreading on to adjacent moorland. Juniper, rowan, aspen and birch are scattered throughout, representing the range of post-glacial colonizing trees. Typical pinewood plants include chickweed wintergreen, and creeping lady's tresses. Crossbill, siskin and capercaillie breed, red squirrel, otter, fox and wildcat are present.

NO480910 at Braeloine, south of B976, 6 miles east of Ballater.

⓮ The Hebridean Machair
Western Isles
Lime-rich shell sand has been blown inland on to low-lying marshes transforming this semi-natural grassland into a magic carpet of botanical interest. The vivid colour patterns of the summer machair vary with the type and intensity of farming. It is difficult to imagine how nature could use the colours to greater effect, varying the shades of hybrid orchids from cream to deep red. Yellow seaside pansies and pink stork's-bill stand out on the sandy patches. The hay meadows and barley fields contain corn marigold, poppies, small bugloss and important populations of corncrake, twite, corn bunting and breeding waders.

NF707707 Balranald RSPB reserve is excellent, west of A865 3 miles north of Bayhead, North Uist.

⑮ Insh Marshes
Highland · RSPB

As you stand on the perimeter road looking down on the most important tract of flood plain mire in northern Britain you will see extensive habitats of lowland fen and marsh with willow carr, small pools and old drainage ditches which fortunately failed to work. Whooper swan and northern sedge are two of the exciting range of northern species.

NN775998 off B970, 1½ miles from Kingussie.

⑯ Loch an Eilein
Highland · SNH

Set in the Cairngorms amidst native pinewoods, this beautiful loch has all the Highland characteristics from white water-lilies to a ruined castle island. Birds feed on the shallow bays and water meadows; brown trout, pike, eels and otters are held in the deeper waters; insects are abundant in the summer warmth.

NH898085 off B970 at Polchar about 2 miles south-east of Craigellachie.

⑰ Morrone Birkwood NNR
Aberdeenshire · SNH

A rare woodland type in Britain today, this is our best sub-alpine birch-juniper woodland with a rich ground flora. There are 280 species of flowering plants and ferns, most notable being those otherwise restricted to open mountains: alpine cinquefoil, Scottish asphodel, alpine rush and hair sedge. Mosses and lichens are numerous in this woodland.

NO143911 off A93 west of Braemar, paths from car park.

⑱ Nigg and Udale Bays
Highland part · SNH

On opposite banks of the Cromarty Firth these bays are part of north-east Scotland's major wintering and migration sites for wildfowl and waders. The estuary flats are extensive and hold good numbers of goldeneye, pintail, scaup, wigeon, whooper and mute swans in winter. Autumn brings roosts of greylag geese from the fertile arable land around.

NH750720/NH710675, view from roads near Barbaraville, Nigg and Balblair, south and east of Invergordon.

⑲ Noss NNR
Shetland · SNH

The view down the sheer 180-metre (600-foot) cliffs, covered in seabirds, is stunning. One of the most spectacular seabird colonies in Europe, there are 10,000 gannets, 20,000 kittiwakes, 63,000 guillemots with fulmars, black guillemots and great and arctic skuas.

HU550400 by boat from Lerwick via Bressay in summer.

⑳ Orkney Cliffs
Orkney · RSPB

Copinsay, Marwick Head and Noup Cliffs form one of the most striking groups of cliffs with breeding seabird colonies. They hold internationally significant numbers of many species; individually they are a most enthralling experience to reward the Orkney visitor. The birds make use of the feeding grounds of the Atlantic, with rich supplies of sand eels for the auks, and are protected by the inaccessible security of high cliff ledges.

Marwick is on western mainland Orkney, Noup Head on Westray, Copinsay on south-east of the mainland, offshore.

㉑ Papa Westray, North Hill
Orkney · RSPB

The heathland of North Hill is brought to life each spring by the return of over 10,000 arctic terns in one unusually large and impressive colony. Gulls, ringed plovers, eiders and dunlins also breed here. The best maritime sedge heath in northern Scotland draws botanists as well as bird-watchers.

HY500550 north part of Westray Island, contact RSPB summer warden before entering the reserve.

㉒ Rum NNR
SNH

In 1957, Rum was sold by the last of the private owners to what is now Scottish Natural Heritage who now manage it as a NNR. Its geology, geomorphology, rich animal life, restored woodlands, heaths, herb-rich grasslands and coastal habitats – make it an ideal island for study and research. By arrangement with SNH it can be visited by anyone keen to see this jewel in Scotland's conservation crown.

NM407992 south of Skye. Pier at Kinloch.

㉓ St Kilda NNR
Western Isles (Eilean Siar, Comhairle nan) · SNH/NTS

St Kilda is the epitome of an oceanic island: isolated, beautiful, rugged, and dominated by the sea. In 1840 it may have been the last refuge of the great auk before extinction. Today it has its own subspecies of wren and long-tailed fieldmouse, feral herds of Soay and blackfaced sheep, and the breeding sites of the rare Leach's, storm petrels and Manx shearwaters. The cliffs drop of over 390 metres (1300 feet), clothed in roseroot, primrose, honeysuckle, moss campion and purple saxifrage. All around is the noise and smell of the largest gannetry in the world, the largest colony of fulmar in Britain and thousands of seabirds of a dozen other species.

41 miles west of North Uist, accessible in the summer months.

㉔ Strathy Bogs NNR
Highland · SNH

To see one of the best remaining blanket bogs in Britain visit this remote land in Scotland now surrounded by commercial afforestation. There are a great variety of bog species, dwarf birch, sundews and bearberry.

NC790550, 8 miles west of B871 on the upper reaches of the River Strathy.

㉕ Torridon
Highland · NTS

Between Lochs Torridon and Maree on Wester Ross is an area of over 380 square kilometres (150 square miles) which is typical of the best of the Highland wilderness, shaped by the power of ice. First appreciating its scale and beauty from a distance, we venture to penetrate this land of rocky coasts, mountains, moorlands, freshwater hill lochs and coastal sea lochs to appreciate the individuality of the Highland wildlife. It seems as though the divers and eagles of Torridon are locked in a time-capsule with the pinewoods and arctic flowers which were obliterated from the warmer south, thousands of years ago. An exciting collection of true Highland habitats not to be missed.

Via A896 and A832 north-west of Achnasheen.

㉖ Ythan Estuary
Aberdeenshire · SNH

The dunes and moorland close to the habitats of the estuary are the perfect combination for the eider ducks to breed in their largest numbers. Shelduck make use of the old rabbit burrows; sandwich, little, arctic and common terns nest on the Sands of Forvie. A marvellous example of a large dune system undisturbed by man.

NK025275 on A975 about 12 miles north of Aberdeen.

2 Central Scotland

If we had to tell the natural history of our islands from one region only it would have been Central Scotland. For here is the drama of mountain scenery with arctic relics, the power of roaring river torrents and the richness of lowland lochs. Remnants of a varied wildwood contrast with the wave-battered oceanic isles. All the shoreline habitats are represented on the east or west coasts. Heather moorlands and upland grasses are grazed by sheep on the rugged hills. Here, the twentieth-century landscapes of coniferous forests are not as new as we may think. There is the essential link between the rich arable land of the lowlands and the wild geese which winter here. Other wildlife species have adjusted to living with man in the great Scottish cities and with our help in new nature reserves.

❶ Ben Lomond
Stirling

With all the splendour of the Highland peaks to the north, Ben Lomond towers over its loch to mark the end of the Lowland hills of Central Scotland. The flora of this mountain is remarkable in its richness. High on the crags and corries are the arctic alpines: fairy flax, alpine meadow-rue, sibbaldia and cyphel. The colourful campions, saxifrage and mountain pansy embellish the highest crags which also support a wealth of mosses, ferns and grasses. The most arctic of our birds, the ptarmigan, is found on the summits with raven and ring ouzel below. Red deer, mountain hare and merlin are also present.

NM370025, a five-hour return trek will take you to the summit, access from Loch Lomond or Queen Elizabeth Forest Park.

❷ Braehead Moss NNR
S. Lanarkshire • SNH

The best local example of both raised and blanket bogs is now a NNR, having been undisturbed by burning, forestry or farming. Rarer species of bog mosses are found among the typical bog plants. The area is open to public access on foot but can be extremely wet. A rare opportunity to appreciate the bog habitats.

NS955510 on B7016 adjacent Braehead village, 6 miles north-east of Lanark.

❸ Clyde Valley Woodlands NNR
S. Lanarkshire • SNH

The upper Clyde Valley has a group of important broadleaved woodlands which feature a wide range of native tree species of oak, elm, ash and alder. Many uncommon plants also grow in these lowland glens including rough horsetail, wood fescue, herb paris, and stone bramble.

NS895455 off minor roads north of Lanark.

❹ Eden Estuary
Fife • Fife C

Common seal will haul out on to the sandbanks between Shelly Point and the mouth of the Eden and their amusing, if somewhat lethargic, antics will brighten any bird-watcher's visit to this estuary. Sheltered with a range of coastal habitats, the Eden attracts godwits, redshank, dunlin and knot in good numbers. Views of the eiders and scoters in St Andrews Bay or the estuary can often be enjoyed more easily than from the Firth of Tay. The black and white

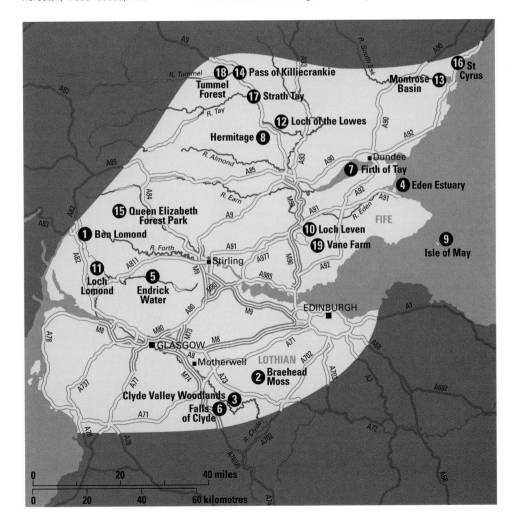

patterns of both shelduck and oystercatchers are always around.

NO455188 main access at Out Head 2 miles north of St Andrews, or from Guardbridge on A919, 4 miles north-west of St Andrews, where there is a visitor centre.

⑤ Endrick Water
Stirling
In its short dash across Central Scotland from the Carleatheran Bog to Loch Lomond, the River Endrick portrays each stage of a river's story through time and space. High in the grouse moors the rills and burns gather speed to erode ravines. The hill streams support brown trout, dipper and grey wagtail. The high waterfall at the Loup of Fintry obstructs the migration of salmon and sea trout further upstream. The lower reaches are subject to sudden spates, from which the river takes its name. There are ox-bow lakes where it slows down. It never reaches the sea but spills out into the fresh-water richness of Loch Lomond where otters and herons fish the mouth of the river.

NS650865 on B818 to NS473875 on A811 south of Drymen.

⑥ Falls of Clyde
S. Lanarkshire · SWT
The power of the Clyde in spate is dramatic indeed, as it roars over a series of falls. It carved the valley and gorge where mink, otter, grey wagtail and dippers now feed. It drove the New Lanark watermills with the crystal-clear waters, still stocked with minnow, trout, grayling, pike and lamprey. The spray-drenched cliffs have developed mosses and ferns and their ledges grow butterwort and purple saxifrage. There are two delightful nature reserves, one on each bank, with excellent flora in woods which are home

to badgers and are rich in birds, including tawny owls and peregrine falcons, insects, which provide food for pipistrelle bats, and fungi.

NS880415 on minor roads south of Lanark.

⑦ Firth of Tay
Dundee City and Angus
Whilst the Firth holds internationally significant numbers of wintering wildfowl and waders, watching for them over this vast expanse of estuary can be a cold and frustrating pastime. The secret is to know when and where to be. Low tide is not a good time as the birds are too far away and too dispersed to identify. Try Kingoodie or Port Allen for autumn waders in Invergowrie Bay, and the minor road from Newburgh to Balmerino for flighting pink-footed and greylag geese, overhead, at dawn and dusk. Diving duck and mute swans collect round the sewage outfall at the Stannergate and near Monifieth. The eider, scoter and divers which normally winter off the Abertay Sands will come close to Tayport and Newport in severe weather.

From Perth to Monifieth (including Dundee, Newburgh, Newport and the Carse of Gowrie).

⑧ Hermitage
Perth and Kinross · NTS
Not all of our coniferous forests are recent and this site is a rare opportunity to illustrate the wildlife, and the amenity, of long-established plantations of Douglas and silver fir, Norway spruce and larch. Alder, birch, oak and wild cherry inevitably find a niche on the river banks, providing food for a wide range of woodland birds. Dipper, grey wagtail and salmon may be seen in the gorge.

NO013423 access directly off A9, 1 mile west of Dunkeld.

⑨ Isle of May NNR
Perth and Kinross · SNH
One of Scotland's premier bird-watching sites, this island in the North Sea, at the mouth of the Firth of Forth, has a growing colony of grey seals on its northern tip. Almost any migrant bird can drop exhausted on to the safety of the rock and the observatory has recorded an amazing species list since its establishment in 1934. The fascination of May, however, is in the dramatic changes in the composition of the seabird colonies. Forty years ago the island was covered in thrift and sea campion with ten times as many breeding terns as gulls. Thirty years later the vegetation was a tangle of chickweed, sorrel and scurvygrass with 40,000 gulls, and no terns. Management now attempts to balance the gull and tern populations but other changes have occurred. Puffin numbers have risen from seven to about 8500 pairs in 30 years and shag increased from six to 1000 pairs in 50 years. The spectacle of this massive colony of oceanic birds is completed with razorbill and guillemot and several thousand pairs of kittiwakes and an expanding population of fulmar.

NT655995 by boat during the summertime from Crail, Anstruther or Pittenweem.

⑩ Loch Leven NNR
Perth and Kinross · SNH
The importance of this region's coastal sites for wintering birds is admirably complemented by the national significance of the breeding duck of Loch Leven. Up to 1000 pairs of duck (about half of them tufted) nest on the shores and islands of this enormous freshwater loch. Waders, especially lapwing, oystercatcher, curlew, snipe and redshank, use the surrounding wetlands for breeding. These species are joined by large numbers of other waders in winter and the

main wildfowl interest is the herds of pink-footed and greylag geese. But the breeding successes are tempered by the significant changes in the loch's water over the last few years. Algal blooms have indicated the increased richness of the water caused by run-off from the agricultural land drained by the Leven's feeder streams. Reedbeds and pondweeds are seriously depleted; stonewort has virtually disappeared along with dragonflies and mayflies. Although the duck's diet of pondweed has declined, the larvae of the chironomid midges is still an abundant food-source.

NO150010 between A911 and M90, access at Kirkgate Park, Findatie, Burleigh Sands and Leven Castle, together with Vane Farm.

⑪ Loch Lomond NNR
Argyll and Bute/Stirling/W. Dunbartonshire · SNH
In the largest freshwater lake in Britain it is not surprising to find a unique aquatic life typified by an unusual fish. The powan, or freshwater herring, is quite rare in Britain and swims with salmon, brown and sea trout in the loch. Roach are confined to the richer waters of the southern end, where the wintering wildfowl also tend to concentrate. Around the edges are fine spreads of reed swamp, lagoons, fen, willow carr and other wetlands. The islands provide ideal sanctuaries for wildlife and the largest, Inchcailloch, has a nature trail with fine sessile oak woodland with alder and birch. During low water levels the exposed shoreline mud attracts a variety of waders. NS420910, the south-east section and islands are the most interesting and include a nature reserve.

B837 off A811 at Drymen. Only 22 miles from the centre of Glasgow.

⑫ Loch of the Lowes

Perth and Kinross • SWT

The wildlife of this very attractive loch is special because it combines, as nowhere else, the species of the Central Lowlands with some from the Highlands. The breeding osprey, red-breasted mergansers, great crested and little grebes are some of Scotland's treasured birds. The shallow waters, woodlands and marsh habitats have a wealth of plant species from the quillwort, shoreweed and bogbean of highland nutrient-poor lochs to the yellow water-lily and amphibious bistort typical of the nutrient-rich waters of the lowlands. Reedbeds hide the secretive water-rail and roe deer. Fringing woodland has the same species composition as the native wildwood with oak, ash, hazel, holly, alder, willow and cherry.

NO050440 south of A923, 1 mile east of Dunkeld.

⑬ Montrose Basin

Angus • SWT

In this great circular basin of estuarine mud the annual cycle of bird migration provides interest for over seven months. Each of the main species reaches peak numbers at a different time, from the curlew in August to the dunlin in February. Oystercatcher, redshank and snipe stay on to breed. While the waders are attracted by the small animals of the mud, the ducks feed on eelgrass and glasswort. Mallard, teal, wigeon and pintail come in large numbers in the winter, as do up to 30,000 pink-footed geese. Eider and shelduck breed. Some of the grey geese which winter in the Central Lowlands will fly into the winter dusk to roost in the basin. Salmon, sea trout, eels and mussels are traditionally harvested in the mouth of the South Esk.

NO694575 west of Montrose.

⑭ Pass of Killiecrankie

Perth and Kinross • NTS

This pass to the Highlands is a dramatic wooded gorge following the River Garry. Oak dominates an attractive forest with bird cherry and a fine ground flora including wood vetch, stone bramble, melancholy thistle, giant bellflower and orchids. Redstart, wood warbler and spotted flycatcher will be seen during the spring and summer when the visitor centre is open to explain the wildlife of the area. The centre also has information for the Linn of Tummel between the pass and Pitlochry with excellent wooded walks.

NN917627 on A9 north of Pitlochry.

⑮ Queen Elizabeth Forest Park

Stirling • FC

A clear impression of the Highland moors to the north can be gained from the open land around Ben Venue. While the oak and conifer woods are the principal interest to the visitor, heather- and bracken-covered moorland rolls for miles around the rising land. Cross-leaved heath is common and the moors are spotted with struggling birch and straggles of bog myrtle. The subtle changes in vegetation over the wetter or rockier patches are reflected in the colour mosaic of the moors. All the birds of the moorland and upland scrub are present with good insect populations in the sheltered parts.

NN520015 Queen Elizabeth Forest Park Centre above Aberfoyle.

⑯ St Cyrus NNR

Aberdeenshire • SNH

This narrow strip of the east coast has a superb range of habitats associated with the shoreline. Of the 350 flowering plants and ferns several are on their northern limit of distribution. The saltmarsh, dunes and cliffs carry typical species with rare examples of the Nottingham catchfly, annual soft clover and rough clover. The dune pastures are still rich in flowers despite the decline of the rabbit population. The tenuous nature of some of the coastal habitats is witnessed by the virtual destruction of the saltmarsh plants following a major sand blow in 1967. Eider ducks and little terns are two of the 47 breeding bird species. Insect populations are also important.

NO745645 at St Cyrus on A92, 5 miles north of Montrose.

⑰ Strath Tay

The rolling landscapes of Central Scotland break at Dunkeld, on the line of the Highland Fault, with a range of low but rugged hills. Three rivers form the complex valley system of Strath Tay, U-shaped in profile with steep sides to a heathery plateau between Dunkeld and Pitlochry. Beyond are the foothills of the Highlands and a narrow gorge through the Pass of Killiecrankie. This area is of outstanding interest for wildlife for it contains many Highland species as well as Lowland plants and animals in extensive forests of exceptional beauty. There are oakwoods and mixed and coniferous plantations, forests planted by the Dukes of Atholl for amenity and timber as far back as 1738. On the shingle islands of the valley floor Scots pine, willow and alder freely regenerate. Many of the steeper and higher sites have held the tree species of the wildwood: birch, juniper, oak and pine. The woodland birds are of particular interest.

A9 from Dunkeld to Blair Atholl, public access by many waymarked trails and paths.

⑱ Tummel Forest

Perth and Kinross • FC

Oak, ash, hazel, alder and birch are the principal species of this deciduous woodland, overlooking Loch Tummel. There are small lochs around the forest which add the interest of waterside plants to those of the forest. Redstart, spotted flycatcher and woodpeckers breed in the broadleaved woods, capercaillie, black grouse and goldcrest in the conifers with mallard, teal and wigeon on the lochs. There is a Forestry Commission information centre at Queens View.

NN865597 off B8019, 5 miles north-west of Pitlochry.

⑲ Vane Farm

Perth and Kinross • RSPB

The close relationship between the wintering herds of geese in the shelter of Central Scotland and the crops of the arable land is well known. For generations the grey geese have flown to these feeding fields beside Loch Leven at dawn, and returned to estuaries, lochs and other safe places at dusk. It is an exciting spectacle when two or three thousand honking geese fly over in wavering echelons in the twilight. They can, however, cause problems for farmers by feeding on growing crops. Here at Vane Farm they are welcomed and the arable land which forms part of the reserve is managed to provide autumn gleanings from barley and potatoes for pink-footed and greylag geese.

NT145987 on B9097, 2 miles east of junction 5 on M90. On the banks of Loch Leven.

3 The Borders

The line of the border between England and Scotland is entirely artificial and ignored by wildlife which spreads across the uplands of Northumberland and the Borders, Dumfries and Galloway. Here the boundaries of the natural habitats do not follow any of the lines we have drawn through history.

The Borders are exciting, their scenery is dramatic and remote, ancient or very recent indeed. The coastline is superb, with some of the finest offshore islands, cliffs and bays in Britain. From the montane flowers of the Cheviots to the submarine kelp forests off St Abb's there is a clear, clean beauty in the region's complex vegetation patterns. The gannets of Bass Rock are no more or less exhilarating than the geese of the Solway Firth. They are different and it is the fact that they both occur here that matters. It is a very special region to those who live here or stay long enough to discover its scenery and wildlife.

❶ Ailsa Craig
S. Ayrshire • Privately owned
As if adrift in an ocean, this rugged island with a 300 metre-high (1000-foot) dome of grassland lies remote and detached from the Clyde Islands and the mainland. Seventy thousand seabirds return from their oceanic wanderings each year to breed on the cliffs. The gannetry has been here at least 400 years, for most of which it was a source of human food. Now 21,000 pairs of protected gannets incubate without the risk of egg gatherers.

NS0200001, 10 miles west of Girvan.

❷ Ballantrae Shingle Beach
S. Ayrshire • SWT
Terns, ringed plover and oystercatcher nest on the spit of flat grey shingles covered in sea campion, sea sandwort and oysterplant. Successive plant associations on the landward side include bird's-foot-trefoil and wild carrot.

NX085825 on A77 between Girvan and Stranraer.

❸ Bass Rock
E. Lothian • Privately owned
Thousands of pairs of *Sula bassana* (the gannet's scientific name is taken from this island) spread up the cliff ledges and on to the summit slopes of Bass Rock. There is still room for kittiwakes, auks, shag and fulmar to breed here too, though they are hardly

noticeable amidst the noise, smell and clamour of the gannetry. The top of the island is one of the best places to to watch the gannets' acrobatic plunges for food beneath the waves.

NT602873 daily summer sailings from North Berwick, subject to weather.

❹ Beltingham
Northumberland • WT
Silt charged with lead and zinc from the northern Pennines' mines has been deposited in the Rivers South Tyne and Allen on to beaches of shingle. The resulting 'heavy metal' vegetation includes mountain pansy, thrift, alpine penny-cress, spring sandwort and alpine scurvygrass. The sites are unique.

NY785641, 3 miles west of Haydon Bridge, turn off A69 and follow signs to Beltingham, then on to the flood plain.

❺ Caerlaverock NNR
Dumfries and Galloway • SNH/WWT
For 6 miles along the Scottish shore of the Solway Firth extends one of the largest unreclaimed saltmarshes in the British Isles. Grazed by cattle and geese the plants also have to withstand regular inundation by salt water. One of the finest sites for our wintering geese (including the entire Spitsbergen population of barnacle geese), the reserve is hunted by harriers and

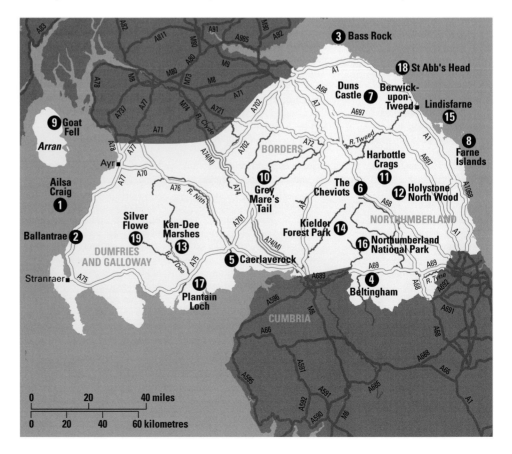

peregrines and used by thousands of migrating ducks and waders. The evening roost flight of geese from the fields to the foreshore is dramatic indeed, with skein after skein of calling geese flying at low level. A thriving population of natterjack toads is also present on the reserve.

NY018653, 7 miles south of Dumfries.

6 The Cheviots

Magnificent views stretch out across the Borders and the Northumberland countryside from the peaks of the Northumberland National Park. Round the summit of the Cheviots grow plants with ingenious ways of surviving the cold, windy and snow-laden peaks. Most important is to stay close to the ground like the parsley fern, dwarf male-fern, chives and maiden pink. Where there are lime-rich rocks on the Cheviots, globeflower, roseroot, alpine saw-wort and mossy saxifrage occur, with hairy stonecrop in wetter patches. All of them have been here for thousands of years, since the arctic tundra of post-glacial Britain.

NT910205 between Wooler on A697 and Carter Bar on A68.

7 Duns Castle
Borders • SWT
In the shelter of the Lammermuir Hills, the wooded surrounds of Duns Castle are picturesque and exceptionally rich in wildlife. Late spring displays carpets of ramsons, bluebells, red campion and purple wood crane's-bill. The show continues through the summer with meadowsweet, foxglove and water avens. Beech, oak and ash are the principal forest trees but poplars add to the amenity and insect habitats. Rarer plants can be found beneath the trees including toothwort, common wintergreen and twayblade.

Tits and pied flycatchers readily occupy the nestboxes. The rides and glades are ideal for butterflies and moths. An artificial loch adds to the richness and beauty of the site.

NT778550 at Duns, 12 miles south-west of Eyemouth.

8 Farne Islands
Northumberland • NT
During all but the highest tides 28 islands stand above the swell of the North Sea. There are low, flat platforms for cormorant or shag to dry out and higher cliffs for the auks and gulls to nest on. The other stars of the Farnes are the grey seals. Their great mottled backs roll beneath the surface and their inquisitive, doleful expressions can be clearly seen as they rise to inspect the passing boats. Noisy, awkward and aggressive on land, they are swift and graceful in the waves. The pups will clamber over the rocks as the cows doze from the security of their rocky shelves.

NU230370 spring and summer boat trips, some with landings on Inner Farne and Staple Island from Seahouses daily, subject to weather.

9 Goat Fell
N. Ayrshire • NTS
Rising to nearly 1000 metres (3000 feet), the scenic ridges and corries of Goat Fell crown the mountain habitats of the Isle of Arran. On the island's granite summits are found arctic alpines: starry saxifrage or mountain sorrel and the alpine buckler-fern. Dwarf junipers survive the cold exposure at higher levels than the birch or oak of Merkland Wood. Raven, golden eagle and golden plover breed in these montane landscapes.

NR990415 on A841 north of Brodick.

10 Grey Mare's Tail
Dumfries and Galloway • NTS
A familiar site with unusual flora. The grasslands of the uplands are grazed by sheep and its surrounding grass-heather moors change on the steep scree to a type of grass heath hard-grazed by multi-coloured feral goats of remarkable agility. But even the goats cannot reach the cliffs of the hanging valley. The sides of the Mare's Tail, a memorable waterfall nearly 60 metres (200 feet) high, have therefore developed a nearly natural flora including roseroot, harebell, wood-rush, scabious, golden rod and wood sage.

NT182150 on A708, 9 miles north-east of Moffat.

11 Harbottle Crags
Northumberland • WT
If you stand on the crags themselves and look down the great sweeps of heather moorland and bogs of sphagnum moss, you will see the result of a programme of regular burning. This apparently drastic action successfully maintains the typical heather cover of an upland grouse moor, long since cleared of its natural oak/birch woodlands. Red and black grouse, meadow pipit, wheatear, whinchat and short-eared owl are typical birds of these moors.

NT927048 turn off B6341 at Flotterton on to minor road via Sharperton and Harbottle.

12 Holystone North Wood
Northumberland • WT
Many of the oaks have a somewhat stunted appearance; others spring from contorted boles, thought to be the result of coppicing many years ago. They are part of an excellent upland sessile oak wood in acid conditions with bracken, mosses, wood sorrel and the rare chickweed wintergreen normally restricted to Scottish

hill pinewoods. Wood warbler and redstart are typical summer visitors.

NT945028 turn off B6341 at Flotterton on to minor roads via Sharperton and Holystone village.

13 Ken-Dee Marshes
Dumfries and Galloway • RSPB
A narrow sinuous loch edged with forest and farmland is an important wintering refuge for wildfowl including the largest mainland flock of Greenland white-fronted geese. The marshes of the River Dee and their associated wet meadows have breeding snipe, curlew, redshank and lapwing with mallard, teal, shoveler, sedge warbler and reed buntings. Tufted duck, goosander and great crested grebe nest on the loch shore.

NX638765 and NX695694 from A713 and A762 south of New Galloway.

14 Kielder Forest Park
Northumberland • FC
This great wilderness of the uplands has the drama and scale of natural landscapes, but is entirely man-made. Kielder reservoir is the largest area of water created by man in western Europe; the Kielder Forest of pine and oak woods, birch and rowan was cleared centuries ago to provide the vast heather moorlands for sheep and grouse. The modern forest park is a huge area of coniferous plantations now forming a structure of different aged blocks. The moors have grouse and merlin, the forest has badger, roe deer and red squirrel, siskin, crossbill and sparrowhawk. The Kielder Forest drive is a toll road and runs through the heart of the forest.

NY633934 turn off B6320 at Bellingham to follow road to Kielder.

⑮ Lindisfarne
Northumberland · EN
The inaccessibility of Holy Island at high tide makes us acutely aware of the importance of tidal movements to the coastal birds. The wildfowl and waders which frequent the fine dunes, saltmarshes and mudflats of Lindisfarne, especially in winter, make it a site of international importance. The largest wintering herd of whooper swans in England and good views of other uncommon wildfowl – eiders, merganers, scaup and brent geese – make an exciting excursion across the causeway, with dunlin, knot and godwits on the shores.

NU095430 off A1 via minor road through Beal across the island causeway.

⑯ Northumberland National Park
Northumberland · NPA
Scattered throughout the National Park are small lakes, or loughs, formed by the glaciers over-deepening the depressions they made in the ground. As the glaciers thawed, the dips filled up with ice-cold water. Some are still open water with sparse or rich vegetation depending on the local soil. Others have naturally infilled with vegetation to form willow-wooded mires. The upland streams may be fed by these loughs or simply charged by the rainwater from the hills. They flow over waterfalls and in powerful torrents where dipper and grey wagtail feed on a wealth of insects. Everywhere the water spreads there are mosses and lichens, sedges and waterside herbs.

NY763796 the Blacka Burn Lough has acid swamp and feeds the Blacka Burn in the conifers of the southern park.

⑰ Plantain Loch
Dumfries and Galloway · FC
The rich delight of this shallow upland loch is its wealth of dragonflies. When they are victims of the many oblong-leaved sundews they can be studied closely. The species include common aeshna and four-spotted libellula, with large red, common ischnura, green lestes and common blue damselflies. These colourful insects are out hunting July to September.

NX841602 near Dalbeattie.

⑱ St Abb's Head
Borders · NTS/SWT
A marvellous day's adventure discovering the wildlife of the sea could start with a visit to the unspoilt fishing village of St Abb's. For generations, fishermen, the last of the real hunters, have harvested the rich marine life of the North Sea. Follow the coast northwards to see how strong tides sweep the shore to keep the submarine kelp forests and rich marine life, including the arctic lumpfish, free of pollution. Upon reaching St Abb's Head you will be struck by the exposures in the rocky cliffs. Not only do they make wonderful coastal scenery but the once horizontal lines of rock planes are now tipped and tilted like crumpled bedclothes to indicate the powerful forces of geological change. The grassland tumbling to the shore and clothing the clifftops is of short turf on different soil types with correspondingly varied floras. Thyme, pink thrift, tormentil and wood sage, unlikely companions, all grow in close proximity. To complete the experience of the sea, over 15,000 seabirds nest on the cliffs, mainly guillemots and kittiwakes.

NT914693 off A1107 at Coldingham, the Head is about 1½ miles north of the village.

⑲ Silver Flowe NNR
Dumfries and Galloway · SNH
On the least disturbed and most varied acidic peatland in southern Scotland an important system of blanket mire has developed. The surface of the bog is extremely sensitive to trampling and no access is provided. However, as you look down from the hillside the seven bog areas are clearly visible, each with its series of shining pools from which the reserve derives its name.

NX470820, fairly remote to the east of Glen Trool in fine walking country.

4 The Pennines

For 150 miles the Pennines form a very distinctive region of uplands, identifiable at any point and yet composed of an extremely complex geology and scenery. The vast peat bogs of the northern uplands contrast with the rich limestone dales of Derbyshire's White Peak. The gritstone plateau of the Kinder is as different a scene from the leafy coastal valley woods of Durham as we could imagine. This fascinating diversity is an essential part of the Pennines' character and leads to a quite outstanding collection of habitats. Some, such as the arctic relics of Upper Teesdale, are fragile and rare. Others lie in endless sweeps over miles of moorland controlled for the grouse and the sheep.

The Pennines dominate the life and landscape of the north. The influence of man is everywhere. His farming and felling, drainage and industries have brought great changes to these impressive hills.

① Asby Scar NNR
Cumbria · EN
The Vale of Eden is lined by a rim of limestone covered by the plant associations of the limestone pavement or by upland grasslands which are grazed by sheep. You can see how the protection of the pavement structure produces a richer flora than the grazed areas of Asby Scar and, indeed, how the exposed grey limestone rocks can be quite bare of any vegetation.

NY648103 on minor roads off B6260, 6 miles south of Appleby Westmorland.

② Castle Eden Dene
Durham · CC/EN/NT
The Denes are coastal valley woods cut into the limestone plateau offering security and shelter for wildlife in quiet and beautiful valleys. A torrent of glacial melt-water from the uplands must have cut its way to the sea through these ravines, now narrowly edged with steep cliffs. Today, the waters rush down to meet the shingle banks thrown up by the North Sea tides. Castle Eden Dene is the finest of these valleys. Clothed with a superb mix of woodland it holds a most outstanding population of birds, insects and mammals. It is the home of the Castle Eden argus butterfly, one of four Lepidoptera species first captured at the Dene.

NZ410387, 3-mile-long valley to North Sea coast immediately south of Peterlee.

③ Fountains Abbey
Yorkshire · NT
Close to the hills of the Yorkshire Dales stands the largest monastic ruin in Britain – a Cistercian monastery founded in 1132. In medieval times the Abbey wielded great power over the management of its vast estates and contributed to the deforestation of the region and to the spread of sheep grazing in the hills. The grounds of the Abbey were landscaped between 1720 and 1740 with a lake and formal water garden, though the estate woods were restocked by informal planting of broadleaved woodland. The deer park remains and the entire area is excellent for woodland and farmland birds.

SE271683, 2 miles west of Ripon off B6265.

④ Hamsterley Forest
Durham · FC
This is an interesting example of modern coniferous plantations where the sheer size of the area has meant the retention of important animal species. Roe deer, red squirrel, badger and fox are all breeding. So are the conifer specialists – crossbill, goldcrest and siskin. Many areas of semi-natural broadleaved woodland were left to grow and Pennington

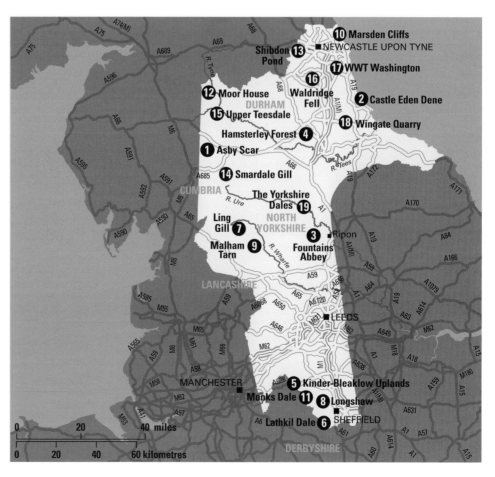

Beechwood is one of the highest beechwoods in the country.

NZ093312 minor roads north of B6282 at Woodland, about 8 miles north of Barnard Castle.

5 Kinder-Bleaklow Uplands
Derbyshire
Conditions are tough for plants and animals on this exposed, high plateau which offers panoramic views across the southern Pennines. But there is still sufficient cover to shelter dunlin, merlin, ring ouzel, golden plover and red grouse. The cloudberry normally favours mountain habitats and it does well here at the limit of its southern range.

SK090929 from A57 east of Glossop.

6 Lathkil Dale NNR
Derbyshire · EN
The Pennine landscapes are remarkably varied, reflecting the different rock formations which have left this spine of uplands down the centre of northern England. At the southern end the millstone grit of the High Peak changes to a soft white landscape of carboniferous limestone. The glacial melt-waters cut deep valleys through the rock with steep slopes, cliffs and crags overlooking much smaller rivers. Broadleaved woodland soon established in the shelter of the valleys but has been depleted by felling. Lathkil Dale, with its rich mixture of grassland and woodland cover, is typical of the White Peak. The river is the only one in the White Peak which originates on limestone; the others flow down from the millstone grit. Purple loose-strife, sedges and marsh-marigold grow on the margins. Grey wagtails feed on the rich insect life.

SK205665 from the village of Over Haddon, 2 miles south-west of Bakewell via B5055.

7 Ling Gill
Yorkshire · EN
You will have to walk a short section of the Pennine Way to reach Ling Gill but a beautiful area of semi-natural woodland rewards the trek. You are free to wander over the boulder-strewn watercourse or the very steep valley sides to gain a marvellous impression of the native ash and elm wood of the limestone gorges of the Dales. Relatively inaccessible, it is virtually unmodified by man or grazing animals. The wood is renowned for its rich ground flora and mosses.

SD803778, 4½ miles from Horton-in-Ribblesdale along Pennine Way towards Hawes in Wensleydale.

8 Longshaw
Derbyshire · NT
Without suffering the exposure of the High Peak we can enjoy the typical acid moorland and heath of the millstone grits at Longshaw. Although it is 300 metres (1000 feet) above sea level this compact series of woods, meadows, pools and open moorland is sheltered by the high moors around and is easily accessible from car parks in the country park.

SK267800 on B6054/6055, 3 miles east of Hathersage.

9 Malham Tarn NNR
Yorkshire · FSC/NT/EN
High above the Dales of Yorkshire you will find a most special tarn – one of only eight upland alkaline lakes in Europe – which has been the subject of intensive field studies by generations of naturalists and which became a Wetland of International Importance in 1993. The tarn is surrounded by a NNR which is a fascinating complex of wetlands, open water, limestone pavements, moors and grasslands. Curlew and lapwing breed in the wetlands while the tarn's resident coot and tufted duck can be viewed from a lakeside bird-hide. Courses run by the Field Study Centre can introduce you to these habitats and their associated flora and fauna. The Pennine Way skirts the eastern and north-eastern shores of the tarn.

SD890672 minor roads north of A65 via Airton and Malham.

10 Marsden Cliffs
S. Tyneside · NT
South of the River Tyne, the limestone rocks of the Pennines outcrop at the coast with a splendid cliff covered in cowslips, rock-rose and thrift. Despite the proximity of the urban conurbation inland, the site forms a most important colony of breeding seabirds. The delightful kittiwakes sit for hours on their nests, providing one of the few opportunities to see these oceanic birds at close range. Fulmars too break their relentless flight to incubate their eggs here. The noisy herring gulls will leave you in no doubt that you are watching sea creatures uneasily holding temporary space on land.

NZ397650 South Shields.

11 Monks Dale
Derbyshire · EN
Since the first clearances of woodland from the Derbyshire Dales rich grasslands have developed on the thin limestone soils. They are full of characteristic species: wild thyme, common rock-rose, marjoram and bird's-foot-trefoil. Where the slopes have a southern aspect there can be over 50 species of plants in a square yard, a profusion of spring and summer colour which adds immensely to our enjoyment of these dales. Towards the top of the slopes the number of species declines with increased acidity and exposure, a subtle transition until dominated by wavy hair-grass, sheep's fescue

and the bilberry and heather of the moors.

SK141735 north of B6049 walking north from Miller's Dale at this point.

12 Moor House NNR
Cumbria · EN
Immediately north-west of the Upper Teesdale Reserve is the largest nature reserve in England, over 10,000 acres (4047 hectares) of blanket bog representative of vast upland areas of the northern Pennines. From 10,000 to 7500 years ago birch and pine spread over these hills. The wetter climate of the next 2000 years meant that bogs overwhelmed the birch, and plant material only partly decomposed forming a layer of peat. The peat accumulated to a depth of 12 feet in places, formed by vegetation similar to that growing on the bog today: heather, cottongrass and sphagnum moss. The peat hags of these uplands are caused by the erosion of the peat by drainage, burning and grazing over the last 2500 years. The typical upland birds are present. Small trout and bullheads are in most of the streams. The reserve is rich in mosses, liverworts and lichens with fungi and algae too.

NY730325 off B6277, 8 miles south-east of Alston.

13 Shibdon Pond
Durham · WT/Gateshead MBC
The subsidence of land has created a rich source of food and shelter for the common and the less familiar of our urban wildlife species. With a carefully managed mix of habitat types ranging from open water to marsh and acid heath to scrub, the reserve attracts an equally varied animal population. The wetlands and water contain eel, coarse fish, frogs, toads, newts and voles. Bats hunt for

the prolific insect life at night; yellow wagtails and warblers do so in the day. Waterfowl are abundant and the secretive water rail is often heard in the reeds.

NZ195628 between Blaydon and Swalwell via A69.

⓮ Smardale Gill NNR
Cumbria · WT
Occupying 3½ miles of disused railway track, this attractive 100 acre (40 hectares) reserve includes steep wooded slopes of the gill carved by Scandal Beck and open countryside typical of the region. Birch, willow and hazel has been allowed to re-colonize the edges of the former track-side where in spring you will encounter many species of woodland flower. Roe deer and red squirrels inhabit these wooded parts and in summer you will hear, and maybe see, wood warblers and pied flycatchers. The grassland is dominated by blue moor grass – rare elsewhere in Britain – on which the rare Scotch argus butterfly lays its eggs, and among which bloody crane's-bill, common rock-rose and various orchids flourish.

Signposted off A685, 1 mile south of Kirkby Stephen. Car park at GR738083

⓯ Upper Teesdale NNR
Durham · EN
This fragile community of flowering plants is unique in western Europe. If you walk from Cow Green Reservoir along the Birkdale Track nature trail to Caldron Snout you pass through an area where arctic plants have grown continuously for 10,000 years. Protected from grazing sheep, the limestone grasslands, flushes and meadows form a colossal carpet of colourful arctic alpine plants such as spring gentian, bird's-eye primrose, alpine bartsia, Scottish asphodel and saxifrages. These survivors are the last of species which were widespread when arctic conditions occurred in Britain at the retreat of the glaciers.

NY815310 off B6277, 16 miles north-west of Barnard Castle. Bowlees visitor centre NY907283.

⓰ Waldridge Fell
Durham · CC
Despite its lowland situation, all the typical plants of the Pennine heaths occur, providing a particularly rich insect population. Here a flora of heather, bell heather, crowberry and bilberry is enriched by bog plants such as bogbean, water horsetail, cottongrass and sedges in the wetter areas. The country park also supports areas of semi-natural broadleaved woodland and is a rich site for insects.

NZ254494 minor roads, 1½ miles west of Chester-le-Street.

⓱ WWT Washington
Tyne and Wear · WWT
An exciting demonstration of how successful nature reserves can be linked to other uses. In the built-up part of the region the waterfowl collection combines the opportunities for visitors to see the tame wildfowl at close quarters and for declining species to be protected. Wild areas with scrapes, ponds, river, reedbeds and woodlands hold important numbers of wildfowl, waders and land birds, many of which use the areas as a stopover while on migration.

NZ330565 south of A1231 at Washington in the Wear valley.

⓲ Wingate Quarry
Durham · CC
The mounds, steep slopes and rocky crags of Wingate were formed by limestone quarrying but support the flora of the magnesian limestone unique to this area. In spring and summer the quarry resembles a wild rock garden with cowslips, bird's-foot-trefoil, knapweed and orchids in flower. Newts, frogs, damselflies and dragonflies are found in the reserve.

NZ373376 south of A181 west of Wingate village.

⓳ The Yorkshire Dales
The heart of the Pennines is formed from a series of limestone and gritstone layers. They are exposed to the wind and rain to form beautiful sweeping uplands with high and dramatic peaks; they are dissected by some of the most picturesque valleys in the British Isles, cut by clear rivers of great force. Every dale is different and each has its own special character, forming a unique blend of farmland, moorland, woodland and river. While many areas are dominated by the rugged beauty of gritstone landscapes, the Dales are also one of our richest compositions of limestone scenery. The remnants of natural woodland and of native plants on the scars and pavements are unequalled. But to most of the Dales' admirers it is the grasslands which make this part of the Pennines distinctive. Each Dale has the combination of open, grazed grassland together with valley bottom meadows enclosed by stone walls. Those meadows which have not been agriculturally improved are managed for hay and support a rich variety of flowering plants, forming some of the most colourful meadows in the country. On the many areas of limestone pavement is semi-natural grassland, untouched by grazing animals, with bloody crane's-bill, zigzag clover and rock-rose on the clints, and wall lettuce, herb Robert, dog's mercury and ferns in the shady and humid fissures.

North-west Yorkshire from Skipton to Richmond crossed by B6160, B6265, A684 and B6270.

5 The Lake District

Lakeland is more than a National Park, more than a landscape, however dramatic and splendid it may be. It is a way of life, a complete story of man and nature sharing the rigours of a hard existence. The story is set in a theatre of majestic beauty and scale. It is a region of moods, created by the scenery and exaggerated by the weather: in the spring sunshine it can be peacefully still, but at other times it can be as wild and inhospitable as anywhere in England.

As the Lakes mirror the mountain's images, so the wildlife reflects the moods and character of the region. The plaintive moorland piping of the golden plover enhances our solitude; the richness of the sheltered lakeside woods rings to the chorus of songbirds. For centuries the Lakes have drawn artists, poets, musicians and naturalists. If you walk from the lake edge to high fell you will know why they came.

❶ Arnside Knott and Heathwaite
Cumbria • NT
Four walks offer sightings of the varied wildlife of this flat-topped limestone hill, including heathland birds in the Higher Pasture and woodcock in the woods. An exceptionally rich population of butterflies includes nationally rare species such as the high brown and Duke of Burgundy fritillary.

SD451773 at Arnside, 3 miles south-west of Milnthorpe.

❷ Claife
Cumbria • NT
Three thousand years ago all but the highest mountains, the bogs and coastal zones of the Lake District were covered in broadleaved woodland. The acid soils were dominated by sessile oak woodland, rich in ferns, mosses and lichens. Redstart, pied flycatcher and wood warbler were some of the special birds in these wildwoods and they still breed around Lake Windermere.

SD388954 end of B5285 on shores of Windermere.

❸ Friars Crag
Cumbria • NT
An important part of the Lakeland character is the combination of woodland and water habitats. Derwent Water has a scatter of wooded islands which can be seen from the Friars Crag nature trail. It runs through mixed woods along the shore where many typical Lakeland birds and plants can be seen.

NY264227 off B5289, 1 mile south of Keswick.

❹ Grizedale Forest
Cumbria • FC
A huge spread of coniferous forest has transformed the area between Coniston and Windermere into a modern landscape on a grand scale. Superimposed on the Lakeland scene, the forest has retained many of the native features, including streams, tarns, bogs an small heaths and pastures. Goldcrest and coal tits call from every part. Deer are present and the information centre will explain about the new forest of Grizedale and its wildlife.

SD336944 from B5285/6 at Hawkshead south to Satterthwaite on minor roads.

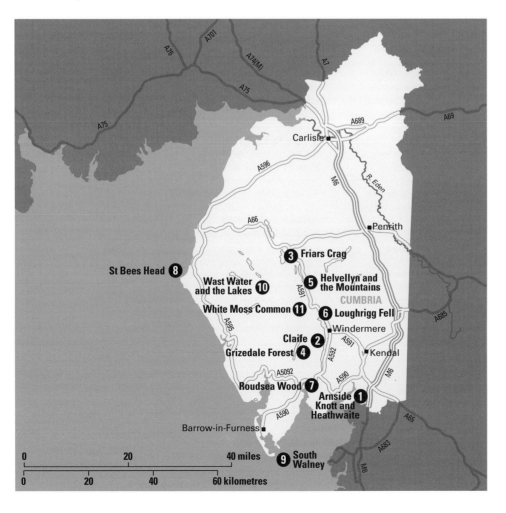

5 Helvellyn and the Mountains
Cumbria • Lake District NPA/NT

From their Icelandic breeding grounds wild whooper swans fly high over the wintry scene. It is covered by the first snows and these arctic migrants will choose to settle on one of the great lakes below them. This complex region was created millions of years ago, when water flowed in all directions from the central heights of a great dome of ancient rocks. These streams were already shed when successive glaciations occurred, completely remodelling the surface of the dome. Stand on Helvellyn's Striding Edge and see to the west how the ice bulldozed the line of the tiny Wyth Burn into a deep valley, scooped a great hole in the valley bottom and, on thawing, dumped the damming moraine and back-filled the depression of Thirlmere with ice-cold water. To the east lies a different view. Here the glaciers ripped two valleys from the side of Helvellyn so close together they left a blade of land with precipitous drops on both sides to form Striding Edge, one of the most dramatic paths in England. Red Tarn remains in the shadow of the mountain as a superb example of a glacial corrie. By the time the glaciers had retreated the Lake District we know had been formed. At first only creatures and plants which could withstand the arctic cold of the tundra survived. Then the climate warmed and plants of the temperate zones spread widely. But winters on the mountains here, where snow can lie for eight months of the year, have an arctic bitterness which enables relics of the post-glacial years to survive. Wherever the sheep cannot graze, on ledges and screes, in cracks and crevices, alpine saw-wort, mossy and starry saxifrage, roseroot and alpine lady's mantle represent some of the arctic flora. A special subspecies of juniper grows on the mountains, severely dwarfed by the exposure. These mountains are the home of golden eagle and peregrine falcon, red grouse, wheatear and ring ouzel. On a sunny June day you may find a Lakeland treasure – on exposed mountainsides over 450 metres (1500 feet) high, the small mountain ringlet butterfly searches the mat-grass for flowering plants. With a larval hibernation of ten months it concentrates the rest of its life into a few weeks in late spring.

NY343153, A591, 5 miles north of Grasmere.

6 Loughrigg Fell
Cumbria • NT

A good walk from Ambleside, across the river and up the sides of Loughrigg to see the patchwork of Lakeland land uses. Grassland and arable fields merge into the upland fell. Woodland and riverside wildlife will also be seen.

NY375047 immediately west of Ambleside.

7 Roudsea Wood NNR
Cumbria • EN

The ideal opportunity to see the difference between the main woodland types of this part of Cumbria, Roudsea provides both acid and limestone woodland. Peatland, saltmarsh and alluvial valley add further habitats to enjoy on this visit. The ridge of carboniferous limestone supports ash and oak, lime, cherry and yew with an understorey of purging buckthorn, spindle, guelder rose and whitebeam. Lily-of-the-valley, columbine and orchids grow among the false brome and dog's mercury on the forest floor. In contrast the sessile oak wood on the slates has birch with rowan and hazel and a poorer field layer dominated by wavy hair-grass. The valley mire between the woods has typical fen species and interesting sedges. The raised mire of Roudsea Mosses is peaty with birch, rowan and pine. Red and roe deer are present and there are occasional sightings of otter, red squirrels, adder and common toads and frogs.

SD335825 from Greenodd on A5092, there is a public footpath across the reserve.

8 St Bees Head
Cumbria • RSPB

The warm red colours of the sandstone cliffs with grassland tumbling over the tops of the weathered rock face make St Bees one of the most attractive of our mainland seabird colonies. Projecting well into the Irish Sea and with just enough gorse scrub to shelter migrants and breeding land birds, the species list is exciting. Manx and sooty shearwaters, red-throated divers, terns, gannets and skuas pass by. Little owl, stone-chat, rock pipit and warblers are among the breeding land birds. The most important users of the cliffs are the auks: razorbill, guillemot and puffin and, on their only English breeding colony, the black guillemot of northern waters. Kittiwakes and fulmars also nest on the ledges.

NX962118 off B5345, 4 miles south of Whitehaven.

9 South Walney
Cumbria • WT

The large gull colony is worth a visit at South Walney. With one of Europe's largest breeding colonies of herring and lesser black-backed gulls, there is also a reserve of many coastal habitats. There are sand dunes with wet and dry meadows, freshwater marsh, open pools, shingle, saltmarsh and mudflats. It is the most southerly breeding site for eiders on the west coast. Mallard, oystercatcher, ringed plover, shelduck and many land-birds nest here. Thousands of waders and wildfowl winter here. The botanical interest is substantial and gravel workings have introduced a fascinating diversity of plants: viper's bugloss, ploughman's spikenard and henbane.

SD215620 Walney Island from Barrow-in-Furness follow Promenade, Ocean Road, Carr Lane, 5 miles to coastguard cottages. Nominal entry charge. Closed Mondays.

10 Wast Water and the Lakes
Cumbria • NT/WT

The deepest of the lakes is surrounded by steep fells, rising almost 900 metres (3000 feet) to the highest point in England, only 2 miles away. The bed of Wast Water was scoured so deeply by the glaciers it now lies over 15 metres (50 feet) below sea level. Charr and whitefish are two of the glacial creatures which have survived being trapped in the lakes. Another relic of glacial lakes, tiny freshwater shrimps, survive in Ennerdale Water. Each lake is different. Some of the shores are fringed with yellow loosestrife and common reed; others have water-lily and quillwort or shoreweed in the shallows. Mallard, teal and tufted ducks, red-breasted mergansers, common sandpipers and grey wagtails breed at Wast Water.

NY145045 Wast Water, minor roads from the south via Nether Wasdale.

11 White Moss Common
Cumbria • NT/Lake District NPA

Between Grasmere and Rydal Water is a good range of typical Lakeland habitats. The lakes, stream and woodland are the main interest but you can see the open fell and pastures.

NY348065 on A591 about 1 mile south of Grasmere.

6 East of the Pennines

If we could follow the water of the Pickering Beck we would experience a journey in time and place. From its source on Lockton High Moor you can see the vast plateau of the North York Moors National Park finally moulded by the glaciers. The beck flows past the bogs and high grouse moors where relic arctic alpines grow at Levisham Moor. There are semi-natural woods and coniferous plantations before the beck runs out into the level plain of the Vale of Pickering. After joining the Rye and the Derwent, it meanders round the Yorkshire Wolds, through the Vale of York, and eventually joins the Humber.

As the great waterway heads for the estuary it collects the Trent from the south and even the rivers draining the arable and grasslands of the north Lincolnshire Wolds. The Humber has a truly remarkable catchment, with a fascinating range of sites to visit. The Humber estuary and its coastal areas also offer a diverse range of habitats from saltmarsh and mudflats to sand dunes and brackish pools.

❶ Axholme Line
Lincolnshire • WT
Lime-rich soils on the site of this disused railway line have produced a splendid colonization of hawthorn, ash, aspen, elder, oak, dog rose and field maple. Birds and butterflies particularly have made full use of the opportunity.

SK773979 off B1396 Blaxton to Haxey Road.

❷ Bardney Limewoods NNR
Lincolnshire • FC
Before the plough had so great an impact on the Lincolnshire landscape extensive broad-leaved forests spread over the lowlands between Lincoln and the Wolds. Bardney Limewoods today is only a small proportion of that former wildwood and is a new landscape of mixed plantations, blended with old woodland. As

you walk the forest trails the ride edges still show evidence of those ancient woods – oak, lime, wych-elm, dogwood, thorns and wild roses in a tangle beneath the woodland canopy.

TF150735 off B1202, 3 miles south of Wragby.

❸ Bempton Cliffs
E. Yorkshire • RSPB
As you stand at the precipitous edge of these spectacular 120 metre-high (400-foot) cliffs, it is easy to forget you are on the British mainland. The drama of the sea, the white cliff faces and the noise of the birds are overwhelming. Indeed, you are looking at the only gannetry and the largest seabird colony on the British mainland. The white chalk cliffs run for 5 miles, and although the reserve is often only a few yards wide, 220 species of plants have been recorded, typically those of the cliff and chalk. The erosion of the soft rock has provided narrow ledges and cracks for 60,000 pairs of kittiwakes, together with fulmar, guillemot, razorbill and puffin, with shag in the caves below. In autumn, shearwaters, skuas and other oceanic birds pass by on their seemingly endless journeys.

TA197741 off B1229, 4 miles north-west of Flamborough Head.

❹ Blacktoft Sands
E. Yorkshire • RSPB
A classical collection of coastal habitats ranging from mudflats to saltmarsh and topped up with a huge reedbed. One hundred pairs of bearded tits and 400 pairs of reed warblers are in their element with water-rails and the occasional pair of marsh harriers. A new lagoon has been created with islands already occupied by gadwall

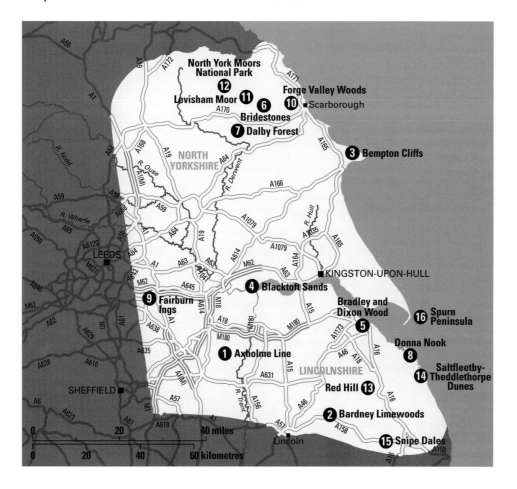

and teal. In the autumn the water levels are lowered to increase the feeding areas for waders passing through.

SE843232 on south bank of Humber, east of Ousefleet off A161.

5 Bradley and Dixon Wood
Lincolnshire • N.E. Lincs. C
Spring and early summer are the seasons to see this local nature reserve at its best, with the cherry and blackthorn blossom, bluebells, orchids and butterflies. There are some coniferous trees amongst the broadleaves but oak, ash and elm dominate.

TA245058 south of A18 beyond the outskirts of Cleethorpes.

6 Bridestones
Yorkshire • WT/NT
Flanked by extensive coniferous plantations, this area of dry moorland with rock outcrops is dominated by heather and bilberry. It is invaded by oak, birch and rowan. Cottongrass reveals the wetter patches. Roe deer, fox and badger are present, no doubt from the forest around.

SE880904 minor roads east of A169 via Low Dalby, 6 miles north-east of Pickering.

7 Dalby Forest
Yorkshire • FC
The extensive forests clothing the hills and moors of the National Park's south-east corner are impressive indeed. They contain a fascinating wildlife, especially on the forest floor, where clearings or ride edges bring light to an understorey, shrub and field layers. Mammals include deer, fox and badger. Predators in the air include peregrine, sparrowhawk and kestrel. Small mammals are numerous and birds surprisingly active. Crossbill, siskin, redpoll, chaffinch and coal tit move

through the crowns of the evergreens. The forest drive needs to be taken slowly to appreciate the detail.

SE857873 Low Dalby Information Centre, then to Hackness on forest drives and minor roads.

8 Donna Nook
Lincolnshire • WT
No better reflection of the diversity of habitats can be shown than to say this site supports breeding red-legged partridge, whitethroat, little grebe and ringed plover. Two hundred and fifty other bird species have been recorded. Along the shore in winter there are delightful bouncing flocks of passerines including shorelark, twite and Lapland bunting. Grey and common seals may be seen. Beware the bombing range which has a flag warning system; otherwise this is a superb variety of dunes, mudflats, saltings and sandflats.

TF421998 off A1031 at North Somercotes, 9 miles north-west of Mablethorpe.

9 Fairburn Ings
Yorkshire • RSPB
Opportunities for wildlife to utilize our developments are never far away. Surrounded by power stations, industry and major roads, a dramatic 2½-mile-long system of subsidence 'flashes' forms an important wetland. Viewed from the adjacent road and paths the shallow pools attract winter wildfowl, breeding and migrating waders and other water-birds in large numbers. The goldeneye and goosander from the north find shelter and security in these pools which are likely to extend as further subsidence occurs.

SE450275 west of A1, 2 miles north of Ferrybridge.

10 Forge Valley Woods NNR
Yorkshire • EN
Hugging the contours of a steep, narrow gorge, you can drive the length of the Forge Valley and see semi-natural woodland all around. Note how the trees change up the valley sides. Oak dominates near the top, ash and wych-elm do well on the shelter lower down, while alder and willow thrive on the wet soils of the valley floor. A good understorey of hazel, holly, elder, hawthorn and rowan attracts the breeding birds. Ferns and mosses are an interesting study. This valley has been wooded for 6000 years but only recently modified by man. The forge which processed local ironstone was fuelled by charcoal timber from the woods.

SE985860 minor road north from East Ayton which is on A170, 3 miles west of Scarborough.

11 Levisham Moor
Yorkshire • NPA
Levisham Moor is part of the central moorland block of the National Park and thus demonstrates its varied natural history. Relic arctic alpines survive high on the moorlands. Specifically, they are the chickweed wintergreen and dwarf cornel, both at their southern range limit and both the last representatives of the cold, bleak days of arctic influence. Large areas of bracken on the moor are coloured with heather, bilberry and crowberry. There is a superb blend of woodlands here too, from thick oakwoods with alder and willow along the streams and birch and rowan at the moorland edge, just the species we would expect in the wildwood of the northern upland. Lower down the slopes lime, maple, guelder rose and gorse are found. Watercress and brooklime edge the streams. Old, rich pastures are grazed by roe deer with ragged

robin and cuckooflower growing in the damp patches.

SE853937 west of A169, 5 miles north of Pickering.

12 North York Moors National Park
Yorkshire • NPA
The most northerly of the waters feeding the Humber estuary rise on the great plateau of the North York Moors. With its source only 3 miles from the coast, the Derwent chooses to wind for over 80 miles through the Vale of Pickering, round the Yorkshire Wolds to join the Ouse, the Wharfe, the Aire and the Trent discharging into the great estuary of Humberside. The high moors of the National Park are cut by many streams all joining forces before Malton. Some of these valleys were cut in post-glacial times when Eskdale was a great lake whose waters, trapped by the ice-laden North Sea, spilled over the moors and raced towards the Vale of York. The huge platform of acid sandstone has produced one of the most distinctive upland areas in Britain. The endless scale of these heather moors is magnificent – they form the largest continuous tract of heather moorland in England. They are managed now as grouse moors and for sheep grazing. The Park is a site of international importance for its breeding birds, in particular merlin and golden plover which, along with curlew and dunlin, breed in the wetter areas of Egton or Danby High Moors. Along with the regular moorland plants are lesser twayblade and common wintergreen. Where other rocks create varied soils, in the deep-cut valleys of Farndale, Bransdale, Rosedale and Westerdale, rare orchids and even wild daffodil fields occur.

SE725960, Rosedale Abbey gives direct access to the central part of the Park.

🔞 Red Hill
Lincolnshire · WT

Probably a remnant of the old Lincolnshire Wold downland the level grassland and the turf on the former quarry area are ablaze in June with lime-loving flowers, kidney vetch, yellow-wort and orchids. The steep red chalk cliff shows the different plants where the site is ungrazed. The rich flora of the lower pastures changes to scrub and rough grassland with fewer flowers.

TF264807 minor roads off A153, 5 miles south-west of Louth.

🔢 Saltfleetby-Theddlethorpe Dunes NNR
Lincolnshire · EN/WT

The shorelines of the Lincolnshire coast have a very distinctive character even if their topography is of low-lying dunes with saltmarsh and mudflats merging into the sea. The waves have no rocks to break them and there is a timeless quality about the coast. The saltmarsh edge has the sea plants – glass-wort and sea-blite; the innumerable creeks have sea-purslane. Here the waders concentrate – dunlin, redshank, oystercatchers and shelduck add splashes of white plumage to the scene. The dunes themselves rise above the marsh, fixed by marram or dense sea-buckthorn in their early years, of particular interest to migrant thrushes and warblers. There is a dramatic increase in the species range as the dunes age: the oldest, most stable dunes can have fine grassland swards with orchids in profusion. Behind the old dunes the freshwater marshes are out of the tidal reach and the waters are excellent for amphibians. Damselflies and dragonflies prey over the dunes and butterflies seek the shelter of these landward habitats.

TF465924 east of A1031 north of Mablethorpe.

🔢 Snipe Dales
Lincolnshire · WT

Grazing has been resumed over large areas of these steep valleys in the Lincolnshire Wolds. Coarser grasses on the higher slopes give way to marshy areas below, with tall ferns and giant horsetail. There was clearly more extensive woodland in the past and its associated flora can still be found in the grass. New plantations have restocked the woodland that has survived. The lowest grassland areas have common spotted-orchid and up to 11 butterfly species.

TF320683 north of A1115, 2 miles from junction with A158 Lincoln to Skegness road.

🔢 Spurn Peninsula
E. Yorkshire · YWT

There can be few other sites in the British Isles as fragile and yet so important as this thread of shingle and sand curving out into the mouth of the Humber. The Spurn we see today is at least the third one there has been – each built and each destroyed by the power of the sea. Today it provides one of our most outstanding observation sites for migrant birds. Here we can see spectacular 'falls' of migrants or individual rarities to add to one of the most impressive species lists in Europe. The site is also notable for its moths and specialist coastal plants.

TA417151 end of B1445, 20 miles south-east of Hull.

7 West of the Pennines

At first glance there appears to be no link between Lancaster and Manchester or between the Wirral and the Forest of Bowland. Blackpool and Chester are very different towns indeed. But they all share the great lowland plains of the Lune, the Ribble and the Mersey, between the Pennines and the Irish Sea. It is a very busy region either side of the M6/M5 corridor and yet solitude and space can be easily found on the fells of Bowland or the shores of Morecambe Bay. There are fine coastal nature reserves on the Ribble saltmarshes, on the Wirral and the dunes near Formby.

Whether you are studying unusual creatures such as the natterjack toad on Ainsdale Dunes or countless thousands of waders and wildfowl on the Dee estuary, this region provides endless opportunities to understand our natural history. If there seems to be an emphasis on watery places then so there should be, for many of the best lie west of the Pennines.

❶ Ainsdale Sand Dunes NNR
Merseyside · EN
A mixture of alien and native woodland species occupies this extensive area of sand dunes. Inland are pinewoods planted earlier this century and management is now creating a mixed woodland with different ages of trees. The wet slacks in the sand dunes are the home of the rare natterjack toads and many species of insects and plants. The dunes were planted with sea-buckthorn in the 1890s and although they stabilized the sand and their orange berries attract many thrush species and other birds in the autumn and winter, they also smother native plant life and are therefore controlled. Watch out for the rare dune and pendulous helleborines.

SD290105 coastal dunes south of Ainsdale, 2 miles south of Southport. Permits required except for public footpath.

❷ Bowland Forest
Lancashire · Various
The loneliest part of this busy region is a wild landscape of sweeping moors, high fells and steep-sided valleys. There is only one road over these hills and you can walk all day meeting only the birds and insects of the uplands. Coniferous forests and reservoirs and the inevitable grouse moors and sheep grazing mark the influence of man. As you stand in the spring sunshine listening to a bubbling curlew consider the

place in a January blizzard, and the glaciers which moulded these hills will not seem so far away.

SD503661 carpark at Dunsop Ridge. Turn off B6478 at Newton for Lancaster.

❸ Cheadle Hulme
Stockport · MBC
Hedgerow plants and animals are the stars of this delightful nature trail. The main structure of the species-rich hedge consists of alder, elder, hawthorn, hazel, holly, oak, rowan and willow. They form the support for climbers including hop, honeysuckle and wild rose. The hedge is thick and offers excellent cover for a number of birds of the farmland and ideal nesting sites for blackbird, chiffchaff, willow warbler, wren and robin. The trail (guide available from

library) also introduces you to the open pasture and the ecology of grasslands.

SJ875855 south of Cheadle, off Hulme Hall Road.

❹ Dibbinsdale
Wirral · MBC/Cheshire WT
The woods lining the valley sides of this delightful reserve are probably relics of the ancient woodland of the Wirral.

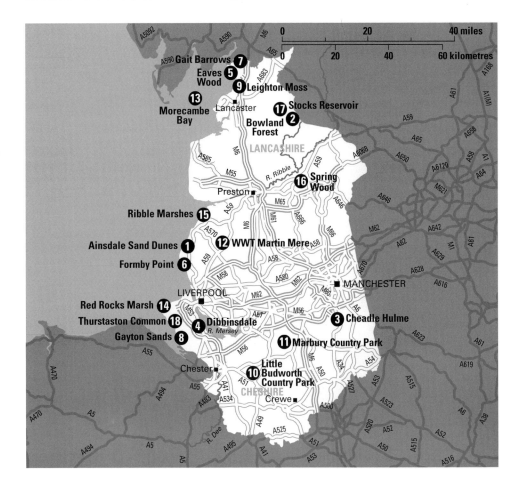

Ash and wych-elm dominate and provide an excellent reserve for woodland birds. Most of the tree specialists breed here including nuthatch, treecreeper, great spotted woodpecker and tawny owl. You will also enjoy meadows, reedbeds and grassland on this site.

SJ345827 south of Bebington on the Wirral.

❺ Eaves Wood
Lancashire · NT
A mosaic of ancient coppice woodland, limestone pavement and grassland which is a refuge for butterflies, especially high brown and pearl-bordered fritillaries. Red squirrels are very localized in this area but do frequent the wood where the mezereon is one of the earliest plants to flower, followed by primroses, wood sorrels and anemones, violets and bluebells.

SD467762 on minor roads south of Arnside.

❻ Formby Point
Merseyside · NT
Part of the fourth largest dune system in Britain, this 200-hectare (494-acre) Merseyside Nature Reserve is made up of roughly equal proportions of dunes and sandflats. Home to the nationally rare natterjack toad, and designated an SSSI and a Ramsar site, the reserve is constantly changing as natural forces mould the mobile dunes and foreshore. Pine woods planted at the turn of the twentieth century in an attempt to stabilize the dunes are home to a red squirrel colony. Many waders, gulls and visiting migrant birds feed on the shoreline, and in the woods, kestrel, treecreeper, wood warbler and greater spotted woodpecker can be seen.

SD275080 west of Formby off A565.

❼ Gait Barrows NNR
Lancashire · EN
One of the best examples of limestone pavement, with its fluted slabs of clint and its grikes where water has dissolved narrow fissures in the rocks, is only one of a range of habitats found in this exceptionally rich reserve. The limestone plants have sheltered in the grikes for thousands of years, secure from grazing animals. The reserve includes wet and dry meadows and a small tarn. The scrub and woods have yew, hazel and juniper among many other species, but the stars of this limestone area are the tutsan, saw-wort, northern bedstraw and rare ferns of the pavement.

SD480772 minor roads 2 miles south-east of Arnside, between Arnside, Silverdale and Beetham.

❽ Gayton Sands
Cheshire · RSPB
The advance of the saltmarsh on to the mudflats is accelerated by the rapid colonization of cord-grass. To ensure their continued spread the saltmarsh plants seed profusely and attract flocks of finches to feed on this harvest of the shore. Shelduck and pintail favour this site particularly and, as you may expect with a reserve surrounded by the estuary of the Dee, vast numbers of other wildfowl and waders winter here. Foxes and weasels chase the large numbers of small mammals and short-eared owls, hen harrier and merlin check this changing shoreline regularly.

SJ273786, between Heswall and Neston off A540.

❾ Leighton Moss
Lancashire · RSPB
This man-made fen is not as old as it looks but is considerably richer than we might imagine. Cut off from the sea by an embankment and sluice, it was drained until only about 70 years ago. Since then the rapid succession of habitats has spread reedbeds into the open water, fen-like marsh into the reedbeds and scrub and woodland into the marsh. Reserve management is essential to maintain the balance of these aquatic habitats and to keep the range of interest for which the reserve is outstanding. Bird life is abundant and includes resident wildfowl, wader migrants, visiting predators and breeding birds of the water's edge, including bittern and bearded tits. Surprisingly, red deer are present as well as otter, mink and smaller mammals. Eels and fish attract the herons. The information centre will explain how annual cutting encourages the diversity of plants in the reedbeds.

SD478751 on minor roads north-west of Carnforth.

❿ Little Budworth Country Park
Cheshire · CC
Here on the great Cheshire plain in an area of rich agricultural land lies a spread of glacial sands which supports a range of different habitats. The drier heath soils are associated with the typical heathland cover of heather, gorse and bracken. The heath is invaded by birch woodland, always the first tree to establish on the heaths with its abundant seed production. In damper places, sphagnum moss has filled the depressions of the bogs, and cottongrass and cranberry vary the plant species present. The variety of insects is outstanding here and an autumn visit will reveal why this heath is well known for its fungi. Tree pipit and redpoll are two of the heathland specialists.

SJ590655 on minor roads east of A49 at Cotebrook.

⓫ Marbury Country Park
Cheshire · CC
The combination of public access to the countryside and the need to protect special wildlife areas from disturbance is well balanced in this country park which is adjacent to Budworth mere. The park offers woodland walks and a mature arboretum, with leaflet guidance. A hide has been constructed to overlook the adjacent Marbury reedbed, avoiding the need for visitors to enter the reserve to enjoy the water, reedbeds and wet woodlands. Coot, moorhen and great crested grebe can be seen going about their daily lives.

SJ651763 access via country park near Comberbach, 2½ miles north of Northwich.

⓬ WWT Martin Mere
Lancashire · WWT
Breeding in the cold northern latitudes of Russia, Iceland or Scandinavia enables many species of birds to exploit a valuable, if temporary, source of food and shelter, without the problems of intense competition. But they cannot survive the rigours of arctic winters and they have to migrate south, thousands at a time, to shelter on the milder wetlands of the British Isles. Extensive marshland, water meadows and open water on this mere provide one of the most spectacular concentrations of wintering birds. There is a special magic in watching the return of Bewick's and whooper swans, pink-footed geese and wigeon. Teal, pintail, mallard, gadwall and many other ducks reach high numbers. Waders change with the seasons too, depending on whether they are breeding, visiting or wintering.

SD428145 on minor roads north of Ormskirk via Burscough Bridge.

13 Morecambe Bay
Lancashire · RSPB

If you find it hard to imagine what a quarter of the total British winter population of bar-tailed godwit, knot, dunlin, oystercatchers and turnstones might look like, then you will have to come to Morecambe Bay and see them. They are there with large numbers of other wader species together with thousands of wildfowl. Without doubt the greatest concentration of wintering shore-birds, their movements up and down the bay in accordance with the tides is one of bird-watching's most thrilling sights.

SD468666, A5105 north of Morecambe.

14 Red Rocks Marsh
Wirral Cheshire · WT

At the very end of the Wirral and overlooking the mouth of the Dee estuary is a compact wetland habitat comprising freshwater and brackish marshland, with dunes and lime-rich grassland nearby. Stabilized by lyme-grass and marram, the foredune has several sea plant species including sea-holly. These merge into grasslands which contain orchids, quaking-grass and kidney vetch with wild asparagus and parsley-piert on the drier areas. Common reed dominates club-rush, gipsywort and yellow iris in the reed-marsh. Clumps of alder and grey willow offer shelter to migrant birds.

SJ204884 on A540 beyond West Kirby.

15 Ribble Marshes NNR
Lancashire · EN

Flat expanses of saltmarsh and mudflats at the mouth of the Ribble provide an impressive and colourful show of typical plants. There are spectacular flocks of waders in spring and autumn, while during the winter, large flocks of wildfowl roost on the mudflats and feed on the saltmarsh. This also provides a largely undisturbed habitat for waders, gulls, terns and finches.

SD360210 view from coastal road Southport north to Crossens.

16 Spring Wood
Lancashire · CC

A tall closed canopy of mixed broadleaved trees provides first-class cover for the a host of resident woodland birds and migrants such as willow warblers and chiffchaffs. Spring brings a chorus of songbirds, and swathes of bluebells and wild garlic. Frogs and newts have colonized the pond.

SD740364 on A671 Accrington Road near junction with A59, 5 miles north-east of Blackburn.

17 Stocks Reservoir
Lancs. · North West Water

Lying at the edge of the Bowland Fells and adjacent to the Gisburn Forest, Stocks Reservoir is set in the rolling farmland of the Hodder Valley. It provides excellent bird watching in most seasons, with winter wildfowl roosts exceeding 1000 birds of at least 10 species. Migrants include waders, terns and Mediterranean gulls which come to breed on the island alongside the resident black-headed gulls. Ospreys, peregrines, hen harriers and buzzards sometimes appear overhead. There is a bird-watching hide and car parking at the northern end and a trout fishery at the southern end.

SD732565 for car park. Access via B6478 from Clitheroe to Slaidburn, then follow signs for Gisburn Forest.

18 Thurstaston Common
Wirral · MBC/NT

An exposure of rocks known as the upper mottled sandstones forms a low ridge exposed here on the Wirral producing an area of acid heathland. Lowland heaths like Thurstaston Common are home to at least 200 flowering plants, many species of moth, bee, ant and dragonfly, and to breeding birds such as the stonechat and the nightjar. The rich insect life is most noticeable in the late summer.

SJ244853 off A540, 2 miles south-east of West Kirby.

8 Cambria

You will find no greater contrast than between the rugged cwms of the Snowdonian peaks and the flat expanse of the Dee estuary's mud and silt. But this part of Wales has its own identity simply because it is the giant rock pile of the Cambrian mountains standing on a narrow coastal plain. The mountains are clear and fresh and wet as witnessed by the superb growth of lichen, moss and fern in the ancient oakwoods of Coed Dinorwig and Coedydd Maentwrog. Water is an integral part of Cambria's regional character and is the source of great rivers such as the Dee, the Wye and the Severn.

The coastal sites at Ynys-hir and South Stack are rich in birdlife; Cors Caron is one of the finest wetlands of its type. As you travel around the Cambrians you will see some of the most dramatic and beautiful wildlife in Britain.

❶ Cader Idris NNR
Gwynedd • CCW

If you want to see glacial relic landscape features and wildlife at their best climb from the Afon Fawnog to the fine corrie of Cwm Cau. With cliffs rising 300 metres (1000 feet) from the Llyn Cau corrie lake to the summit of Penygadair, the power of the glaciers becomes apparent. Ravens wheel round on the air currents which rise up the cliff faces, too steep to be grazed. There on the Cader Idris, having been undisturbed for thousands of years, are moss campion, globeflower, Welsh poppy and purple saxifrage. The isolation and exposure of Britain's high mountain habitats is one of the most demanding environments for plants and yet one of the most enduring.

SH730114 off B4405, 8 miles along A487 south of Dolgellau.

❷ Cemlyn
Anglesey • NWWT

Winter storms and spring tides add a colourful variety of stones to the shingle bar of this storm beach. This harsh environment drenched with winter salt spray and baked in the summer sun is colonized by specialized plants such as sea-kale, sea-beet, scurvygrass and thrift. Behind the shingle bank a brackish pool attracts winter wildfowl and shelduck breed in old rabbit burrows in the dunes.

SH336932 minor roads west of A5025, 6 miles west of Amlwch, Anglesey.

❸ Coed Dinorwig
Gwynedd • C

While most of the Welsh hill oakwoods have been grazed, this ancient oak forest on the slopes of Padarn Country Park was fenced. It shows clearly how attractive the natural flora of the wildwood must have been. A curious mixture of species from the wood, the heath and the moorland communities form a tangled undergrowth ranging from bramble to wood-rush and from hazel to parsley fern. Native hunters include buzzard, sparrowhawk and polecat.

SH586603 Padarn Country Park, 6 miles east of Caernarfon.

❹ Coedydd Aber NNR
Gwynedd • CCW

Although it is clear that man has been present in the Aber Valley since Iron Age times, these ancient oakwoods have survived the clearance of surrounding forests, probably because they were too steep and inaccessible. As the trail leads up to the Aber Falls so the composition of the

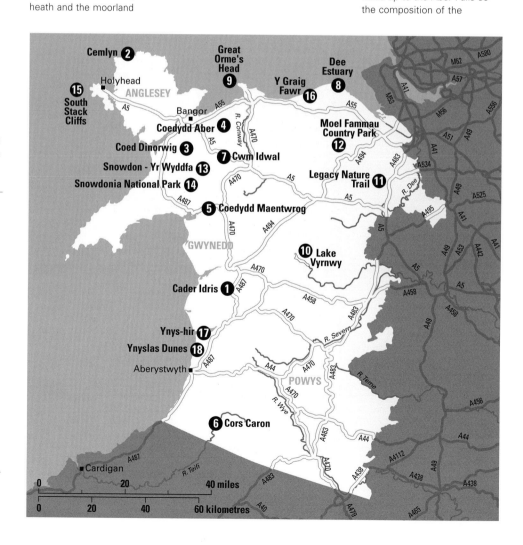

woodland changes with varying site conditions. Alder and goat-willow are in the open, wet patches; ash, elm and hazel on the lower slopes; and rugged rowan, birch and twisted oaks on the high, steep cliffs by the falls. Typically the woods are rich in lichens, mosses and ferns. Redstart, pied flycatcher and warblers are all present.

SH662720 turn off A55 in Aber, 8 miles from Conwy.

5 Coedydd Maentwrog NNR
Gwynedd · CCW

The oaks in the high woodland of Coed Llyn Mair are covered with lichens, mosses and ivy, with ferns all around. This is one of a group of three woods, forming one reserve and representing the natural oakwoods of Wales – wet, shady places where pied flycatchers and mottled umber moths are part of a rich insect and bird fauna. In pockets too wet for even the oaks to grow are rushes and willows. Clearings are dominated by bracken or purple moor-grass showing how very close we are to the uplands.

SH652414 on B4410, 3 miles west of Ffestiniog.

6 Cors Caron NNR
Ceredigion · CCW

If you find the process of change from water to raised bog difficult to understand, then this site will reveal nature's techniques. Originally a shallow lake trapped by a moraine in the Teifi valley, the flood plain mire spread over the valley floor. Plants and organic material filled the water to produce a rain-fed mire above the river level. The river divides the bog, which is clearly visible by its cover of purple moor-grass, heather, cottongrass and deergrass, from the rising land either side of the valley. Sphagnum moss inevitably covers the highest points, where adder, lizard and

slow-worm may occasionally be tracked by polecat. The wetter areas where winter floods occur may have water voles and otters to observe. The variety of habitats, including willow scrub, attracts many breeding and wintering birds. Water rail, willow tits and wintering hen harriers are typical of this very important wetland.

SN696632 between A485 and B4343, north of Tregaron.

7 Cwm Idwal NNR
Gwynedd · CCW

There could be no better way to understand the character of these mountains than to follow the Cwm Idwal nature trail around the first Welsh NNR. Explained and set before you in panoramic views are the formation of cwms and corrie lakes, together with the structure and complexity of these unique rocks. In total contrast, the trail also directs your attention to the lives of individual plants, how they survive, why they are there, and why their conservation is important to the story of Snowdonia.

SH640590 off A5, 6 miles west of Capel Curig.

8 Dee Estuary

The estuary started with the melt-waters from the glaciers depositing material washed down from the Cheshire Plain. As the climate warmed, the sea level rose and drowned the river mouth to start another process of deposition. The silts and sands of this massive estuary system attract so many waders in autumn and winter that counting them seems pointless. But why do tens of thousands of these delightful birds of the water's edge come to the Dee? Incomprehensible numbers of tiny crustaceans and worms are packed into the estuarine silts and muds. The waders are especially

adapted to find and eat them. In summer as many as 200 grey seals may congregate and other sea mammals are seen – dolphin, porpoise and killer whales. But the drama is in the autumn flocks of waders as they rise like billowing smoke clouds to fly the tideline in search of a secure resting place.

SH125847 the entire estuary can be good but Point of Ayr is a reliable observation point. North of A548, 4 miles east of Prestatyn.

9 Great Orme's Head
Conwy · CB

The fine North Wales coastline has its share of rugged cliff scenery. Here on the peninsula beyond Llandudno, the cliffs support a varied flora with such lime-loving plants as common rock-rose, dropwort and quaking-grass growing alongside coastal wild flowers which include sea-pink, spring squill and wild cabbage. Colonies of kittiwakes, guillemots and razorbills share the sea cliffs with jackdaws, ravens and rock pipits. During the winter months, the headland plays host to snow buntings and chough, and red-throated divers may be seen close inshore.

SH780832 on Marine Drive, Llandudno.

10 Lake Vyrnwy
Powys · RSPB

Part of the most extensive heather moor in Wales and complemented by thousands of acres of grass moorland and mire, the moors are grazed by many hundreds of mountain sheep and are periodically burnt to improve the heather. Red grouse, curlew and whinchat breed on this extensive managed moorland. Coniferous forest adjacent has red squirrel and polecat. Newts and frogs are found in the mire pools and several fritillary

species in the broadleaved woodland.

SH985215, B4393 from Llanfyllin.

11 Legacy Nature Trail
Wrexham Maelor · NGC/ Groundwork Wrexham

The mounds were constructed to help screen the substation and blend this piece of twentieth-century technology into an attractive landscape. There is now a nature trail specifically laid out to demonstrate the colonization of man-made habitats. Marsh and grassland have been deliberately introduced to diversify the habitats available.

SJ295483 off A483 immediately south-west of Wrexham.

12 Moel Fammau Country Park
Denbighshire · CC

High, rolling, heather grouse moor conjures a picture which Moel Fammau will fit very well. It is a superb example of a widespread and important habitat of the uplands. Heather, bilberry and bracken are the familiar plants but there are delightful new ones to discover too, including marsh pennywort and cross-leaved heath.

SJ171611 north of A494, 4 miles from Ruthin.

13 Snowdon – Yr Wyddfa NNR
Gwynedd/Conway · CCW

Even if you do not climb to the summit of Yr Wyddfa it is worthwhile walking the Miners' Track from Pen-y-Pass to Llyn Llydaw. Constructed to serve the copper mines of the nineteenth century, this route tells us much about Snowdon's history and wildlife, for example, how the sheep pastures of the lower land are like a lawn of mat-grass but how the older grasslands which are not grazed are richer and more colourful. Towards the lake appear small bogs coloured with sphagnum moss and bog asphodel. Insectivorous plants such as the sundew and butter-wort are poised to consume passing insects to supplement their poor diet from the soil. The bright red bills and legs of the choughs are visible as they perform aerobatics above this wild mountain landscape.

SH630530 off A4086 at Llanberis Pass.

⑭ Snowdonia National Park
Gwyned/Conway • NPA
Imagine, for a moment, that you could see the mountains through the eyes of a merlin. With the speed of this falcon's low-level flight, the scale and beauty of wild mountain tops, sheer cliffs, tumbling screes and the knife-edge ridges of the cwms would spin and roll beneath you. The spectacular corrie lakes and the glistening white torrents of the waterfalls would be impressive indeed. The glaciers scraped and smoothed, crushed and fractured the rocks into these shapes and features. As the merlin drops on to the cold, north-facing peaks it settles among relic plants of the

mountain tundra. The arctic alpine plants include the Snowdon lily, found nowhere else in the British Isles and associated abroad with permanent snow-fields. Alpine species of saxifrage, meadow-rue, mouse-ear and cinquefoil have occupied their niches in these mountains since the last glaciation. As the climate warmed and the light grey, almost lifeless tundra soils slowly built up their organic material, other plants moved up the slopes. Tough, stunted colonizers of birch and pine, and grass and heather were followed 5000 years later by wet oak forests with a rich fauna. Between the mountain tops and the farmland of the valleys and lowlands are vast expanses of grass moorland with heather and bracken in which the merlin and its main prey, the meadow pipit, breed. Raven and wheatears are also found here.

SH720580 north and west of Capel Curig.

⑮ South Stack Cliffs
Anglesey • RSPB
As you look down on the sea over 90 metres (300 feet) below, you will not fail to be impressed by the spectacle of seabird colonies on these famous cliffs. Every tiny ledge is packed with a family of hungry guillemots, razorbills, puffins, kittiwakes or fulmars. The parents make constant journeys to and from the sea to bring food to the young so precariously balanced above the waves. From these delicate perches the young auks must eventually make their maiden flight down to the waves where they will live until they return to nest on the stacks.

SH205823, 3 miles west of Holyhead, Anglesey.

⑯ Y Graig Fawr
Denbighshire • NT
Overlooking the Vale of Clwyd, this limestone hill supports many lime-loving plants including the small scabious and lady's bedstraw. The hoary rock-rose grows on the steeper western face. Many butterflies are associated with the limestone flora, including the common blue.

SJ064800, A547 south from Prestatyn.

⑰ Ynys-hir
Ceredigion • RSPB
While the woods and moorland of the reserve are bird habitats of considerable importance, the estuary and saltmarsh of Ynys-hir are special. Forming a flat coastal plain in a beautiful mountainous landscape, they attract, among other wintering ducks, wigeon, teal, red-breasted merganser and goldeneye. The Greenland white-fronted geese visit the saltmarsh and hen harriers and peregrine falcons check for unwary prey.

SN683963 off A487 in Furnace village.

⑱ Ynyslas Dunes
Ceredigion • CCW
The greatest threat to this fragile system of dunes is from the 300,000 visitors who come to enjoy this part of the Dyfi estuary as part of their summer holiday. The flora and fauna of the dunes and slacks are well worth a visit during the week. But the reserve has much more to offer the inquisitive naturalist with estuary birds and a sunken forest.

SN610940 off B4353, 8 miles north of Aberystwyth.

9 The Severn

Between the rugged splendour of the Cambrians and the industrial development of the Midlands spread soft, rich lowlands with reminders of the adjacent landscapes. The Malverns and the Long Mynd reflect the ancient uplands of Wales. There are splashes of industry in the Shropshire countryside where disused canals and quarries record 300 years of industry. The timber of the royal forests of Dean and Wyre were exploited for construction and charcoal burning, whereas the present-day plantations of Chaddesley and Wentwood will supply some of our modern needs for timber.

The region is warm and sheltered and the farmland very productive. The Vale of Evesham is distinctive and contrasts sharply with heathlands at Hartlebury Common and the Devil's Spittleful. The rivers all have a story to tell, but none so dramatic as the winding gorge of the Wye. Despite its narrow neck of industrialized coastline, this region, the lowland catchments of the Severn and the Wye, contains a marvellous range of shoreline habitats.

❶ Brown Moss
Shropshire • CC
The influence of man's drainage and peat cutting has extended the natural changes in this former bog to create an area of dry, acid heath around a series of pools. Nevertheless, thirty species of birds breed here and uncommon wetland plants include floating water-plantain, floating club-rush, water-violet and orange foxtail.

SJ564394 on minor roads less than 2 miles south-east of Whitchurch.

❷ Chaddesley Woods NNR
Worcestershire • EN/Worcs. WT
The combination of wildwood species including small-leaved lime, wild service-tree, hazel, oak and birch indicate that parts of Chaddesley are of ancient origin. Elsewhere, there are recent conifer plantations. The importance of this particular reserve is how its management demonstrates that the pursuit of commercial forestry need not necessarily be contrary to the aims of nature conservation.

SO914736 off A448, 6 miles south-east of Kidderminster.

❸ Colemere Nature Reserve
Shropshire • CC
North of Shrewsbury, glaciers spread great volumes of sand, gravel and clays from the hills and valleys they scoured. The depressions in these mounds filled with melt-water and in turn the succession of vegetation either built up the pools to make bogs or fringed the lakes with a wealth of aquatic plants. Here at Colemere the open water remains with woods and meadows down to the water's edge. Water birds are always present but at migration times there are also passage terns and waders.

SJ434328 on minor roads off A528, 14 miles north-west of Shrewsbury.

❹ The Devil's Spittleful
Worcestershire • WT
Occasional fires have resulted in a varied age structure of ling on this spread of lowland heath. Areas of open heather intermingle with birch woodland and hawthorn scrub,

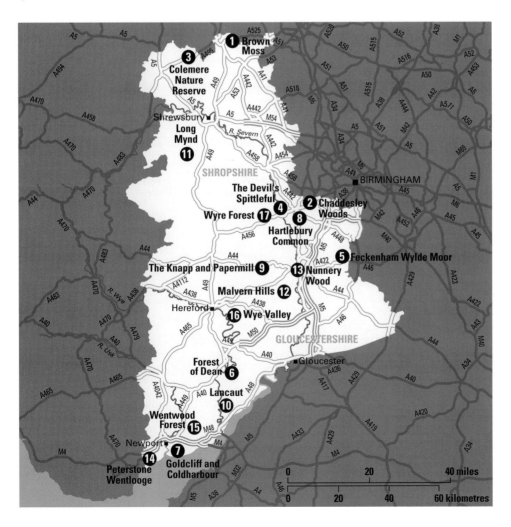

creating a mosaic which supports a wide variety of heathland plants and animals.

SO810747 on A456 between Bewdley and Kidderminster.

❺ Feckenham Wylde Moor
Worcestershire · WT
This 11.5 hectare (28-acre) fen marsh has extensive beds of reeds, rush and sedge, with grazed and mown wet meadows and a lake. A hide is open to the public and snipe are usually to be seen as they breed and winter here.

SP012603, B4090, 8 miles east of Droitwich.

❻ Forest of Dean
Gloucestershire · FC
In the quiet arboreal calm of England's first national forest park you can reflect on the character that makes each of our woodlands distinctive. You will sense the passage of time in the age of the trees in the different parts of the forest. You can follow the mixture of species as you pass from one part to another over changing soils. You will see the drastic influences of man's management in the Saxon clearances and the medieval coppicing. Alien species were introduced to increase the volume of timber which the forest is capable of growing. Above all, you can enjoy the wildlife. From the oaks, limes, elm and cherry of the wildwood to the spruce and larch of recent decades, there are homes for half the British butterfly species, including brown argus, grayling and pearl-bordered fritillary. The Dean is most important as the representative of the wildwood for our familiar native woodland wildlife. It has the uncommon too: there are hawfinch, crossbill and tree pipits.

SO615080 Parkend is a useful starting point on B4234 or B4431.

❼ Goldcliff and Coldharbour
Gwent · WT
Long recognized as a major flight path for our millions of migrating birds, the Severn Estuary invariably carries good numbers of all birds of travelling species. Here on an estuary foreshore, waders and wildfowl congregate in the autumn and winter as they move south ahead of the cold.

ST385825 via minor roads south of Newport.

❽ Hartlebury Common
Worcestershire · CC
This site embraces the open heathland and woodland of Hartlebury Common local nature reserve and Hillditch Pool and Coppice. The sandy heathland supports buckshorn plantain, shepherd's cress and, in damp areas, marsh cinquefoil and bogbean. Insect life is plentiful. Emperor and fox moths fly by day, along with green hairstreak, small copper and small heath butterflies. Common lizards and grass snakes can also be seen. Tree pipits, whitethroats and redpolls perch in the three species of heather and two of gorse.

SO820705 off B4195 Stourport to Hartlebury Road.

❾ The Knapp and Papermill
Worcestershire · WT
The habitats of this delightful reserve include woodland, orchard, meadow and brook which demonstrate very clearly the effects of management on the natural woodland cover as well as many of the traditional techniques. While the crack willow by the water are pollarded, the alder and ash there are coppiced. The wooded slopes of the valley have areas of oak, lime and wild service-tree, which have been coppiced, and fine stands of oak and ash over coppiced hazel. In the dampness of the lower land are ferns, orchids,

butterbur and comfrey. On the drier banks are cowslip and primrose. The site is occupied by uncommon silver cloud and wave-backed moths. Some 30 species of butterfly have been recorded and 20 mammal species enjoy the shelter of this woodland scene.

SO748522 on minor roads near Alfrick off A4103, 3½ miles west of Worcester.

❿ Lancaut
Gloucestershire · WT
In a typically spectacular curve of the Wye, Lancaut Reserve embraces natural and man-made habitats of great contrast: from the deep tidal waters and the mud and saltmarsh of the valley floor, up steep gorge sides where woodland contains all the species of the wildwood, to the little chapel and the Offa's Dyke at the top of the cliffs where ancient man has left his marks. The river terrace has been quarried and colonized by limestone grassland with many of its delightful flowering plants: St John's-wort, yellow-wort, hairy violet and lesser calamint.

ST539967 on B4228 north of Woodcroft, 1 mile or so north of Chepstow.

⓫ Long Mynd
Shropshire · NT
This softly rounded mass of rocks has continued to be changed through many geological eras, culminating in the crushing weight of the Pleistocene ice. The glaciers rubbed the hills to a whale-backed plateau still over 450 metres (1500 feet) above sea level. The post-glacial pinewoods gave way to a natural cover of broadleaves but man soon cleared the Mynd and used it for sheep grazing. In the worst of the winter months the streams are again recharged with melt-water, to cut ever deeper,

winding valleys down the slopes. These clear, fresh waters are rich in insect life and attract the dipper which will breed on these uplands with the ring ouzel and wheatear. The former mountain habitats have all but gone, leaving an extensive heather moorland with a regular bracken-mowing programme.

SO425945 west of Church Stretton on A49, 12 miles south of Shrewsbury.

⓬ Malvern Hills
Hereford and Worcs.
Do not be tempted to view the Malverns only from the farmland below. The best way to sense the character of this intricate mass of ancient rocks is to walk across and over it and to look down from its summits on to the mosaic of habitats. The influence of the grazing animals is a transition from grassland to scrub or woodland. Woods run up the shallow valleys and between the mounds. The slopes and cliffs are scattered with gorse and broom. Even the exposed rock patches have stonecrops, mosses, lichens and ferns.

SO768454 immediately south-west of Great Malvern on A449.

⓭ Nunnery Wood
Worcestershire · CC
For centuries these ancient woodlands have been managed to allow light in, encouraging bluebells and wood anemones to carpet the ground in spring. The tree and shrub re-growth (which includes birch, aspen, hornbeam and wild service) provides dense thickets for birds and mammals.

SO877543 off A422, 2 miles east of Worcester.

⓮ Peterstone Wentlooge
Gwent • WT
You will appreciate how the sea wall has created a diversity of habitats by controlling the influence of salt water on the new land. The mudflats and saltmarsh are excellent, attracting dunlin and knot among many other waders. Unusual winter visitors include long-tailed duck and common scoter but the sight of a dashing peregrine or a short-eared owl slowly quartering the reserve will never fail to delight. Behind the sea wall are grassland and scrub, adding shelter and food sources for smaller birds passing through.

ST278807, B4239 midway between Newport and Cardiff.

⓯ Wentwood Forest
Newport • FC
An ideal opportunity to compare the wildlife of the ancient broadleaved woods of oak and beech to the twentieth-century plantations of larch. As you wind through the trails, the forest provides a mixture of tree species and ages which offer a range of habitats from the open clearings for nightjar to the mature conifers for crossbills. Amphibians do well in the pools. Raven, buzzard and sparrowhawk are three of the predators breeding here.

ST436936 off A449, 4 miles north-east of Newport.

⓰ Wye Valley
No other river in England or Wales retains its natural character as dramatically as the Wye. From its source in the Cambrian mountains to the Severn estuary, it winds through narrow gorges with spectacular wooded cliffs. Originally on a slow and wandering course over a level plateau, the river then had to excavate a deeper channel to compensate for a fall in sea level. Rejuvenated by the massive volume of melt-water from the Welsh glaciers the river retained its meandering course but cut deep into the rocks like a young stream. So the autumn landscape of the Wye Valley can be stunning. The colourful woods and clear, clean waters provide exceptional habitats for wildlife. The individuality of the Wye is typified by the rare and delicate upright spurge which occurs nowhere else in the British Isles.

The entire valley from Builth Wells to Chepstow is well served by public roads.

⓱ Wyre Forest NNR
Hereford and Worcs. • EN/FC
With its distinctive appearance and variety of woodland types the Wyre brings the wildlife of the uplands close to the West Midlands conurbation. In places it is like the damp oak coppices of Wales but elsewhere the woods resemble the native forest of the Midland clays. Remnants of ancient oak woodland are set among modern plantations and the fast-flowing Dowles Brook is a great attraction. In the older parts, the woodland flora is mixed and colourful, the invertebrate populations are exceptional and the range of moth species alone could provide a lifetime's study here. Woodpeckers, woodcock and owls are present with redstarts, tits, warblers and many other woodland birds. The mammals, too, have survived the forest's changes and all the usual species can be found together with the rarer dormouse. The continuity of woodland cover, once protected by royal forest laws, has provided one of our most precious lowland woods.

SO759766 north-west of Bewdley, 4 miles from Kidderminster.

10 The English Midlands

You might have expected that, in the wake of industrial innovation and expansion, traces of the former landscapes would be obliterated and animals and plants of the wildwood and heath would be absent. The forests and heaths of Sherwood, Rockingham, Cannock and Charnwood are indispensable refuges for wildlife and essential escapes for urban man.

The fox is the symbol of Midland wildlife. It hunts the heaths adjacent to Sherwood Forest and the shores of Rutland Water; it is resourceful enough to use urban sites such as the wetlands of Martin's Pond. For centuries it has been pursued over the woods and fields of north Leicestershire. The countryside of the Quorn hunt is a fine example of enclosure landscapes. The open fields at Laxton, though, give us a clear impression of the Midland farmland and its wildlife of 600 years ago.

Compare the rushing glacial streams of the Coombes and Manifold Valley to the impressive new water parks on the Trent and Tame. You will then have the essence of the Midlands' variety.

❶ Beacon Hill
Leicestershire • CC
On the edge of Charnwood Forest, 241 metres (802 feet) above sea level, the rocky summit of Beacon Hill is the highest point in Leicestershire and has outstanding panoramic views from the remains of the massive ramparts of the Bronze Age Fort. On the hillside, heathland is actively maintained by grazing with rare breeds of sheep and tree pipits have recently colonized. The birch and oak woodlands are attractive to green wood-peckers and pied flycatchers.

There is a special collection of native tree species growing on the lower, eastern slopes.

SK51148 just east of M1 between Junctions 22/23, off B591, on the edge of Woodhouse Eaves, 3 miles north of Bradgate Park.

❷ Bradgate Park
Leicestershire • CC
Dramatic Charnwood heathland on the land overlooking the ancient Swithland Woods and the recent Cropston Reservoir. As we escape to an expanse of heath with grassland and bracken we can see close views of grazing deer. Many trees are scattered over the hillsides. The reservoir holds good numbers of wintering wildfowl; wigeon and teal round the edges, with goldeneye and tufted duck on the deeper water.

SK523116 off B5330, 3 miles west of Rothley.

❸ Cannock Chase
Staffordshire • CC
Look carefully across the heathland landscape and you will see all the features which you need to build the history of Cannock. Scattered oak and birch are the remnants of the wildwood. The chase was protected by forest laws, then depleted by felling for charcoal burning in the ironworks of the West Midlands. Deer and rabbit can still be seen and it was these animals, together with sheep, that prevented the regeneration of the forest trees and so created the heathland of today. Along the sky lines are twentieth-century forestry plantations. The valley mires have northern plants at their southern limit (marsh hawk's-beard) and southern plants

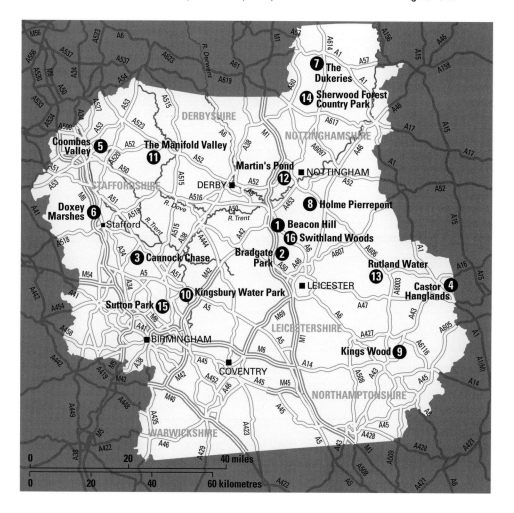

(southern marsh-orchid) at their northern limit. They also have round-leaved sundews, cranberries and grass-of-Parnassus. The most distinguished characters of Cannock, though, are the nightjars and the deer – many fallow but small numbers of red and muntjac too.

SJ971160 follow the signs on to minor roads south-west from Rugeley.

❹ Castor Hanglands NNR
Cambridgeshire · EN
Your visit to this NNR would be justified to see any one of four main habitats: woodland, grassland, scrub or wetland. But the grassland is of special interest. Common grazing ceased in the 1930s when mixed scrub immediately invaded, only to be cleared by the Ministry of Defence during the Second World War when it was used as a bombing range. Parts are now cut for hay, swiped or grazed in different combinations. This variety of management is carefully compiled to produce the best range of flora and fauna. Many birds and insects benefit particularly from the coarser, longer grass areas. The reserve offers a remarkable habitat range.

TF118023, take Helpston Road north of A47 at Ailsworth, 4 miles west of Peterborough.

❺ Coombes Valley
Staffordshire · RSPB
Charged with the gushing meltwater of post-glacial thaws, the stream cut and plunged down its steep-sided valley soon to be covered in oak woodland. The character of the reserve today still holds these important elements – the uplands, the brook and the woodland. There are beech, oak, ash and birch with a superb range of woodland and grassland plants. Insect populations are high; reptiles

include common lizards and adders. The birds are the highlight of this rich display. Redstarts and tree pipits of the oakwoods and grey wagtails and dippers of the upland stream are examples of the full list of 130 species, half of which breed here.

SK005530 on minor road to Apesford off A523, 4 miles south of Leek.

❻ Doxey Marshes
Staffordshire · WT
The River Sow flows through a 123-hectare (300-acre) wetland and grassland reserve which is bordered by Stafford and the M6, and through which runs the main-line railway. A hide overlooks artificial scrapes which attract a variety of birdlife including heron, redshank, snipe, lapwing, golden plover and pochard. Swallows roost in the reedbeds and sparrowhawks and short-eared owls hunt through the reserve. The disused railway that cuts across the south-eastern corner of the marshes attracts butterflies and other insects. Doxey is the epitome of what can be done to encourage wildlife in a patch of damp, rough ground hemmed in by a motorway, a railway and suburbia.

SJ903250 access from car park at the bottom of Cresswell Farm Drive off the Eccleshall Road from junction 14 of M6.

❼ The Dukeries
Nottinghamshire · NT/CC
So much of the north-east section of Sherwood Forest was enclosed to form private estates that the concentration of magnificent parkland bears the popular name of 'The Dukeries'. They are splendid examples of the English Landscape Movement's fashion to create informal and romantic settings to the ducal homes of the eighteenth century. They provide a range of mixed

woodland, farmland, heathland and lakes. The rivers were dammed to create landscape features which now hold important winter wildfowl stocks. The woodlands are particularly rich in bird life. Ancient oaks, reminding us of the former forest, have been retained, together with their invaluable invertebrate populations.

SK615730 between A60 and A614. Clumber and Rufford Parks have straightforward public access.

❽ Holme Pierrepont
Nottinghamshire · CC
An ambitious programme of gravel extraction and land reclamation has produced the National Water Sports Centre, an Olympic-sized rowing course, a country park and nature reserve. The attraction to water birds is increased by the presence of flooded gravel lagoons on the opposite bank of the Trent at Colwick. The winter gull roost numbers thousands of birds and wandering skuas chase terns down the course. Little ringed plovers may be found regularly in the summer when common sandpipers dip and call along the shores of the pits.

SK615390 off A52 immediately east of West Bridgford on the outskirts of Nottingham.

❾ Kings Wood
Northamptonshire · DC/WT
This ancient Midland forest was extensive in area and rich in wildlife as we can witness from the evidence of Kings Wood. Ash and many old oaks stand over hazel with impressive displays of bluebell, wood sorrel and sanicle. Orchids show in early spring and the woodland is one of the best in the area for lichens.

SP864874 off A6003 south of Corby.

❿ Kingsbury Water Park
Warwickshire · CC
Old gravel workings in the Tame Valley are the origin of this 254-hectare (620-acre) Water Park, north-east of Birmingham. Part of the park is now a nature reserve with areas of alder and willow carr which shelter woodland birds. In spring, the songs of nine species of warblers may be heard, including blackcap, lesser whitethroat and grasshopper warblers. The reserve also offers excellent views of some of Britain's rarer passage waders.

SP204958 off A51, 4 miles south of Tamworth.

⓫ The Manifold Valley
Staffordshire · NT/CC
In summer, the river in the Manifold disappears down 'swallet' holes in the limestone and the bed dries out. In winter, though, the volume of water carries on over the holes and follows a dramatic fall past meadow, limestone grassland, woodland slopes and craggy cliffs. A range of limestone plants which enjoy damp or dry conditions thrive. Mountain currant drapes the rocks, kingfishers and dippers feed on the clear water and the damper patches display water avens, comfrey and valerian.

SK100543 on minor roads above Ilam, 4 miles north-west of Ashbourne (Derbys.).

⓬ Martin's Pond
Notts · City Council/WT
This pond with marsh and scrub habitats is remarkably rich in wildlife. A walk takes you past the pond and the reserve through bulrushes and willow scrub, open water and marsh. There is colourful and lush plant growth, breeding and wintering birds, insects, amphibians and mammals.

SK526402 off A609, Ilkeston Road in Wollaton, Notts.

⓭ Rutland Water

Leicestershire · WT/AW

You will enjoy a site planned and designed for wildlife as part of the awe-inspiring enterprise of creating Britain's second largest man-made lake. The sheer scale of Rutland Water reminds us, and apparently the birds too, of the sea. Cormorants, gulls and other seabirds are common. Around the edge, the treatment and management of the shore provide ideal conditions for wetland and water species of all kinds. On the migration routes of the Nene and Welland the reservoir is already of national significance to wildfowl. Large flocks of ruddy duck are to be seen among 20 other regular ducks, swan and geese species. For an inland water, spring and autumn passage is outstanding and comfortably observed from a number of well-sited hides. This new landscape will continue to grow in stature and is already one of Britain's outstanding water areas.

SK897049 off A6003, 2 miles south of Oakham.

⓮ Sherwood Forest Country Park

Nottinghamshire · CC

If you stand beneath the 'blasted oaks' it is not difficult to imagine the forest of medieval times when some of these ancient giants were mere seedlings in the bracken. Protected by forest laws these woods of oak and birch high forest were never cleared though they were often stripped of their best-quality timber. Assarts would have been cleared and farmed before reverting back to heath, then forest. Since the spread of the two oak species (both of which are present in the same proportion), the continuity of forest cover has endowed this legendary place with an invertebrate population of international significance. Fungi too are outstanding. An early autumn visit will show you an ancient, dry oak forest in all its regal splendour.

SK627677 on B6034 just north of Edwinstowe.

⓯ Sutton Park NNR

Birmingham · CC

Somehow this vast heath has escaped the spread of urban development to form a popular open space and a fine example of natural features surviving intensive public use. The oak-holly-birch-rowan woods are clearly of ancient origin. Grassland, bracken, bilberry and heather heaths have been invaded by birch. Wetter patches discourage public trampling and alder carr, purple moor-grass, cottongrass and sphagnum mosses mark the wetland. Moths and other insects are less disturbed by the public access than the birds.

SP103963 west of Sutton Coldfield.

⓰ Swithland Woods

Leicestershire · CC

The variety of soil types must have given Charnwood a wider range of native trees. Indeed, the remnant of that ancient forest has many of the wildwood species still present. Oak, ash and small-leaved lime form the high forest but hazel, birch and alder are here too. Regular coppicing was abandoned 100 years ago. The plants of the forest floor have found sufficient light to survive and range from grasses to bluebells and yellow pimpernel to pendulous sedge. A true mixed woodland with its roots in the wildwood of 2000 years ago.

SK538129 off B5330, 3 miles west of Rothley.

11 East Anglia

Since Bronze Age man worked the flints of Grimes Graves in present-day Norfolk, the area we now call East Anglia has always had a most distinctive character. The Broads cover 570 square kilometres (220 square miles) of Norfolk and north Suffolk, comprising England's largest wetland area. This wetland landscape is rich in wildlife, but is also a popular holiday destination. The Broads area has National Park Status, and the Broads Authority, the statutory body, works closely with organizations such as the Norfolk Wildlife Trust, the RSPB and the National Trust to enhance the nature conservation value of the area and balance the needs of nature conservation with tourism.

To win the richest dark soils of Britain, men have battled to drain the Fens, destroying almost all of the varied wildlife they once supported. Much energy and cost has been expended on a task which nature, in time, would have completed for us. Through natural habitat succession, much of the fen, marsh and swamp would, without our intervention, now be high and dry. Instead, the people of the Fens are committed to perpetual pumping to preserve the agricultural land.

But, in so doing, they have created new wetlands, as on the Ouse Washes, with new wildlife associations. The coasts too are always changing, yet they are still of international wildlife significance. The beauty of the Norfolk estates, the intimate Suffolk lanes and the mysterious solitude of dawn on the Fens combine to create the unique East Anglian character.

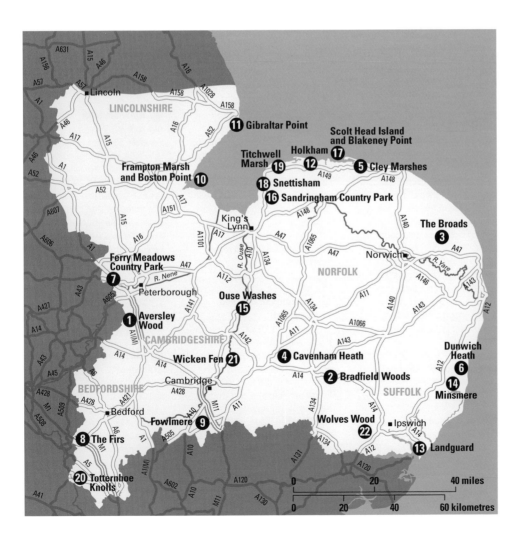

❶ Aversley Wood
Cambridgeshire · WdT
The structure of this beautiful ancient woodland includes mature ash/oak/maple with a high number of wild service-trees and a wide range of woodland flora. Grassland flora thrives along the wide rides.

TL158815 entrance a short walk from Sawtry on A1, where there is car parking.

❷ Bradfield Woods
Suffolk · WT
One of the finest examples of traditional woodland management, this ancient wood shows the stages of coppicing and pollarding. Bradfield is unique in having an unbroken record of coppicing since the 1200s; a visit is a practical introduction to woodland history. It is renowned for its nightingales and the best range of plant life in East Anglia.

TL935581 minor roads east of A134, 4 miles south-east of Bury St Edmunds.

❸ The Broads NP
Broads Authority/WT
The flooded remains of peat pits dug out by the inhabitants of East Anglia during medieval times are the origin of the newest member of the National Park family, a watery tapestry of waterways, marshes, tangled woodlands and reed-fringed lakes. Stretching from Norwich in the west to Great Yarmouth on the coast, the 40 or so broads provide homes for a wealth of spectacular wildlife, including species such as bitterns, marsh harriers, swallowtail butterflies and the rare Norfolk hawker dragonfly.

TG357149 the Broadland Conservation Centre at Ranworth Broad (Norfolk WT) provides a duckboarded trail through woodland, reedbed and open water. TG428222 Hickling Broad NNR (Norfolk WT) has a water trail and a series of connecting footpaths from which dragonflies and swallowtail butterflies can be seen in summer.

❹ Cavenham Heath NNR
Suffolk · EN
This is the most dramatic of the remaining Breckland Heaths. The plants have to survive acidic and dry conditions, binding a thin, sandy soil. Historically, the Brecklands have been farmed with difficulty. Their heaths and forests are incongruous landscapes in a region of otherwise intensively-farmed land. An impressive range of plants, birds, butterflies and moths can be found. Look for the resident herd of roe deer and watch for adders, too.

TL757727 off A1101, 8 miles north-west of Bury St Edmunds.

❺ Cley Marshes
Norfolk · WT
The oldest and one of the best known of the Wildlife Trust reserves. A mix of scrapes, reedbed, shingle bank and grazing marsh attracts early spring migrants such as chiffchaffs, wheatears and sandwich terns – followed by a succession of reed and sedge warblers, parties of ruff and black-tailed godwits and even arctic-bound waders such as the Kentish plover and Temminck's stint. Other rarities such as bee-eaters and spoonbills have turned up at Cley in June adding to the avian glamour of the avocets, bitterns and bearded tits that regularly breed there. The autumn migration continues almost until early December when most of the winter wildfowl visitors arrive.

TG054441 for visitor centre opposite the reserve, 9 miles west of Sheringham on the A149 coast road just before Cley.

❻ Dunwich Heath
Suffolk · NT
Near to Minsmere, this coastal heathland tells a long story of Suffolk's natural history. These heather-covered 'sandlings' are remnants of once extensive sheep-grazed heaths which now support an exceptionally fine collection of grass species, owing to the distribution of wetter areas. There are low, sandy cliffs down to the pebble beach where shingle plants, like the sea pea and yellow horned-poppy, add further colour and botanical interest to the site.

TM476685 off B1125, 7 miles north-east of Saxmundham.

❼ Ferry Meadows Country Park
Cambridgeshire · Nene Park Trust
Lying in a floodplain of the River Nene, this country park, which is part of the Nene Park, has a wide range of habitats, including flooded gravel workings, old woodlands, wet meadows and marshland. There are two wader scrapes where feeding birds can be observed from hides.

TL145975, north of Oundle Road (A605) 3½ miles west of Peterborough.

❽ The Firs
Bedfordshire · CC
The Firs has all the facets of heathland habitats with a mixture of heather, broom, gorse, grasses and bracken. In the wetter patches watch out for gipsywort, and marsh violet and a further range of plants.

TL028376 off A530 west of Ampthill.

❾ Fowlmere
Cambridgeshire · RSPB
These derelict watercress beds are now one of the finest reedbeds in the region. Reed warblers add to a splendid spring chorus of songbirds. Water forget-me-not is one of the water-loving plants which grow in profusion here. Ducks and waders shelter during the winter with species of birds not usually associated with aquatic habitats, including corn bunting and thrushes.

TL407462 off B1368, 8 miles south of Cambridge.

❿ Frampton Marsh and Boston Point
Lincolnshire · WT
If you want to view the massive expanses of the Wash and its coastal mudflats and saltmarshes, the long walk to Frampton Reserve and Boston Point is rewarding. In this dramatic seascape, there is a continuous movement of gulls across the area. Waders will rest and feed here on migration and winter wildfowl provide encouragement for those who will brave the exposure.

TF390385, 4 miles south-east of Boston. Beware tides.

⓫ Gibraltar Point NNR
Lincolnshire · WT
The stretch of coastline out to Gibraltar Point provides one of the best places in Britain to see the accumulation of new land from the sea. The progression from tidelines and windblown sand to dunes clothed in dense shrubs can be followed, with each stage marked by its distinctive plants and animals. The marram grass and sea-buckthorn play vital roles in the seaward extension of dry land. A nationally outstanding list of migrant and resident bird species includes those normally associated with woodland and heath as well as the coast and the sea. The natural history of this part of the coast is explained by the information centre.

TF556581, 3 miles south of Skegness, follow signs to Seacroft.

⓬ Holkham NNR
Norfolk · EN
For over 20 miles most of the land adjacent to the north Norfolk coast, from Holme to Cley, is protected as nature reserves. Holkham has dunes (stabilized by Corsican pine), saltmarsh, sandflats, mudflats and farmland. It has all the special plants of these habitats including marsh helleborine and orchid species.

TF892447 north of A149, 2 miles west of Wells.

⓭ Landguard
Suffolk · WT/CC
This is a fascinating reserve with a fine pebble beach backed by a broadly level shingle plain and then a wooded bank with Landguard Fort watching over Harwich Harbour entrance. The plain has subtle vegetation changes in its many shallow depressions, but it is the migrants for which the site is famous. Once we waited and watched for enemies, now

we search for the arrival of butterflies and birds from another continent.

TM285319, A14 from Felixstowe via private road to Dock Viewing area.

⑭ Minsmere
Suffolk • RSPB
This must be one of the world's most famous nature reserves, yet there is so much more to Minsmere than the story of the avocets. It would rank among the best of the British sites even without these delicate and beautiful waders. Coastal flora includes the enormous marsh sow-thistle and hemp-agrimony. The entire site is a paradise for naturalists.

TM473672 off B1122, 6 miles north-east of Saxmundham.

⑮ Ouse Washes
Cambridgeshire • RSPB/ WWT/WT
Created in the seventeenth century to store the surplus winter floodwaters of the River Great Ouse, the Washes are a major contribution to the maintenance of the arable land of the fens. The grasslands and ditches are carefully nurtured to encourage their nationally important ornithological and botanical interest. In summer, when the water level is down, the cattle share their pastures with breeding redshanks and lapwings – and there may be ruff and black-tailed godwit. But you will see the Washes at their most spectacular in the wintry evening light, when waving skeins of whooper and

Bewick's swans fly over the banks to splash down among the tens of thousands of wintering wildfowl, roosting and feeding on the flooded grasslands.

TL500880 on B1411 or TL470860 off B1093, east of Manea.

⑯ Sandringham Country Park
Norfolk • SE
This famous estate has a most attractive Country Park where the nineteenth-century estate woodlands provide homes for a range of fauna. Squirrels, redpolls, jays and nuthatches are some of the arboreal creatures you can find regularly, but the resident flocks of crossbills are elusive. The patches of heathland attract breeding nightjars. Follow marked trails to enjoy the quieter areas and see the full range of woodland habitats.

TF689287 turn east off A149, 2 miles south of Dersingham.

⑰ Scolt Head Island NNR and Blakeney Point NNR
Norfolk • EN/NT/WT
In a wild and open landscape of their own making, these sites belong to the sea. The shingle banks are covered by sand, then successions of dune vegetation. Accessible by boat, they are worthwhile visiting not simply for their bird life but also to witness the power of the sea and the wind in creating and destroying our land.

TF805465 and TG001464 north of A149, by boat or a long walk. Beware tides.

⑱ Snettisham
Norfolk • RSPB
This is the place to see one of the country's greatest wildlife spectacles. As the tide rises and covers the Wash, hundreds of thousands of wading birds, as well as ducks and geese, gradually move up to pools in front of the reserve's hides. The best time is autumn and winter when the knot and other waders jostle for space at high tide, and Impressive skeins of pink-footed geese fly over in the early morning and evening. Best to check the local tide table to work out the best day-light hours to visit.

TF647335 Signposted from A149 at Snettisham, between King's Lynn and Hunstanton.

⑲ Titchwell Marsh
Norfolk • RSPB
Like Holkham, Titchwell is a coastal reserve but here the sandy beach is fringed with reedbeds, freshwater marshes and scrub. Birds, invertebrates and amphibians abound. An exciting day for the expert, it also provides interest and information for the casual visitor too. The call of bearded tits across the reedbeds and the marsh harrier overhead are as unmistakably East Anglian as the Norfolk dialect.

TF750436 on A149, 6 miles east of Hunstanton.

⑳ Totternhoe Knolls
Bedfordshire • CC
The story of the Knolls reflects the changing influence of man's use of the site since he built a Norman castle on the highest point. The gentle chalkhills were cleared of woodland and grazed by sheep for centuries. Then the layers

of harder Totternhoe Stone were quarried leaving a topography of hills and holes, now with a thin turf and a beautiful range of chalkland plants. Orchid species and clustered bellflower are among the less common flowers on the grasslands. The scrub contains ash, privet and spindle; the woodland is dominated by beech. Many of the downland butterflies and moths are present.

SP979220 via B489, 2 miles west of Dunstable.

㉑ Wicken Fen NNR
Cambridgeshire • NT
This superb example of relic fenland contains all the habitats associated with the succession of changes through reedbed, sedges, alder buckthorn thickets, mixed scrub and wet woodland. The management of each stage has produced a beautifully rich flora and a high population of birds, insects and other invertebrates linked with the fens. One of the oldest reserves in Britain, it provides a rare opportunity to view the fenland habitats once common in East Anglia.

TL563705 off A1123, 8 miles north-west of Newmarket.

㉒ Wolves Wood
Suffolk • RSPB
An outstanding example of traditional management encouraging a fine woodland flora and fauna. The soils are wet clays and ponds diversify the natural history interest of this attractive oak/ash/maple woodland. A hornbeam coppice is an unusual feature.

TM054436 north of A1071, 8 miles west of Ipswich.

12 South Wales

What is it that unites the wild sandstone landscape of the Brecon Beacons and the beauty of the Pembrokeshire Coast? What links the complex habitats at Oxwich, on the Gower, with the breathtaking gannetry on Grassholm? It is not geology or soils, climate or vegetation, because this region has an extremely diverse collection of different habitats. It is the sense of place which sets this region apart. It is an intangible feature of every site, felt most strongly by the local people and respected by the visitor.

The following selection is intended to show how this part of South Wales is at once romantic and dramatic. The memories of your visits to sites such as Taf Fechan and Castle Woods will evoke the senses of wonder and delight which you felt when you first saw them. They may travel the oceans but the seals of Ramsey Island and the petrels and shearwaters of Skomer are as Welsh as the ravens on the Brecon Beacons.

❶ Afan Argoed Forest Park
Glamorgan • CBC
Coniferous forests cover a significant part of this region and the pine and larch forests on the steep valley slopes of Afan Argoed are typical of these quiet, evergreen woods. Pockets of much older woodland occur in the plantations which hold many of the plant and animal species that do well in the shade.

SS821951 off A4107, 6 miles north-east of Port Talbot.

❷ Afon Tywi
Carmarthenshire
This region of coastal cliffs and heaths, of exposed moors and mountainsides, supports a relatively small proportion of arable land. If you follow the Afon Tywi up its valley you will see the ploughland along the coastal plains change to small fields clinging to the lower valley slopes and eventually disappear as the Beacons are approached. Relying heavily on their animals, the farmers have always supplemented

their produce from the sea and the rivers. Here on the Tywi they still launch coracles to net the salmon and trout. Notice how the fields change shape and size as the valley grows steeper and higher and the land becomes too poor to plough.

SN420200 following A40 from Carmarthen to Llandovery, then minor roads into the hills.

❸ Bosherston Ponds
Pembrokeshire • NT
One of the region's few large areas of open freshwater was created as recently as 1790 to 1840, when three narrow limestone valleys were dammed. The drowned valleys are edged with yellow iris, reedbeds and water mint, together with extensive beds of white water-lilies and stonewort. Fed by streams, these clear waters support a variety of aquatic insects and birds such as the reed warbler. Otters and wintering wildfowl add further interest to the ponds which form part of Stackpole NNR, a reserve which ranges from wooded limestone slopes through thorn scrub to sand dunes and sea cliffs which have breeding choughs and a colony of auks and kittiwakes.

SR966948 south of B4319 via Bosherston or Stackpole, 4 miles south of Pembroke.

❹ Brecon Beacons National Park
Powys • NPA
From the highest peaks of this wild landscape, you can see the results of massive forces of heat and ice which have modelled the old red sandstones. The glaciers created corrie lakes and scraped the edges of sheer mountainsides. The rivers which swelled as the ice melted cut steep gorges, now wooded, where the grazing sheep and ponies cannot reach them. On the inaccessible

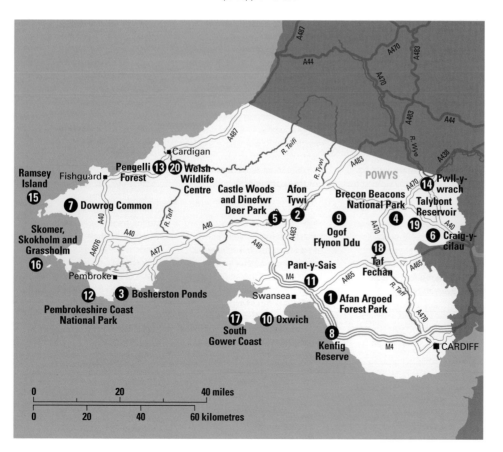

ledges of the cliffs grow relics of Brecon's former vegetation: globeflower, purple and mossy saxifrage and great woodrush on the lower slopes. Elsewhere, the moors of heather and bilberry have been transformed by grazing sheep to smooth sweeps of grassland. This dramatic landscape is accessible by car with many roads over the National Park. The Brecon Beacons are renowned for their upland birds; watch for the flashing white rumps of the wheatears, and for ring ouzel, raven and the rare merlin.

SO050290 roads from Brecon in all directions.

❺ Castle Woods and Dinefwr Deer Park
Carmarthenshire • WTWW
This is one of the most exciting woodlands in South Wales and is on a limestone bluff above the Afon Tywi. The woodland is primarily oak, holly, cherry and ash. The shrub and ground cover is outstanding, with hazel, spindle, dog-violet and the parasitic toothwort. Lichen communities are of importance and include the rare lungwort. Overlooked by the romantic castle of Dinefwr, the fine, old parkland has herds of fallow deer. The mature trees attract woodpeckers, redstarts and pied flycatchers. In winter the water meadows draw large numbers of ducks. Lichens are a speciality.

SN627220 off A40 through the town park at Llandeilo.

❻ Craig-y-cilau NNR
Powys • CCW
The sweep of pale cliffs at Craig-y-cilau gives away the change to limestone rocks and a unique flora. Five exceptionally rare whitebeams with elm, oak, yew and beech are scattered over the steep slopes above a bog. Here in a glacial depression is a small raised bog with round-leaved

sundew at the edges. The gushing melt-waters cut out a cave system beneath the crags which is used for hibernation by lesser horseshoe bats.

SO188159 minor roads off A4077, 6 miles west of Abergavenny.

❼ Dowrog Common
Pembrokeshire • WTWW
The pattern of different plants growing in the varying soils and wet and dry conditions is very apparent on this lowland heath with pools. The wealth of flowering plants include a number of scarcer species and the pools provide an excellent habitat for dragonflies and the rare marsh fritillary. The wintering birds are regularly joined by wildfowl and hen harrier.

SM769268 minor road from A487 crosses the common 2 miles north-east of St David's and provides a good vantage point.

❽ Kenfig Reserve
Glamorgan • CCW
The fact that 500 flowering plants have been recorded on this coastal reserve is sufficient to indicate its importance and richness. There is a full range of dune vegetation types. A clean reed-fringed pool provides a comprehensive range of wetland habitats too, from open water to willow and birch woodland. A botanist's delight, this site will reward those looking for birds and insects too. It tells its own story of how the habitats and wildlife are constantly developing and changing.

SS802815 Kenfig village, 3 miles north of Porthcawl on minor roads.

❾ Ogof Ffynnon Ddu
Powys • CCW
These spectacular limestone caves form one of the longest

and deepest cave systems in Britain (a permit is required to enter them). Elsewhere on this site are relic plants surviving in the 'grikes' or narrow slits between the stones of the limestone pavement (you can even see which way the glaciers moved). Secure from grazing sheep are green spleenwort, lily-of-the-valley and mountain melick.

SN867155 off A4067, 15 miles north of Neath.

❿ Oxwich NNR
Swansea • CCW
If you want to follow the natural progression of almost all the coastal plant communities from the tidal zone to the clifftop then Oxwich is the site to visit. A trail leads you from the sea-holly and saltwort of the sandy beach, through marram-grass dunes and calcium-rich, damp hollows with common centaury and dune gentian. On the more stable slopes bracken grows where rain has washed out the calcium – wild privet and carline thistle prosper where it hasn't. Before the woodland trail is a grass sward with clover and then the scrub of hawthorn and gorse maturing to tall oak and ash woods before the rising land levels off to clifftop grassland. This wonderland of habitat progression supports an equally varied fauna of reptiles, mammals and birds.

SS501865 immediately south of A4118 on Gower Peninsula, 9 miles west of Swansea.

⓫ Pant-y-Sais Fen
Glamorgan • CBC
Close to the modern industrial landscape of Neath is a narrow strip of rich fen, one of the few remaining wetlands in the region. From trees to aquatic plants this local nature reserve, which can be explored along boardwalks, offers an important sanctuary for a wide range

of plants and their associated insects. The adjacent Tennant Canal provides delightful towpath strolls.

SS713939 between Neath and Swansea off B4290.

⓬ Pembrokeshire Coast National Park
NPA
The smallest and only truly coastal of our National Parks is all the more appealing because its wide range of habitats are to be found in such a concentrated area. The coastal scenery ranks among the finest in the British Isles and the bays and drowned valleys have rafts of scoters, other sea-ducks and auks. The estuaries offer sheltered accommodation for west-coast migrant insects and birds, and the dunes, farmland and cliffs seen from the 299-kilometre (186-mile) Pembrokeshire Coast Path National Trail provide enjoyable and fascinating walks at any time of year – particularly in spring when the coastal flora is at its best.

Pembrokeshire Coast Path from St Dogmalls near Cardigan to Amroth.

⓭ Pengelli Forest
Pembrokeshire • WTWW
Seventy years ago these woods were clear-felled for charcoal and mining timber. The trees have regrown from coppice stools to form an attractive habitat with a most distinctive flora and fauna. Polecats, badgers, frogs, lizards and slow-worms are among the inhabitants of this maturing forest, which remains the largest block of ancient woodland in the area. It is an example of how the continuity of woodlands can survive the axe if the axe is not followed by the plough.

SN124395 off minor roads from A487, 10 miles north-east of Fishguard.

⓮ Pwll-y-wrach
Powys · Brecknock WT
Here you will find woodland which is very like the former natural cover of the steep river valleys of the Brecon Beacons. The upper slopes of sandstone are dominated by tall oak with a good understorey lower down on the harder shelf of limestone. By the waterfall there is ash and spindle. Part of the area is now being coppiced and this attracts speckled wood, comma and fritillary butterflies. The carpet of woodland flowers beneath the oak is best in the spring. Recently an easy access trail has been established.

SO163327 on minor roads, 1 mile south-east of Talgarth.

⓯ Ramsey Island
Pembrokeshire · RSPB
Of all the ocean mammals the grey seal is the one which affords us the best opportunity to study at close range. On the northern tip of St Bride's Bay and standing the full force of the Atlantic gales, this inshore island has the most important colonies of chough and grey seals in Wales.

SM700235, daily boats from St Justinian's, June to September.

⓰ Skomer, Skokholm and Grassholm
Pembrokeshire · WTWW
Three of the most spectacular seabird colonies on the British coast, these islands will eventually draw every bird-watcher to view the spectacle. On Grassholm – an almost bare rock in the Atlantic managed by the RSPB – there are puffin, guillemot and razorbill. Summertime visiting migrants include the white-throated robin, desert wheatear, booted warbler and black stork. Skomer, the largest of the

three, is a NNR. Deeply intersected by the sea, most notably at North and South Havens, where puffins raft in their hundreds, and at the Wick, one of the finest cliff seabird colonies in north-west Europe. The island's breeding birds include kittiwake, fulmar, wheatear, short-eared owl and chough. The 100,000 pairs of Manx shearwaters remain in their burrows during the day. A new micro camera inside one of these burrows provides the world's first magical insight into this bird's life underground. The thunder of waves and screams of the seabirds should not distract the visitor entirely from carpets of wild flowers including bluebells, thrift and campions, followed in the late summer by the heathers. The Skomer vole is unique to the island, being larger and lighter in colour than its mainland relative, the bank vole. Grey seals can be seen from the clifftops, as can porpoise and dolphin, and there are some 30,000 pairs of noisy, aggressive gannets, which comprise the second largest gannetry in the world, fighting to protect their mini territories. Skokholm is larger, more accessible and closer to land with a dazzling display of wild flowers in the summer. The most maritime of all our seabirds nest here and so we have the perfect opportunity to see them – Manx shearwater and storm petrel, feed in the tide races around the head-lands. Skomer and the Marloes Peninsula are surrounded by a marine nature reserve where a wealth of marine species are protected. All three islands form an important part of the Pembrokeshire Coast National Park.

There is no access on Grassholm – the birds can be viewed from boats – but Skokholm has holiday

accommodation and limited day trips from Martinshaven. Daily trips to Skomer in summer, weather permitting.

⓱ South Gower Coast
Swansea · CCW/Glamorgan WT
If you can visit the Gower when it is free of the crowds of holiday-makers, you will find a wild landscape of natural beauty with a great deal of wildlife interest. The cliffs and shallow limestone grasslands have a comprehensive list of plant species including small rest-harrow and goldilocks aster. Incapable of spreading, even in suitable habitats, these plants must be the survivors which weathered the glaciers on these ice-free cliffs but which could not spread, like the other plants, when the grip of the Ice Age was released. The coastal sites are of exceptional interest for their flora and fauna.

SS470840 at Port Eynon (A4118), then east to Mumbles Head and north to Whiteford Point.

⓲ Taf Fechan Woodlands
Merthyr Tydfil · Glamorgan CBC/Glamorgan WT
In this steep valley is a delightful collection of habitats derived from the influences of water, and then man. Flowing over acidic grits and softer limestones, the ice was followed by a torrential river cutting a deep section through the rocks. Where they are hard and wet grow liverworts, mosses and ferns. At the water's edge are sedges and figworts. After the limestone quarries were abandoned hawthorn, fairy flax and wild thyme took over. The valley bottom ranges from alder swamp to wet meadows. The water is full of insect larvae

feeding brown trout, dippers and wagtails.

SO045097 at Cefn-coed-y-cymmer on A470, 1 mile north-west of Merthyr Tydfil.

⓳ Talybont Reservoir
Powys · Brecknock WT/NPA
A long, deep reservoir high in the Brecon Beacons and lying in a steep-sided valley. The greatest attraction for the visitor to this man-made landscape feature is the huge flocks of wintering wildfowl: dabbling ducks, mallard, wigeon and teal around the edge; diving duck, including tufted and goldeneye, in the deeper waters. Other occasional visitors include the osprey.

SO098190 turn off B4558 at Talybont, 5 miles south-east of Brecon.

⓴ Welsh Wildlife Centre and Teifi Marshes
Ceredigion · WTWW
The reserve includes extensive salt-water reedbeds, meadows, ponds and part of the tidal reaches of the River Teifi, the second longest river in Wales. The marshes are renowned for their bird life – especially Cetti's warblers, kingfishers, geese, waders and a variety of ducks. Overhead soar buzzards and the area is a stronghold for otters and for eight species of bat, including the especially rare lesser horseshoe and Natterer's bats. There are seven permanent viewing hides and a visitor centre with pro-active exhibits and panoramic views over the reedbeds. Open April – October.

SN188452 access at Cilgerran, 1½ miles south of Cardigan on A478.

13 The Chilterns and Cotswolds

Perhaps your favourite impressions of these hill ranges in southern England are of their villages, some of the most picturesque in the country. Perhaps, though, you remember the gentle hills of chalk and limestone, dry valleys, beechwoods and rolling downland. The colourful downland turfs and rich woodlands are full of song and the activities of birds and butterflies.

Exceptionally rare plants have drawn botanists to the Avon Gorge for over a century, and it is still the plants and their associated insects which attract naturalists to the Cotswolds and Chilterns today. There are other fascinating sites, including a magnificent park at Blenheim, the world's greatest wildfowl collection at Slimbridge, outstanding coastal habitats at Brean Down and new wetlands at the Cotswold Water Park and Stony Stratford.

❶ Ashton Court Estate
N. Somerset • Bristol City Council
This attractive parkland, landscaped by Repton, spreads over lime-rich soils which support a range of plants associated with the limestone scrub or grassland such as the common rock-rose, green hellebore and green-winged orchids. The park is famous for its ancient pollarded oaks and there are several exotic species as well as many native trees and shrubs. A walk round the parkland may provide close views of fallow and red deer and sunny summer days can be excellent for seeing butterflies.

ST55472 6 off A369 on western outskirts of Bristol.

❷ Aston Rowant NNR
Oxfordshire • EN
Despite being severed by the construction of the M40 motorway, this NNR retains its importance as the finest example of the vegetation of the Chilterns. Over one-third of the reserve is covered with the superb ancient downland turf including the rare Chiltern gentian and pale toadflax. Insects are exceptional too with dark green fritillaries and rarer skippers. Beech woodland and scrub widen the reserve's appeal, particularly for the birds.

SU741967 north of A40, 6 miles south-west of Princes Risborough.

❸ Avon Gorge NNR
Bristol/N. Somerset
This deep, narrow gorge has long been famous for its unique botanical interest. The carboniferous limestones are exposed on steep cliffs and the woods have an international botanical importance. The Bristol whitebeam is found nowhere else in the world. There are many other exceptionally rare species, including Bristol rock-cress and some rare sedges. These plants have evolved in the isolation of the gorge, relatively secure from the changes around. Man's influence has been present but was limited to the Iron Age hill fort and woodland management, including the coppicing of hazel which continues today.

ST5513731 off A369 at Clifton Bridge.

❹ Blenheim Park
Oxfordshire • DOM
Blenheim's many ancient oaks predate the gift of the 900-hectare (2223-acre) Park by Queen Anne to the 1st Duke of Marlborough in 1704. The straight lines of trees in the two main avenues reveal the original formal plantings of Henry Wise in the early eighteenth century – his elms have since been replaced with limes and planes. Today the Park and Lake stand as fine

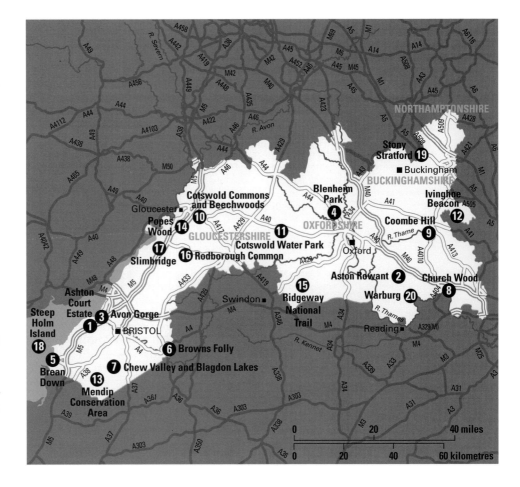

examples of how wildlife has occupied the new opportunities of amenity plantings in the eighteenth century and earlier. A nature trail leads around the Lake and the bird life throughout is outstanding.

SP442168 off A34 at Woodstock.

❺ Brean Down
N. Somerset • NT
An extension to the Mendip Hills jutting out into the southern estuary, Brean Down is a massive ridge of limestone. You will find the south slope is steeper, with jackdaws, kestrels and rock pipits on rocky ledges, while to the east there is an estuary with mudflats and saltmarsh. Peak migration times bring thousands of birds to the reserve and nearby coastline.

ST296586 off A370 south of Weston-super-Mare.

❻ Browns Folly
Bath and N.E. Somerset • Avon WT
You can sit on the terraces of limestone downland and see over the canopy of mixed woodland around. Browns Folly is an isolated building standing on a massive rock high above the Avon. From here was once quarried the famous stone of Bath but the woodland and grassland now cover the old quarries. Woolly thistle and agrimony are found in the grassy spaces.

ST798664 off A363, 3 miles north-west of Bradford-on-Avon.

❼ Chew Valley and Blagdon Lakes
N. Somerset • Bristol Water
These large reservoirs attract huge numbers of water-birds in the winter including shoveler, gadwall, wigeon, teal and goosander. Their natural bankside vegetation, which

includes reedbeds, provides ideal nesting sites for reed warbler, great crested grebe and water rail. Surrounding grassland, hedges and woods are managed for wildlife and support many wild flowers, notably green-winged orchids, as well as butterflies and dragonfly populations. Nature trails provide interesting walks and birds can be observed from hides.

Chew ST570600 north of A368, 14 miles west of Bath. Blagdon ST510600 6 miles further west.

❽ Church Wood
Buckinghamshire • RSPB
Where two of the region's main rock types merge near the surface, the resulting woodlands are very varied. Church Wood has a mixture of beech, hornbeam and yew on the chalk with oak and birch on the more acidic flinty clays. Two hundred plants and 80 species of birds tell their own story about the richness of wildlife here. White admiral and purple and whiteletter hairstreak butterflies enjoy the woody clearings and rides. The dense cover of shrub species attract nesting warblers.

SU973873 off A355, 2 miles south of junction 2 of M40.

❾ Coombe Hill Nature Trail
Buckinghamshire • NT
In a region centred on the chalk and limestone soils, acidic heaths are uncommon but form an important contrast to the lime-loving species elsewhere. Along this nature trail you will see the difference between the chalk slopes with juniper, yew and whitebearn and the clay with flints on the hilltops where broom, gorse and heather flourish. The walk to the top is rewarded by panoramic views to the Cotswolds and the Berkshire downs.

SP849066 1½ miles west of Wendover, west of A4134.

❿ Cotswold Commons and Beechwoods
Gloucestershire • EN/Various
If you would like to see how the Cotswolds looked before their thin limestone soils were cleared and farmed, then this string of woodlands on the steeper slopes will provide the answer. Although they were coppiced once, present-day management tends to recreate the natural woodland of 5000 years ago. This is beech high forest with a rich flora associated with limestone. Amongst the carpet of brambles, ivy, dog's mercury, sanicle and wood spurge are the rarer bird's-nest orchid and the common wintergreen.

Buckholt Wood (WT) SO894131 off A46, 6 miles south of Cheltenham.

⓫ Cotswold Water Park
Gloucestershire/Wiltshire • CWPS/Glos.WT
When we see nature reserves in the making we can feel the sense of optimism and excitement as we witness the creation of valuable new habitats. After excavating the valley terraces for their gravel we have left a series of shallow, lime-rich pools of fresh water. This type of lake is nationally scarce and supports a distinctive aquatic plant community. The lakes also support large numbers of wintering waterfowl, including great crested grebe, gadwall, pochard, tufted duck and coot. The Park contains several important grassland sites where snake's-head fritillaries, meadowsweet and orchids thrive.

SP215007 off A361, just north of Lechlade.

⓬ Ivinghoe Beacon
Buckinghamshire • NT
The views from these hills attract many visitors and the chalky slopes are well trodden. Nevertheless, there are quieter

areas where steeper slopes, thinner soils and fewer feet allow the typical chalkland flowers to survive: kidney and horseshoe vetches, bird's-foot-trefoil, milkwort with yellow rattle and orchids. Grazing is used in order to keep the grasslands clear of the invading scrub, where trampling feet do not suppress its growth.

SP961168 off B489, 5 miles south of Leighton Buzzard.

⓭ Mendip Conservation Area
N. Somerset • WT
No one can fail to be impressed by the richness and diversity of these two reserves in the Mendips. Velvet Bottom is pitted by the lead workings from pre-Roman times to the 1880s and now forms flower-rich grassland and scrub. The broadleaved woodland and limestone grassland of Black Rock are excellent for flowers and butterflies.

ST482545 off B3135 near Cheddar, for the Black Rock reserve. ST503556 for Velvet Bottom.

⓮ Popes Wood
Gloucestershire • WT
A mature beech woodland which dispels the idea that beechwoods have uninteresting ground cover. Green hellebores, spurge-laurels and orchid species are all present and there is plenty of cover for a good range of woodland songbirds.

SO875128 off A46, 7 miles south of Cheltenham.

⓯ The Ridgeway National Trail
CC/HA
Starting at the World Heritage Site near Avebury in Wiltshire, this 137-kilometre (85-mile) Trail follows mainly ancient tracks along the chalk ridge as it travels through five counties to Ivinghoe Beacon in

Buckinghamshire. Traversing two distinctive landscapes – open chalk downland in the west and the more intimate beech-clad Chiltern Hills in the east – the Ridgeway passes through several nature reserves and other pockets of unimproved chalk downland rich in flowers, insects and birds. Sightings of red kite are likely in the Chilterns.

SU118681 to SP961168.

⑯ Rodborough Common
Gloucestershire • NT
This famous common is recognized for the importance of its wildlife, and among the many flowers and grasses are the common rock-rose, eyebright, cowslip, pyramidal and common spotted orchids, stemless thistle and bird's-foot-trefoil. Butterflies include chalkhill and small blues, dark green fritillary and Duke of Burgundy. Dog's mercury and bluebell flourish in the ash, oak and beech woodland remnants. The small coombes and spurs of Rodborough Common support a wide range of plants and associated invertebrates.

The site is famous for its orchid displays.

S0852035 off A419 near Stroud.

⑰ WWT Slimbridge
Gloucestershire • WWT
The world's most comprehensive collection of wildfowl also ranks as one of the region's most important estuary sites. Vast expanses of mudflats, saltmarsh, grazing meadows and lagoons can be viewed. They hold nationally important populations of waders as well as geese and ducks. The largest winter flocks of Bewick's swans and white-fronted geese in Britain can assemble on this part of the Severn Estuary at Slimbridge. Migration and population studies carried out from here are explained at the Trust's centre.

SO723048 off A38, 7 miles west of Stroud.

⑱ Steep Holm Island
N. Somerset • KAMT
You can visit this offshore island sanctuary by boat from

Weston-super-Mare and find the most remarkable range of wildlife species. Cormorants, gulls and other seabirds breed here, with slow-worms and muntjac deer. Many migrant birds also occur. An incongruous mixture of creatures from the land and the sea, which is complemented by the plants including the rare wild peony and wild leeks.

5 miles offshore by boat from Weston-super-Mare, from April to October.

⑲ Stony Stratford
Buckinghamshire • BBONT
The river valley water conservation area was established in 1980 specifically as a new nature reserve following the extraction of sand and gravel for the construction of the new A5. Primarily, it provides breeding grounds for waders but open water and islands are also available. The establishment of a good aquatic vegetation cover has been assisted by transferring water plants from the nearby canal. Wildfowl, redshank, ringed plover and kingfisher

have all established themselves at this new site.

SP785412 off A5 west of Milton Keynes.

⑳ Warburg
Oxfordshire • BBONT
For its size and diversity the woodland habitat of Warburg is outstanding. You will find open chalk grassland, old meadows, banks and scrub, but the woodland dominates. The tall trees include beech, yew, sycamore, and sweet chestnut and conifers. The understorey shrubs and trees include dogwood, privet, spindle, field maple and wayfaring tree. Woodcock, wood warbler and willow tit are three examples from the wood's long list of breeding birds and the moths have some fascinating names: maple prominent, scarce footman, clay triple lines and map-winged swift moths.

SU720880 off A423 near Bix, 3 miles north-west of Henley-on-Thames.

14 South-east England

It is interesting to consider the impact of one of the greatest cities in the world spreading out over the heaths, forests, marshes and downs. But even as London sprawled, pockets of countryside were left. Greatly modified by their urban surroundings, Epping Forest, Regent's Park and Wimbledon Common are valuable reminders of the former scene. Now the cycle of urban development has come full circle. On the derelict banks of canals at Carnley Street and St Pancras, conservationists are creating new urban habitats.

Despite being so densely populated, the south-east has a complex pattern of many types of countryside, accessible to the visitor and liberally distributed across its landscapes. You may choose the popular Box Hill – a splendid downland site – or you may prefer the fascination of Kentish wetlands at Stodmarsh. Thursley (a Surrey heath), and The Men's (ancient Sussex woodland) are other representatives of these special retreats now protected so we can enjoy the countryside and its wildlife.

❶ Box Hill
Surrey · NT
Box Hill is first and foremost a marvellous open space for everyone to enjoy. It also happens to be a very good example of chalk downland and woodland. There are several woodland types but the most notable is full of box and yew.

The scrub on the edges of the woods contains whitebeam, dogwood and wayfaring tree while the wild cherry adds a splash of colour in the spring. The open downland, created by centuries of animal grazing, has a full range of chalkland butterflies and contains nearly 400 species of plants

including many types of orchid. Intensive public access has not destroyed the wildlife value of this splendid natural playground.

TQ179513, 1 mile north-east of Dorking on A24.

❷ Camley Street Natural Park
London · London WT
Sometimes the natural colonization of derelict land can form the basis of a new future for the wildlife of the city. On a piece of derelict land adjacent to the canal in Camden, the Camley Street Natural Park has been created. It is a wildlife refuge and a place where people can go to enjoy nature in the city centre. The pond supports aquatic plants and amphibians while reedbeds and marsh provide breeding areas for birds and food for dragonflies. Meadow plants support butterflies and bees in the summer months, while many species of birds can feed from the scrub surrounding the whole park. Alder and willow complement the buddleia which existed here prior to the construction of the park. There is also a visitor centre.

Camley Street, London NW1.

❸ Colne Estuary NNR
Essex · EN/WT
The wide spreads of colour over the saltmarsh remind us that these coastal estuaries can be both beautiful and interesting for their plants as well as their birds. Sea-blite, sea-beet and sea wormwood indicate the maritime origins of the plants. The tidal mudflats attract the brent geese and thousands of waders.

TM085154 off B1027 through St Osyth to sea wall and creek.

4 Cuckmere Haven
Sussex · E. Sussex CC
The Cuckmere Valley itself is attractive downland but from the Haven to Beachy Head and the famous Seven Sisters is some of the best chalk coast in the country. The whole area is defined as the Seven Sisters Heritage Coast and is renowned for its chalk downland plants, including such rarities as the burnt orchid and early spider orchid. Fulmar nest on the cliffs, and terns and ringed plovers on the shore.

TV518995 south of A259 between Eastbourne and Seaford.

5 Dungeness
Kent · RSPB
Probably the largest shingle ridge in Europe, the scale of this massive heap of stones dumped by the sea is awe-inspiring. Within is an intricate range of habitats from small pools to pockets of grassland. Altogether it is one of the most exciting bird-watching sites in the country. It is migration that makes Dungeness spectacular, as it is the first landfall for birds such as the wryneck and bluethroat and for clouded yellow butterflies.

TR063196 minor roads to Dungeness, 4 miles south-east of Lydd.

6 Epping Forest
Essex · Corporation of London
Much of Epping Forest, a 2460-hectare (6000-acre) open space north of the capital, is ancient woodland with some fine old pollarded oaks, beeches and hornbeams. The woodlands are noted for their birds, deer, beetles and fungi. There are also open grassy areas as well as many ponds with rich aquatic life.

TQ412981 on A104 between Chingford and Epping. Queen

Elizabeth's Hunting Lodge, Rangers Road, Chingford is open to the public Wednesdays to Sundays; the Epping Forest Information Centre, High Beach, Loughton is open all week.

7 Ham Street Woods NNR
Kent · EN
On the southern edge of the Weald clay, where it slopes down to the flat expanse of Romney Marsh, you will find a large area of damp oak woodlands managed under the traditional coppice with standards system. The diversity of woodland habitats provide for a superb range of woodland birds, from the tits in the high crowns of the trees to wrens and dunnocks on the forest floor.

TRO10340, 1 mile north of Ham Street village on A2070, 4 miles south of Ashford.

8 Kingley Vale NNR
Sussex · EN
In the beautiful chalk valley of Kingley Vale is one of the finest yew woodlands in Europe. There is no better place to see what a mature yew wood looks like. It is a strange and magical place. For over 500 years these ancient, twisted trees have slowly welded a canopy of dark green foliage, so dense and cool it has excluded all but a handful of plants beneath. On the slopes are younger trees, only 50 to 250 years old, with ash where the yew have slipped from the hill to create a gap. Elsewhere the woodland cover of the reserve changes to oak and ash, with holly, buckthorn, spindle and dogwood.

SU824088 near West Stoke off A286, 4 miles north-west of Chichester.

9 London Parks
For Londoners, Regent's Park and others like it are indispensable. The hand-fed

chaffinches, squirrels and pigeons are only the more obvious tip of a much larger proportion of species relying on man's urban environment. Each park is different, with its own character and its own distinctive blend of wildlife. Resident or migrant visitors, native or introduced species, however well-adjusted the animals may be, they will eventually need to seek the water, shelter, security or food supply of the urban parklands. The range of habitats and species is surprising; we have underestimated how nature can adjust to even our harshest environment in the centre of our greatest city.

Central London: Hyde, Regent's, Richmond and St James's Parks.

10 The Men's
Sussex · WT
You will find that the Men's group of woodlands are remarkable by any standards. They are, to most visitors, a beautiful and emotive image of true woodland. They are also of immense historical importance and you will not be in them for long before you realize they have a wealth of wildlife interest too. This combination is not by chance. It is through man's continuous influence on the native woodland which must have been here 3000 years ago. Trees in the Men's had to be pollarded or left to grow as high forest because grazing animals would have destroyed the traditional coppice growth of other Sussex woods. More than any other, the Men's looks like the native wildwood of Sussex. The full range of woodland plants and animals are therefore able to find a home. Deer and fungi are outstanding but the entire woodland ecology is of importance.

TQ024236 on A272, 3 miles east of Petworth.

11 Nunhead Cemetery
London · Southwark C./Friends of Nunhead Cemetery
You can find little gems of nature hidden all over the city but this small reserve in a Peckham cemetery is truly curious. Dominated by the prolific growth of the sycamore and ash which thrive in these tough urban spaces, over 100 other plants have started their process of colonization. Watch for woodland birds, butterflies and, in the evening, foxes.

Linden Grove, Peckham, London SE15.

12 Pulborough Brooks/Amberley Wild Brooks
W. Sussex · RSPB/WT
In the scenic Arun valley between Pulborough and Amberley the RSPB and the Sussex WT have restored wet grassy meadows which, with controlled flooding in winter, offer refuge for thousands of ducks, geese and wading birds. In spring and summer, the ditches are rich in plant and invertebrate life and many bird species breed along them and in the wet meadows. Fringing woodland harbours many songbirds, including nightingales. The RSPB has converted a traditional Sussex barn into a comprehensive visitor centre from which a circular trail leads to several spacious hides overlooking the valley.

TQ059164 signposted on A283, 2 miles south-east of Pulborough towards Storrington.

13 Queensdown Warren
Kent · WT
From its origins as a commercial rabbit warren over 700 years ago, the continuous grazing and nibbling of the grass has provided the short turf suited to rock-rose, wild thyme and marjoram. Occasionally a beech seedling

survived the grazing, or was deliberately planted and these stand over the pastures. The scrub and wood indicate where grazing once stopped. Chalkhill blue butterflies and grasshoppers are not difficult to find in summer.

TQ827629, 2 miles north-west of A249 about 5 miles west of Sittingbourne.

⑭ Rye House Marsh
Hertfordshire · RSPB
This marsh is rich in plant species and full of insects on which feed a splendid range of wetland birds. From the warblers in the reedbeds to the swallows and swifts catching the insects in flight, the intricate food-chains are beautifully illustrated by the variety of bird species, each having adapted to its own food-source. Hides provide excellent viewing and your bird-watching will be made more exciting by the terns which stay to breed and migrants which briefly pass through. The marsh also provides winter quarters for water rail, snipe and ducks.

TL386100 by the river Lee at Hoddesdon off AI0.

⑮ Selsey Bill
Sussex
Projecting out into the English Channel this area has been swamped by development yet still holds its place as a favourite haunt of seabird watchers. The oceanic species pass by and the divers and grebes, which resort to the sea in winter, gather in flocks off the Bill.

SX860925 at the end of B2145, 8 miles south of Chichester.

⑯ Stodmarsh NNR
Kent · NCC
The wetlands of the Stour Valley had all but disappeared through drainage schemes when subsidence, due to underground coal workings, recreated the marshland of the past. Lagoons and reedbeds are full of reed and bulrush, dykes have bogbean and spearwort and elsewhere are typical plant communities of the bank and wet scrub. The rare bittern, bearded tit, Cetti's and Savi's warblers are here. In winter the watery habitats attract ducks. Many migrant birds regularly use the marsh as a resting and feeding station. Flooded meadows with mare's-tail and sea club-rush provide food for wildfowl.

TR222607 walk along the Lampen wall or the river wall. On minor roads 5 miles north-cast of Canterbury.

⑰ Sydenham Hill Wood
London
The largest remaining fragment of the old Great North Wood, Sydenham Hill Wood has been managed as a wildlife sanctuary by the London Wildlife Trust since 1982. A unique mix of old woodland, Victorian garden survivors and secondary woodland, it is very rich in invertebrates – notably stag beetles and purple hairstreak butterflies. The mainly oak and hornbeam trees support over 70 bird species (including lesser spotted woodpeckers, treecreepers, sparrowhawks and tawny owls), 200 different plants and 200 species of fungi.

TQ344726 entrance on Crescent Wood Road off Sydenham Hill, SE26.

⑱ Thursley NNR
Surrey · EN
There is a special story of man and wildlife on Thursley. The mists of time still roll across one of the most important lowland heath and bog sites in southern England. They must have shrouded the first farmers who felled the wildwood, covered the exhausted farmland as it reverted to heath and then concealed a continuing history of human enterprise: peat digging, iron working, grazing, burning, wildfowling, military training and, finally, conserving this valuable site. There is a quite outstanding range of plants and animals in the heath, pools, scrub and bog. You can experience for yourself the true character of rich and ancient heathland

SU915400 is the access gate on the A3. 2½ miles south-west of Milford.

⑲ Wimbledon Common
London · WPCC
Of immense value owing to its accessibility, this heath is also very interesting because of its range of habitats. Higher, gravelly areas are grass with gorse and birch scrub; oak, beech and hornbeams do well on the clay slopes and bogbean is found in the valley bogs. Reptiles are always a surprise to find – lizards are present.

TO231725 carpark at windmill on the common. London SW19.

⑳ Wye and Crundale Downs NNR
Kent · EN
If you stand on the edge of Coomb Head and look down the steep-sided valley of the Devil's Kneading Trough you will see a dramatic sweep of lush grassland and farmland beyond. But 12,000 years ago this same site was a frozen waste. You are standing on a thin layer of soil over a massive thickness of chalk. Even the soft chalks are harder rocks than the clays of the Weald around and have withstood the erosion of wind and rain and scraping glaciers. About 10,000 years ago, at the end of the Ice Age, the surface of these chalky hills was shattered by the constant freezing and thawing of the tundra soils as the influence of the ice diminished. During the thaws, gushing melt-water from the ice and snow on the Downs where you are standing pushed the broken earth down to the plain below. Thus the dry valley, or Coomb, you can see was created. Plants took a foothold in the shallow soils. Grazing animals, first wild deer and then sheep and cattle, trampled out the narrow 'terracettes' on the sides of the Kneading Trough. These animals prevented the invasion of woodland and scrub and the specialist grassland plants could thrive, including sheep's fescue, hoary plantain and dwarf thistle. Today the site is outstanding for orchids. Uncommon species include the musk orchid in the short turf, and fly orchid in longer grass.

TR077455 on minor roads 4 miles north-cast of Ashford.

㉑ Yockletts Bank
Kent · WT
If you want to see chalk woodland and its grassy glades at their best this site is a classic. Ash, oak, beech and hornbeam grow over shrubs which include dogwood, maple and the wayfaring tree. These are crowned by a superb display of common spotted, early purple, fly and pyramidal orchids and other spring flowers. Badgers and nightingales represent two species of the many mammals and birds on the reserve.

TR125467 on minor roads east of B2068, 8 miles south of Canterbury.

15 Wessex

From the high, rolling downs to the Somerset levels there is a richness of colour and activity, variety of habitats and finely balanced enjoyment of the rare and the familiar. Throughout this region the antiquity of man's presence and the evidence people have left behind are strikingly clear. From the Iron Age tracks of Wiltshire to the motorway in Berkshire the passage of man and his influence on the wildlife around him is apparent. The entire region is like a living museum and a very impressive one too. Who could fail to admire the phenomena of Chesil Bank or the Needles, or wonder at the natural history of the New Forest. Who could not share Gilbert White's enthusiasm for the beechwoods, or Thomas Hardy's respect for the heaths? Most of this region lies in the area which Hardy called Wessex and we could not think of a better name for this romantic region.

❶ Brownsea Island and Poole Harbour
Dorset • WT/NT
This intriguing gravel island stands in the complex estuary and harbour of Poole, now heavily used for sport and recreation. However, there is still room for the birds which have always frequented the bays and the reserve on the island itself is important, with freshwater pools and reedbeds. The many seabirds are joined by herons from one of our largest heronries and the woods provide a secure stronghold for the red squirrel.

SZ032877 by boat from Poole Quay or Sandbanks Ferry.

❷ Chesil Bank and the Fleet
Dorset • Ilchester Estate
You can wonder at the spectacle of Chesil Bank, one of Europe's five largest shingle banks, and the Fleet, a saline lagoon, at any time of the year. The Fleet is important for its marine life and supporting thousands of wintering wildfowl, particularly brent geese, wigeon and mute swans which feed on the eelgrass. Hundreds of the swans are resident, breeding in colonies at Abbotsbury where they can be visited from March to October.

SY578840 off B3157 Bridport to Weymouth.

❸ Ham Hill Country Park
Somerset • S. Somerset DC
Spectacular views across the Somerset countryside can be

enjoyed from the top of this huge Iron Age hillfort. You will find the disused limestone quarries well concealed by a vigorous colonization of plants and animals.

ST478167 just off A303 between Ilchester and Ilminster.

❹ Kingcombe Meadows
Dorset • WT
The meadows, marshy ground, hedgerows and woodland around the hamlet of Lower

Kingcombe are a legacy of farming practices carried out for centuries up to today – without the use of pesticides or artificial fertilizers. The distinctive patchwork of small fields of 'unimproved' grassland stands out from much of the surrounding countryside, and is maintained by a regime of grazing and hay cutting which promotes the various grassland habitats and their wildlife communities. Over 150 plant species can be found, including lady's mantle, pepper saxifrage and devil's-bit

scabious. In early summer the marshy areas are coloured by flag iris, ragged-robin and water forget-me-nots. Thirty-six butterfly species have been seen on the reserve. Ravens and buzzards are a frequent feature of this agricultural 'oasis'.

Turn south off A356 halfway between Dorchester and Crewkerne to Toller Porcorum and Lower Kingcombe to find Pound Cottage Information Centre at SY554990.

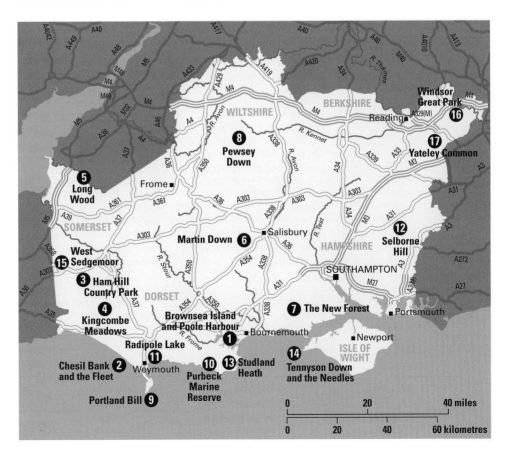

5 Long Wood
Somerset • WT
Above the Cheddar Gorge, Long Wood occupies the head of a steep limestone valley. The wood was originally of ash and oak with an understorey of hazel and a rich ground flora. The wood was clear-felled in the 1950s and planted with beech, which is shading out the native plants. The beech is being removed to re-establish the oak and ash of the ancient wood.

ST487551, B3135 east of Cheddar.

6 Martin Down
Hampshire • EN/CC
By manipulating the grazing patterns of the sheep, a mosaic of short and long grassland can be created. Uncontrolled scrub growth would spread rapidly, as shown by the five types already present on the reserve, including chalk scrub species of ash, buckthorn, privet and spindle. Dogwood grows where the downs were ploughed during the Second World War, and elder is strongly associated with the disturbed soils of the earthworks. Butterflies are outstanding with rare silver-spotted skippers and adonis blues, hairstreaks and fritillaries.

SU058192, A354, 10 miles south-west of Salisbury.

7 The New Forest
Hampshire • FC/Various
Each part of the New Forest is a rich historical record with a very special woodland ecology. As a whole it is one of Europe's most extensive and most important ancient lowland forests. For 2000 years the woodland has been adapted to suit the needs of man. It has been used as a source of food or fuel, material for building homes or ships or for early industries. The forestry cycles of management have been completed time and again over generations but still the sense of a natural woodland prevails. Once a wildwood of oak, hazel, lime and elm, the New Forest now has superb mature beech and oak woodland with many other species present. The grazing beneath limits the ground cover and, not surprisingly, holly forms one of the main shrub layers. Elsewhere, the variety of soil and drainage conditions gives a mixture of other plant associations with the trees. Roe and fallow deer are present in good numbers with a few red and sika. The lawns, damp open clearings of grass and moss, are special places at dawn when the birds and animals of the forest cautiously work their way into the open while undisturbed. There are many areas of heathland, too, and these complement the insect and bird populations of the forest. All three British sundews are here in the heaths. The wettest 'lawns' and valley bottoms in the forest have marshland habitats which attract redshank and snipe. Other New Forest birds include the nightjar, stonechat, hen harrier, hobby, merlin and many more. The appearance of the area today is the result of man's sometimes ruthless exploitation of New Forest timber but the continuity of habitats through history allows us to enjoy a very beautiful place, with a most distinctive character and natural history.

SU300080, A337 and minor roads out from Lyndhurst and Brockenhurst.

8 Pewsey Down
Wiltshire • EN
To see this expansive sweep of short-grazed chalk downland is a memorable experience. High on the slopes there is a spring carpet of flowers in the ancient turf, known to be one of the longest grazed of the few large downland sites now left. Chalk milkwort, bastard-toadflax and field fleawort are survivors from the ancient pastures. Pewsey Downs are free of the invading scrub because of the continuity of grazing management. Many individual plants, especially burnt and bee orchids, are stunning but it is the overall impression of this ideal example of downland which remains.

SU115635 on minor roads between Marlborough and Devizes.

9 Portland Bill
Dorset
Projecting far into the English Channel, the Bill grants an exciting day's bird-watching throughout the year. At peak migration times in spring and autumn the birds of the ocean pass by. There are ducks, divers and waders, terns harried by the skuas, and shearwaters, auks and scoters which are so accustomed to the sea they seek land only for nesting sites. Rarities can be expected.

SY680685 beyond Weymouth off A354 to the Bill.

10 Purbeck Marine Reserve
Dorset • WT
This was the first marine reserve to be established on the British mainland and shows the value of this area of Kimmeridge Bay. Clear, shallow waters allow us to glimpse the life of the sea beyond the tidal zone. The interpretative centre helps to reveal a colourful and fascinating world of plants and creatures that we rarely see.

SY909788 on Isle of Purbeck via minor roads off A351.

11 Radipole Lake
Dorset • RSPB
Changes in wetland habitats can be surprisingly fast and take place for many different reasons. This freshwater lake and reedbed was part of the tidal estuary of the River Wey only 60 years ago. Then sluices prevented the inundation by salt water and the ecology quickly changed. Now it is managed as a valuable feeding and resting place for migrant birds. Reedbeds have colonized since 1945. The airborne migrants include swallows, martins and swifts. The reedbeds have attracted breeding bearded tits and Cetti's and sedge warblers. You may notice the garden plants, buddleia and bramble among the waterside vegetation – they arrived with the building rubble from the housing areas in Weymouth which was used to make the easy access paths.

SY676796 in the centre of Weymouth town.

12 Selborne Hill
Hampshire • NT
Encompassing some fine examples of beech 'hanger' woodlands on the chalk escarpments of east Hampshire, these fragments of ancient landscape around Selborne are of great ecological importance. The observations of the Rev. Gilbert White, pastor and naturalist, published in *The Natural History and Antiquities of Selborne* in 1788, are an invaluable and fascinating record, with lists and locations of individual scarce plants, of the ancient hangers, the valleys of the Short and Long Lythes, the historic wood pasture, chalk grassland and mixed woodland of Selborne Hill and Common. His famous zigzag path to the top of the beech hanger on Selborne Hill is still in use.

SU735337, B3006, 3 miles south-east of Alton.

13 Studland Heath NNR
Dorset • EN/NT
This heath is where you can find all six British reptiles in a series of dunes and heaths with pools and slacks. Lesser

dodder is a parasite growing on heather and gorse on the drier ridges. Elsewhere, in damper places, are round-leaved sundew and bog myrtle with cottongrass. The heath is a site for dragonflies and many other insects and for Dartford warblers. Beware the extreme fire risk.

SX034836 off B3351, Studland on the Isle of Purbeck.

⑭ Tennyson Down and the Needles
Isle of Wight • NT

It is the atmospheric location of this important range of downland and scrub habitats that makes it both interesting and dramatic. The sheer chalk white cliffs drop 144 metres (480 feet) to the sea below and provide nesting sites for cormorants, shags, razorbills and fulmars. Even the shortest grassland herbs suffer from the exposure but short-stemmed harebells and dwarf thistles are well adapted. The scrub is rich in shrub species with unusual combinations including gorse, blackthorn and privet growing together.

SU324855 follow B3322 to the most westerly point of the Isle of Wight.

⑮ West Sedgemoor
Somerset • RSPB

The Somerset Levels and Moors are one of England's largest surviving wet meadow systems, managed by farmers and various local and national conservation organizations to enhance its wildlife value. The RSPB's reserve at West Sedgemoor covers 582 hectares (1420 acres) and comprises damp grasslands, cattle droves and drainage ditches bordered by deciduous woodland on the southern scarp. Swell Wood has one of Britain's largest heronries with about 100 pairs, best visited between March and June. Blackcaps, marsh tits and nightingales breed nearby. Along the ditch edges, the sedge warbler is the most conspicuous and typical bird. On the moor, lapwings, redshanks, curlews, snipe, whinchats and quails nest and whimbrels pass through on passage north. The winter floods attract Bewick's swans, teal, wigeon, golden plovers and lapwings.

ST361238 signposted off A378 from Taunton to Langport, 1 mile east of Fivehead village.

⑯ Windsor Great Park
Berkshire • CEC

There are very few opportunities for us to experience the character and feeling of a particularly ancient woodland. The oldest stands of open high oak forest, with their grand old trees, dignified even in decay, give us a dramatic impression of one type of wildwood in Britain. Even here the woodlands have been protected and managed as royal hunting park, estate woodland and productive forests. Nevertheless, the continuity of oak forest cover and the presence of the ancient trees have ensured the survival of hundreds of species of animals and plants that rely on the oak forest. Invertebrate populations are of international significance with some 2000 species of spiders and beetles. The Park also harbours 30 butterfly species and four species of deer. Birds include hobbies, nightjars and woodpeckers.

SU953735 south of Windsor.

⑰ Yateley Common
Hampshire • CC

This country park offers a network of paths through heathland habitats, including wet and dry heaths with pools. Gorse, broom, birch and pine form good scrub cover for the birds. Heather and purple moor-grass give way to sphagnum and acid bog plants or to rich marshland in the pools. Bulrush, yellow iris and water-lilies are easily recognized but look also for the less familiar plants and the butterflies, including silver-studded blues.

SU822597 at Yateley, 3 miles north-west of Fleet.

16 The South-west Peninsula

The forces of the wild Atlantic impress themselves on some of the most dramatic coastal scenery in the British Isles. This peninsula of hard rocks is exposed to the sea and yet in the lush, green, sunken lanes of Devon, you may feel as safe and sheltered as anywhere. There are wonderful wildlife contrasts within this region's differing habitats. It provides a richness and interest of its own. On the estuaries we find wild, open spaces; in the rock pools there are intimate details to enjoy. The delicate and rare butterflies in the Devonshire woodlands and the seemingly indestructible seabirds battered by the ocean gales tell their own story of the south-west.

The beauty of the scenery and the special nature of the wildlife will never fail to draw its visitors, annually seeking their own experience of this part of wild Britain.

❶ Berry Head Country Park
Devon • Torbay C
Near the popular seaside resorts of Tor Bay this remarkable nature reserve doubles as a country park for the enjoyment of visitors. The value of its superb range of habitats is increased by its dual role. The headland is topped with scrub, heathland and grassland supporting many rare species. The strikingly-coloured stonechat males can be seen on the tops of the bushes and the headland forms a landfall for migrant passerines including black redstarts. Further interest for the bird-watcher is provided by the cliff-nesting guillemots, fulmars and kittiwakes which breed in very few other places on our south coasts. The birds can be viewed from the Head's vantage point above the waves.

SX943564 east of Brixham.

❷ Cabilla and Redrice Woods
Cornwall • WT
Together, these mainly broadleaved woodlands cover 190 acres (77 hectares). The nature trail takes about two hours to complete and passes through a pond area, alder coppice and beech plantation – and a large woodland glade where on sunny summer days adders, common lizards and slow-worms can be glimpsed basking and pearl-bordered fritillaries are on the wing laying eggs on the dog violets which grow in profusion. You will see evidence of charcoal burning and iron working from earlier centuries.

SW129652 off A38, 3 miles east of Bodmin, take turning north towards Cardinham, cross bridge over River Fowey. Access via track on right after sawmill.

❸ Chudleigh Knighton Heath
Devon • WT
An important example of lowland heath in the south-west, this site has dry and wet heathland with small ponds. Invertebrates do well in the scrub and woodland habitats and, on the heath, attract a range of songbirds.

SX837776 west of A38, 10 miles south-west of Exeter. Access by public rights of way only.

❹ Dart Valley
Devon • NPA/WT
From the rain-soaked bogs of the uplands, the Dartmoor rivers flow through steep-sided, often wooded valleys and through heaths of gorse and grasses. The combination of woodlands and streams near to these extensive heaths results in a distinctive species list of birds. In this typical valley are the dipper and grey wagtail, buzzard, redstart and whinchat. Fox and badger hunt the banks, and salmon and brown trout breed in the river.

SX680727, take B3357 to Dartmeet and follow the valley.

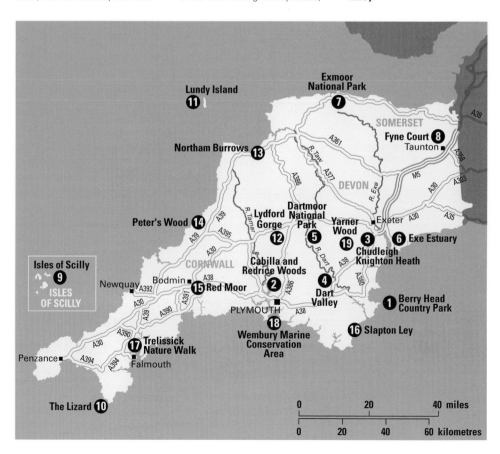

⑤ Dartmoor National Park
Devon • NPA
Climb the granite tors of Dartmoor and you will see how screes called 'clitters' have been formed when huge boulders were split from the tors by ice. The ancient woodlands, which once covered the hills, are now only small relics. The small farms concentrate in the sheltered valleys with the fields on the slopes and the open land on the moors. At the prehistoric enclosure of Grimspound, where the remains of 24 stone houses can still be traced, we can see a timely reminder that thousands of years ago early farmers lived up here on the moors, retreating to the lower land as the climate cooled and poor soils became exhausted.

Grimspound SX705815 off B3212, 7 miles north-east of Two Bridges.

⑥ Exe Estuary
Devon • WT/RSPB/MOD
You should try to visit this huge estuary in the winter as well as the summer for it is then that the wildfowl are at their most spectacular. Large flocks of brent geese, mallard, shelduck, teal and wigeon are found on the shore, while the sea has rafts of sea-duck including eiders and scoters. Autumn, too, is worthwhile as the flocks of waders comb the estuary. Sandflats, mudflats and saltmarsh can be overlooked from footpaths on both shores.

SX980785 south of Exeter, footpaths from SX973845 north of Powderham and SX99236 south of Lympstone.

⑦ Exmoor National Park
Somerset and Devon • NPA
With its dramatic coastline, open windswept moorland, steep wooded hillsides and villages nestling in sheltered valleys, Exmoor is a place of contrasts. The 54-kilometre (34-mile) coastline boasts England's highest cliffs, rising to 433 metres (1420 feet), and its longest stretch of coastal woodland. On the gently undulating hills are large areas of uncultivated moorland – an open, treeless landscape of peaty soils. Clinging to the steep valley sides and cliffs are extensive areas of broadleaved woodland. Standing among the branches dripping with ferns, mosses and lichens, you can feel the antiquity. Yet these apparently wild places have been influenced by countless generations of people who have lived and worked on Exmoor. Other survivors of Exmoor's past are the remarkable Exmoor ponies which have been in these uplands since prehistoric times. Red deer also roam the moors.

Dunkery Beacon, at 519 metres (1702 feet) the highest point in the National Park, is just a short walk from car parks on a minor road between Wheddon Cross (10 miles north of Dulverton) and Luccombe (6 miles south-west of Minehead) at SS892417.

⑧ Fyne Court
Somerset • WT/NT
The Somerset WT headquarters offers a good example of the wildlife habitats of the Quantocks, some of which are being restored and managed within the grounds. Woodland and ponds, together with an old quarry, provide the basis of habitats to be developed in the future for studying and enjoyment.

ST223321 minor roads 6 miles north of Taunton.

⑨ Isles of Scilly
Cornwall • DOC/IOSET/EN
The story of the sea is encapsulated in these beautiful isles. Only five of the islands are inhabited although another 40 have land vegetation above a variable sea level. Once joined to Cornwall and wooded with oak and hazel the central plateau was drowned by a gradual rise in sea level over the centuries and only the rim of the land mass now stands above the waves as a group of islands. The Atlantic dominates the scene, the air is clean, the waters clear. As a landfall for migrating birds the islands are famous, but the sea itself is rich with colourful marine life including corals, sea snails and sea anemones. The elegant featherstar is a deep-water creature but here in the Scillies can be found in the shallows.

By air or by ferry, Easter to October, from Penzance.

⑩ The Lizard
Cornwall • EN/NT/WT/others
The rare and complicated geology of this most southerly peninsula creates unusual habitats ranging from coastal cliffs to a unique type of heathland. The cliffs at Predannack face the full force of the Atlantic westerlies. Plants survive the exposure only in stunted forms (ox-eye daisy, knapweed and scabious), or by growing flat (prostrate forms of broom, privet and juniper can be found). Cornish heath, which is restricted to this county, is readily found here. Other unusual plants include dwarf and pygmy rushes. Spring squill and dog-violets provide colourful seasonal displays.

SW701140, A3083 south from Helston.

⑪ Lundy Island MNR
Devon • LT
By the time the boat reaches Lundy from the mainland you will have been drawn to the character of this granite outcrop: the smell of the sea, the grandeur of the cliffs and the sound of the wheeling seabirds. The East Side landing gives views of the gentler, more sheltered side of the island where maritime flowers abound during spring and summer, including the unique Lundy cabbage. The top of the island opens out onto heathland and a short walk takes you to the towering cliffs of the West Side where thousands of seabirds can be seen nesting on the tiniest ledges. But that is only half the story. Below the waves is the fascinating world of the first Marine Nature Reserve to be designated in Britain. Here creatures such as sea fans and other corals normally associated with the Mediterranean thrive in Lundy's warm waters.

SS143437 by boat from Bideford or Ilfracombe or by helicopter at Abbotsham.

⑫ Lydford Gorge
Devon • NT
The gorge is a dramatic illustration of the powerful forces which created the character of the south-west. This famous ravine scooped out by the River Lyd is 1½ miles long. It is a series of pools and falls leading to the 27-metre-high (90-foot) White Lady Waterfall. The steep, rocky cliffs of the gorge are covered in beautiful oak woodland. Plants such as lady, male and hart's tongue ferns, woodrush, ramsons and ivy cover the gorge, and the rocks are coated with many types of rare mosses, lichens and liverworts. Kingfishers, herons, grey wagtails and dippers feed along the river, and greater spotted woodpeckers, tree-creepers, pied flycatchers and nuthatches can be seen among the trees.

SX509846 west of A386, 6 miles south of Okehampton.

⑬ Northam Burrows
Devon • CC/Torridge DC
If you want to compare all of the major habitats of the shoreline in one area, they are here at the mouth of the rivers Taw and Torridge. You will find

rock pools with crabs; sandy beaches and mud with sandwort and sea spurge; and sand dunes with blue and brown butterfly species. Out on the estuary are curlew, ringed plover and shelduck.

SS444298 from Northam, 2 miles north of Bideford.

⑭ Peter's Wood
Cornwall · NT
Many of the narrow, steep river valleys of the north Cornwall coast provide shelter for small pockets of woodland. Too steep to farm, they have been little used by man and parts of Peter's Wood are of ancient origin. The plants – for example, great wood-rush and hard fern – indicate wet, acidic conditions. A wide range of plants is established, including the unusual royal fern and Tunbridge filmy-fern. There are sufficient invertebrates to provide food for three different resident bat species and the river itself attracts dippers.

SX113910 off B3263 near Boscastle.

⑮ Red Moor
Cornwall · WT
This delightful mosaic of habitats combines wetland, heath scrub and woodland like pieces in a jigsaw. The former working of alluvial tin has created a compact reserve demonstrating how a range of species from lichens and heather to linnets and spiders has moved in where man moved out.

SX077622 off B3269, 4 miles south of Bodmin.

⑯ Slapton Ley NNR
Devon · FSC
A freshwater wetland complex, impounded by a 4-kilometre-long (2½-mile) shingle bar which is a blaze of colour in the summer, with plants such as yellow-horned poppy and viper's bugloss. The lagoon attracts breeding and wintering wildfowl, and reedbed birds include the Cetti's warbler. The seabirds at Start Bay add to the bird life, especially during migration periods. The NNR is used as an 'outdoor laboratory' by students from the nearby Field Centre.

SX828442, A379 8 miles from Kingsbridge.

⑰ Trelissick Nature Walk
Cornwall · NT
You will enjoy this beautiful woodland and parkland walk for pastoral scenery, woodland and coast. The trail will take you to a viewpoint overlooking the man-made parkland on the slopes of the River Fal. It is an impressive example of dramatic landscape enhancement and wildlife interest.

SW837396, B3289, 4 miles south of Truro.

⑱ Wembury Marine Conservation Area
Devon · WT/MOD/NT
This fascinating rocky shore provides an opportunity for studying the richness of the shallows below the level of low tide, as well as the tidal rocks and pools. Wembury Point is a useful location for watching waders such as redshank and greenshank, and sighting migrating birds. Wembury Marine Centre (open April to September) organizes popular rock pool rambles.

SX517484 6 miles east of Plymouth on road to Kingsbridge.

⑲ Yarner Wood NNR
Devon · EN
The oaks of Yarner Wood lie in a sheltered valley, partly on disused farmland. It is a very attractive wood indeed with pied flycatchers and wood warblers, and a wealth of fungi and invertebrate species. You will not fail to be intrigued by the nest constructions of the wood ants. An integral part of this woodland ecology, there may be 800 nests occupied by 200 million ants.

SX785788 on B3344, 2 miles north-west of Bovey Tracey.

PICTURE CREDITS

The three principal photographers who have contributed to this book live and work in three distinctly different parts of Britain.

NIALL BENVIE'S home is in Angus, Scotland where he has been a full-time writer and wildlife photographer since 1993, specializing in Scottish and Norwegian topics. His pictures appear regularly in *Amateur Photographer* and *BBC Wildlife*. His latest book *The Art of Nature Photography* is to be published in spring 2000.

MARK HAMBLIN lives in Sheffield near the heart of the English Peak District where his passion for bird watching led him to become a professional wildlife photographer in 1995, specializing in British birds and mammals. He contributes to national publications including *BBC Wildlife and RSPB Birds*.

COLIN VARNDELL lives in south-west England, in a Dorset village where, since 1982, he has been a professional wildlife photographer. His speciality is landscape photography and garden and woodland plants and animals. His first book *Wildlife in West Country* was published in 1994. Colin regularly contributes to national and local wildlife and photographic magazines.

BBC Worldwide would like to thank the following photographers for providing photographs and for permission to reproduce copyright material. While every effort has been made to trace and acknowledge all copyright holders, we apologize for any errors or omissions.

INDEX

This book is published to accompany
the BBC television series entitled *Living
Britain*, produced by the Natural History
Unit at BBC Bristol and first broadcast
in 1999.

Series written and produced by:
Peter Crawford
Producers: Yvonne Ellis, Mark Jacobs

Published by BBC Worldwide Ltd,
Woodlands, 80 Wood Lane,
London W12 OTT

First published in 1999
Copyright © Peter Crawford 1999
The moral right of the author has
been asserted.

Photographs copyright
© The photographers 1999.
For a full list of photographic credits,
please see page 283

ISBN 0 563 38476 X

Commissioning Editor: Vivien Bowler
Project Editor: Lara Speicher
Copy Editor: Anne Gatti
Art Director: Linda Blakemore
Designer: Janet James
Maps: Angela Wilson, All Terrain Mapping

Text set in Bembo

Printed and bound in France by
Imprimerie Pollina s.a.

Colour separations by Radstock
Reproductions Ltd, Midsomer Norton

Jacket printed by Imprimerie Pollina s.a.